MACMILLAN INTERNATIONAL POLITICAL ECONOMY SERIES

General Editor: Timothy M. Shaw, Professor of Political Science and International Development Studies, Dalhousie University, Nova Scotia

The global political economy is in a profound crisis at the levels of both production and policy. This series provides overviews and case studies of states and sectors, classes and companies in the new international division of labour. These embrace political economy as both focus and mode of analysis; they advance radical scholarship and scenarios.

The series treats polity–economy dialectics at global, regional and national levels and examines novel contradictions and coalitions between and within each. There is a special emphasis on national bourgeoisies and capitalisms, on newly industrial or influential countries, and on novel strategies and technologies. The concentration throughout is on uneven patterns of power and production, authority and distribution, hegemony and reaction. Attention will be paid to redefinitions of class and security, basic needs and self-reliance and the range of critical analysis will include gender, population, resources, environment, militarization, food and finance. This series constitutes a timely and distinctive response to the continuing intellectual and existential world crisis.

Recent titles:

William D. Graf (*editor*)
THE INTERNATIONALIZATION OF THE GERMAN POLITICAL ECONOMY

Betty J. Harris
THE POLITICAL ECONOMY OF THE SOUTHERN AFRICAN PERIPHERY

Richard Higgott
AUSTRALIA IN THE GLOBAL ECONOMIC ORDER

Steven Kendall Holloway
THE ALUMINIUM MULTINATIONALS AND THE BAUXITE CARTEL

Guy Martin
THE EUROPEAN COMMUNITY AND THE THIRD WORLD AFTER 1992

Matthew Martin
THE CRUMBLING FAÇADE OF AFRICAN DEBT NEGOTIATIONS

Marjorie Mbilinyi
WORKING ON PLANTATIONS AND PEASANT FARMS

James H. Mittelman
OUT FROM UNDERDEVELOPMENT

Dennis C. Pirages and Christine Sylvester (*editors*)
TRANSFORMATIONS IN THE GLOBAL POLITICAL ECONOMY

John Ravenhill (*editor*)
AFRICA IN ECONOMIC CRISIS

Stephen Riley (*editor*)
THE POLITICS OF GLOBAL DEBT

Garry Rodan
THE POLITICAL ECONOMY OF SINGAPORE'S INDUSTRIALIZATION

Ennio Rodríguez and Stephany Griffith-Jones (*editors*)
CROSS-CONDITIONALITY, BANKING REGULATION AND THIRD-WORLD DEBT

Jorge Rodríguez Beruff, J. Peter Figueroa and J. Edward Greene (*editors*)
CONFLICT, PEACE AND DEVELOPMENT IN THE CARIBBEAN

Patricia Ruffin
CAPITALISM AND SOCIALISM IN CUBA

Roger Southall (*editor*)
LABOUR AND UNIONS IN ASIA AND AFRICA

Frederick Stapenhurst
POLITICAL RISK ANALYSIS AROUND THE NORTH ATLANTIC

Sharon B. Stichter and Jane L. Parpart (*editors*)
WOMEN, EMPLOYMENT AND THE FAMILY IN THE INTERNATIONAL DIVISION OF LABOUR

Arno Tausch
TOWARDS A SOCIO-LIBERAL THEORY OF WORLD DEVELOPMENT

Fiona Wilson
SWEATERS: GENDER, CLASS AND WORKSHOP-BASED INDUSTRY IN MEXICO

David Wurfel and Bruce Burton (*editors*)
THE POLITICAL ECONOMY OF FOREIGN POLICY IN SOUTHEAST ASIA

Workers in Third-World Industrialization

Edited by
Inga Brandell
Research Coordinator
AKUT (Working Group for the Study of Development Strategies)
University of Uppsala, Sweden

MACMILLAN

First published 1991

Published by
MACMILLAN ACADEMIC AND PROFESSIONAL LTD
Houndmills, Basingstoke, Hampshire RG21 2XS
and London
Companies and representatives
throughout the world

Edited and typeset by Povey/Edmondson
Okehampton and Rochdale, England

Printed in Hong Kong

British Library Cataloguing in Publication Data
Brandell, Inga
Workers in third-world industrialization.—(Macmillan
international political economy).
1. Developing countries. Industrialization. Effects on employment
I. Title
338.091724
ISBN 0–333–54547–8

Series Standing Order (International Political Economy)

If you would like to receive future titles in this series as they
are published, you can make use of our standing order
facility. To place a standing order please contact your
bookseller or, in case of difficulty, write to us at the address
below with your name and address and the name of the
series. Please state with which title you wish to begin your
standing order. (If you live outside the UK we may not have
the rights for your area, in which case we will forward your
order to the publisher concerned.)

Standing Order Service, Macmillan Distribution Ltd,
Houndmills, Basingstoke, Hampshire, RG21 2XS, England

Contents

List of Maps

Preface and Acknowledgements

Industrial workers in the Third World are neither pawns in the hands of transnational companies and authoritarian governments, nor heroes of the future just waiting for an order to move forward. Still, what they do matters: it matters for the economic development of each country and for the ongoing constitution and reconstitution of political and social forces within and beyond the limits given by the legitimacy of national development and welfare.

Some of the chapters in this book focus on single events in a factory, others on a branch or a region in a long term perspective. Some constitute the first appearance of a piece of original empirical research; in others the authors have seized the chance to return to previously presented research data. They all contribute to the continuing empirical and theoretical investigation of the impact of industrial workers' actions on societies in transition. They also share the same urge to look beneath the surface in order to find the unnamed, and to understand how they make history.

The opportunity of bringing together the authors in this book was given by a research programme, 'Labour and democracy – economic transformation and popular struggles', initiated by AKUT (Working group for the study of development strategies) and funded by Uppsala University and SAREC (Swedish agency for research cooperation with developing countries). Two international seminars devoted to such labour issues were held in 1986 and 1987, thus introducing experiences and analyses from several continents which have been subsequently revised for this collection.

Naturally many persons beside the authors have been involved in the work. Gunnel Cederlöf made the index. Anu-Mai Köll translated Chapter 2 from French and Daniel Moore Chapter 8 from Spanish. Lars Rudebeck, with his sense of conceptual and linguistic nuances, did a lot to help out in this transposition into English. Gunilla Andrae and Björn Beckman both participated in every step of the project; their perseverance helped to overcome occasional standstills. Initially Owen Laws and then Gabriella Boström, never hesitated in typing and retyping the text, arranging and rearranging end-notes and references. Peter van Gylswyk prepared the maps. Rosemary Galli, Arne Tostensen and Timothy M. Shaw provided incisive comments. Any shortcomings remain, as usual in these cases, the responsibility of the editor.

INGA BRANDELL

Notes on the Contributors

Gunilla Andræ is a researcher at the Department of Economic Geography at Stockholm University. She has worked primarily on industrial development in West Africa and has published *Industry in Ghana: Production, Form and Spatial Structure*. Together with Björn Beckman Andrae has authored *The Wheat Trap: Bread and Underdevelopment in Nigeria* and *Industry Goes Farming: The Nigerian Raw Materials Crisis and the Case of Textiles and Cotton*.

Giovanni Arrighi is Professor of Sociology at the State University of New York at Binghamton and a board member of the Fernand Braudel Center. He is author of *The Geometry of Imperialism* and co-author of *Dynamics of Global Crisis* and *Transforming the Revolution: Social Movements and the World System*.

Yusuf Bangura is a research fellow at UNRISD (United Nations Research Institute for Social Development), coordinating the project on Crisis, Adjustment and Social Change. He was formerly a lecturer in Political Science at Ahmadu Bello University (1980–8) and visiting researcher at AKUT, Uppsala University (1988–9). He has contributed in many journals and books on the issues relating to labour, crisis, democracy and international economic relations, and is author of *Britain and Commonwealth Africa: The Politics of Economic Relations (1951–75)*.

Björn Beckman is Associate Professor at the Department of Political Science at Stockholm University and was previously lecturing at the Ahmadu Bello University, Zaria, Nigeria. His research has concerned problems of state and political economy of West Africa. He has published *Organising the Farmers: Cocoa Politics and National Development in Ghana* and is a frequent contributor to and overseas editor of the *Review of African Political Economy*. Beckman has also co-authored two books with G. Andrae (see above).

Inga Brandell is a political scientist and research coordinator of AKUT (Working group for the study of development strategies), Uppsala University. She is the author of *Les rapports franco-algériens*

– *du pétrole et des hommes*. Her research has concerned labour, migration, industrialization and international relations.

Said Chikhi is Lecturer at the Institute of Sociology at the University of Algiers and researcher at CREAD (Centre de Recherche en Economie Appliquée pour le Développement). He is a specialist on labour sociology, and has written several works in that field, including *Question ouvrière et rapports sociaux en Algérie*. At present, he is researching social movements and democracy in Africa.

Ali El Kenz is Lecturer at the Institute of Sociology at the University of Algiers and research director at CREAD. He has published several studies on industrial and labour sociology, for example *Le complexe sidérurgique d'El-Hadjar – une expérience industrielle en Algérie*. His research includes a wider reflection on theories of development.

Jeff Guy is a South African who worked in the Department of History of the National University of Lesotho from 1971 to 1985. He has published articles and books, *The Destruction of the Zulu Kingdom* and *The Heretic*, on the history of Natal and Zululand, and articles on oral history and Southern African mine labour. At present he works in the Department of History at the University of Trondheim, Norway.

Bosco Parra is a Chilean lawyer and social scientist. He is a former member of the political committee of the Popular Front under Allende's government and is today a research fellow with AKUT at Uppsala University. In connection with the strategical problems facing the Chilean popular movement he has written 'Fuerza civil, fuerza militar' in *Cuadernos Americanos* and *Dimensión operacional del proceso de democratización en Chile*.

Fortunata Piselli is Professor of Sociology at the University of Calabria, Italy. She has contributed to many scholarly journals, and is the author of *La donna che lavora* and *Parentela ed emigrazione*.

Beverly Silver is a research associate at the Fernand Braudel Center, State University of New York at Binghampton. She has published several articles on labour in the world economy and in particular countries. She is currently completing a long-term, large-scale analysis of the world labour movement.

Motlatsi Thabane is Lecturer in the Department of History at the National University of Lesotho, where he is also a researcher in the Oral History Project of the Institute of Southern African Studies. At present he is researching the history of mining in Southern Africa with emphasis on diamond mining in Lesotho.

Fiona Wilson is a Research Director in Women's Studies at the Centre for Development Research, Copenhagen. She has written on changing social relations in the Peruvian Andes during the nineteenth and early twentieth centuries and on agrarian change and women's labour in Latin America. Her most recent work is *Sweaters: Gender, Class and Workshop-based Industry in Mexico*.

1 Practices and Strategies – Workers in Third-World Industrialization: An Introduction

Inga Brandell

A NEW PERSPECTIVE ON A CLASSICAL SUBJECT

This book addresses a classical and central topic in the social sciences – wage-labour in an industrial and capitalist work organization – in fact the very focus of social science theory for authors otherwise as different as Karl Marx, Emile Durkheim and Max Weber. As Claus Offe (1985: 2061) puts it:

> Wage work, separated from the home and from traditional communitary forms, without political protection and integrated into the capitalist organisation of work, into the impoverishment, the alienation and the rationalisation which have an impact on it, has clearly constituted the center around which all research and all theory in social science have been organised. Together with the forms of economic, political and cultural resistance developed by labour (with or without organisations) or on the contrary the forms for its social integration, all other aspects of society – politics and culture of knowledge, family and moral systems, forms of living and religion – have found their theoretical development there.

However, the classical vision, built on the experience of proletarianization and industrialization in the European and North American contexts, has been challenged in the last decades by new knowledge about the origins of capitalist industry in the west as well as by research findings from other parts of the world, where wage work and industry have been introduced under different circumstances than those prevailing in the first case. In fact, the process of proletarianization resulting in the creation of a free and mobile wage-earning

1

labour force implying a different rationality of economics, followed by the independent organization of labour in the twin organizations of trade unions and workers' political parties, with a subsequent profound change in political and social systems, did not unfold systematically in third-world countries.

To begin with, proletarianization in a third-world colonial context has been shown to have been a process characterized by a high degree of coercion, and also a very slow one, sometimes never leading to full proletarianization; that is, wage work has been only temporary and a certain access to land has been maintained (Arrighi, 1973; Munck, 1988: 60). As a result, migrant temporary labour has in some cases, especially in Southern Africa, been considered the dominant form of labour. Authors like Claude Meillassoux have even offered a theoretical explanation which makes migration the basic form for the integration of labour into the capitalist process of production in the phase of imperialism (Meillassoux, 1981).

From another view-point, even in those third-world countries where proletarianization is most advanced, the effects have been questioned: because of the higher productivity of modern industrial technology, the spread of wage-earning underway will never lead to a nucleus of industrial wage labour as great as that in Europe and the United States, where as much as 50 per cent of the labour force was at one point employed in industry. That level will probably never be attained in the industrializing third world, and this has led to the suggestion that the industrial working class will not have such a unifying and dominant role in the whole labour movement there as was the case in early industrialized countries (Palloix, 1981; Brandell, 1982). The issue of the impact of industrialized labour in the third-world societies has of course become even more crucial when signs of '*deindustrialization*' occurred in several countries hit by economic recession.

Migration and the continued reproduction of the labour force outside the fully capitalist industrial sector had evident effects for the rationality of economics, in principle by limiting the expansion and growth of a capitalist consumer market. The pattern of trade-unionism has been questioned with regard to its economic as well as political effects. In many African countries, for example, trade unions during colonialism became an integral part of the movement for national liberation which, for evident reasons, was understood as the primary goal also for organized labour. This was also the case in parts of Asia (Southall, 1988a). After independence, trade unions were, as a consequence, much more linked to the state than their North American or European equivalents at their early age (Freund, 1984: 7–10). In Latin America, on the other hand, where independence preceded the rise of trade unions by a long time, the latter for other reasons did not often become strong socio-political actors with a real independence from the state: sometimes they developed under the protection of nationalist regimes, as in the case of Brazil and Bolivia, with subsequent periods of heavy repression, or were at least partly coopted by the state as was the case in Argentina under Peronism. The defence of relative autonomy has also in some cases led Latin American trade unions to retreat from the national political scene (Feuer, 1987).

Not only the linkage to a nationalist developmentalist state distinguishes the situation of emergent third-world trade unions from that of their European or North American counterparts. The timing of the formal recognition of political rights, especially the right to vote, and the right of organization and expression, also matters in this context. Regimes in newly independent countries in the twentieth century have all formally recognized those rights as part of independence and the victory over colonialism. In some cases those rights are respected, but even where dictatorship have suppressed them, trade unions have generally not become the central actor in the transition from more authoritarian rule to at least formal democracy. Yet this was a process central to the growth of European trade unionism. By contrast, in Latin America, where democracy has by no means been respected, trade unions have only sometimes, but not systematically, been at the forefront of the resistance towards dictatorship and of the struggle for the restoration of democracy (Therborn, 1979; Feuer, 1987).

The links between the developmentalist state and the trade unions, on the one hand, and the relatively better economic situation for the workers in industry and mining as compared to the majority of unemployed population in towns and in the countryside on the other, gave rise to a debate both in Latin America in the 1960s and in Africa in the early 1970s on the character of the industrial working class, defined as a *labour aristocracy* (Munck, 1988: 53–5; Arrighi, 1973). Positions in the debate were divergent but the implicit conclusions concerning the classical formulations of social science were the same: under the international and national circumstances accompanying the introduction of capitalist production in developing countries, the central elements of social science theory on labour were not of any immediate and direct use. Generalizing from the free worker – homogenization of the category of labour and the labour market – the introduction of a new economic and technical rationality could simply not be taken for granted. Neither did the historical experience adapt to the assumed impact of those elements: rise and unification of trade unions and workers' parties, democratization, with their decisive consequences for politics and society in general.

But elements of classical theories have been questioned also from within the highly industrialized societies. Historical studies of labour in Europe and the United States stressed the lack of unification of the labour market. Women, children, ethnic minorities and immigrants had experienced and continued to experience different working conditions. They were not part of the same labour market, and sometimes even not admitted into trade unions (Roth, 1974; Piore 1980). A perspective on labour and labour history, confined neither to 'industrial relations' nor to the official history of trade unions, put the focus on earlier neglected forms for labour resistance: absenteeism, going slow, wild-cat strikes, which not only seriously disturbed industrial production in Europe and the United States in recent times, but also could be discovered during earlier periods.

Some authors stressed the link between workers' resistance in the factories and the life and tradition of workers' communities (Thompson, 1968), while others put the relations at the workplace at the center of analysis (Quaderni Rossi), in both cases moving outside the framework given by workers' own official organizations. The technical rationality of the industrial labour process was put in a social and political perspective in the works by Braverman on the dequalification of labour (1974), by Coriat on the introduction of Taylorism and Fordism (1976, 1979), and by Arrighi and Silver on the different impact of the craft workers' and the skilled workers' 'market bargaining power' on the one hand and the 'workplace bargaining power' of the workers on the line on the other (1984, 1985).

The last decades' important contributions to the labour history of industrialized as well as third-world countries, and the debate over the impact of current industrialization have opened up possibilities for a new perspective, to which this book seeks to contribute. It is a perspective which often has its point of anchorage in the concrete labour process and the relations at the workplace. It also seeks a broad understanding of the relation between the labour process and the workplace, on the one hand, and the wider organizational, cultural, political and economical setting of society on the other hand. The perspective permits rich empirical studies which also raise important methodological and theoretical issues.

PRACTICES AND STRATEGIES

Once research on labour goes beyond statistical recording and the technicalities of labour and production processes, it enters into the complex of workers' attitudes, behaviour and actions. One set of questions concerns what explains attitudes and actions: are these determined by the actor's position as wage labour in an industrial setting, or are they a result of other patterns to be found in the individual or in society as a whole? Is, for example, absenteeism to be explained most coherently as resistance to working conditions, or as a result of workers' involvement in other activities outside the factory? Absenteeism may even be necessitated by the conditions for reproduction, obliging workers to be absent to take care of different aspects of life. Another set of questions has to do with the social forms and expressions used to legitimate or explain attitudes and actions. Grievances and demands addressed to the factory management may, for instance, be presented in religious or ethnic terms. How should these be understood? If there is a demand for respect for religious duties during the working day, should it be looked upon as traditional resistance to industrial production or an attempt to reduce the work effort?

Said Chikhi and Ali El Kenz, authors of Chapter 2, 'Workers' perceptions and practices in Algeria', have recently published monographs on the two largest Algerian industrial plants at least measured in terms of the number of employed workers: the industrial vehicle plant in Rouiba outside Algiers (Chikhi, 1986), and the huge iron and steel works at El Hadjar, outside Annaba in the east of the country (El Kenz, 1987). Their contribution to this volume summarizes some of their findings within a conceptual framework evolving around the concept of strategy. According to them it is inappropriate to use this concept in dealing with the industrial labour force in Algeria, and probably also in other third-world contexts.

Against the background of an Algerian society in rapid change, where industrialization has increased the proportion of workers in the employed population from 13 per cent in 1969 to 29 per cent in 1983, the two authors draw an image of an industrial world in constant turmoil because of high levels of labour turnover and absenteeism coupled in the case of the truck factory with almost constant go slows and strike periods. In the case of the iron and steel works at El Hadjar, the first big industrial project launched after independence, it is possible to distinguish several periods in industrial relations: from the early euphoric unity between managers and workers to today's profound disillusionment and the penetration into the factory of all kinds of regional and religious cleavages and patron–client relationships.

The high levels of absenteeism and labour turnover have marked effects on the performance of the factories. In the ongoing Algerian debate on the relative failures of the ambitious industrialization project, some authors argue that for historical and current reasons neither the logic of capital nor that of productive work have imposed themselves on Algerian society (Henni, 1984). Chikhi and El Kenz stress, in particular, that the instability of the population of workers and their refusal to fully integrate themselves into the factory and to adopt the values linked to the domain of industry are all symptoms of a lack of homogeneity and collective identity. *In this situation there can of course be action; but no action as a social and collective calculation keeping in mind the means, the goals and the reactions of other social actors, which would be action as part of a strategy* (p. 32). Thus, Chikhi and El Kenz consider it consequently more accurate to speak of workers' practices than strategies.

In the case of Basotho men working in the South African mines in the inter-war period, their actions most commonly take form and legitimation in an ethnic and community context. Yet Jeff Guy and Motlatsi Thabane, in Chapter 4 of this volume, 'Basotho miners, ethnicity and workers' strategies', claim that ethnicity in this case should be considered a workers' strategy. Operating under extremely repressive working conditions, these workers tried to ameliorate their situation in a way 'which indicates that [they] have projected their predicament into the future as a means of gaining some control over it', which means – according to the authors – that this was not just resistance but a strategy. Evidence drawn from the life stories of the miners, collected by Thabane in an extensive oral history project on migrant workers from Lesotho, suggests that there is 'one overwhelming "strategy" . . . [which] is based on the sense of ethnic commonality . . . of being a worker amongst other workers from the same background, with a shared history and language; of coming from a country which resisted the attacks of the Boers and

which had not been incorporated into the Union of South Africa . . .'
(pp. 81–2). In the South African situation there were alternative
strategies – the authors name the broad-based nationalism of the
African National Congress, the unity in class struggle called for by
trade unionists and communists, as well as the liberal demand for
political equality – which all were influential at times. However, the
'ethnic identity has remained a powerful force coming time and again
to the fore during crisis and struggle' (p. 83).

The point here is that ethnic identity, which in the South African
context is commonly understood as management's device to divide
and rule over miners, is shown in Guy and Thabane's analysis also to
have been used by workers *against* management. The authors do not
deny that ethnicity is manipulated by management and the state, but
they stress the more hidden use of ethnicity by the workers for their
own purposes in the compounds and in the workplace. The Basotho
miners had a specific role in the labour process of shaft-sinking which
gives the issue of ethnic identity a basis in the workplace and the
labour process. It is hence not 'beyond the arena of production' and it
can therefore not be claimed in this case, as in Michael Burawoy's
(1985:87) critique of E. P. Thompson: that tradition and community
as bastions of resistance have mostly been 'closely bound up with
threats to production and to the control exercised by the direct
producer'.

This is clearly not the case here: as described in Chapter 4, the use
of the community organization and identity does not have any
particular connection either to threats to production or to control
exercised by direct producers. On the contrary, the Basotho men are
involved in an expanding production, where their control over one
particularly difficult part of the production process is not questioned
during the period under study. But, certainly, the lines between ethnic
identity, used as a workers' strategy at the workplace, or as a
community strategy in the compound, or even as an individual
strategy, are not easily drawn; as shown in the remarkable life-story
of the miner Rantao, which concludes Thabane and Guy's essay.

Fiona Wilson's contribution to this book, 'Day-to-day struggles in
Mexican workshop production', analyses workers' actions in a way
which calls into question the distinction between strategies and
practices and their opposition. We are here learning about the
incorporation of a mostly, but not only, female labour force into
small-scale textile industry and the efforts undertaken by the workers
to improve their situation. The context is a hitherto predominantly

agrarian region where male emigration has become extensive. The chapter follows the evolution of work relations from an early period with no or simple machinery, characterized by family-like relationships between workers and workshop owners, to later, more capital-intensive production, characterized by a slow evolution towards less family-like, more Taylorist, work relations. To these changes in work relations and in use of machinery correspond also changes in the payment system, which in turn intervenes in determining the forms of action chosen by the workers.

With the exception of one large and unsuccessful strike, the actions recorded and analysed in Chapter 3 all involve one workshop, and sometimes one individual. However, by a careful account of the context, each action, even by one individual, is shown to have its roots in the evolution of the labour market, in the technological conditions, and in the process of incorporation of labour. We also see how such action *affects all these domains*. To each step in the incorporation of labour correspond concrete limits on the management's handling of the labour force; and the transgression of those limits is under all the different circumstances met with resistance. The forms taken by the resistance point not only to the social limits of the prevailing relations of production, but also in the direction of possible change. The workers who take up the fight for job security, the application of the legal minimum wage or for health insurance not only set examples to others, they also create precedence. The issues may be dealt with in a way that is positive or negative for the worker, they may be addressed implicitly or explicitly, but the issues are there. In this sense the actions may have a strategic importance, even when undertaken by an individual, outside the scope of a collective social project, and independently of the individual's understanding of his or her own action.

The diffused character of industrialization in this rural Mexican setting with its exclusive reliance on the local labour market, gives a unique opportunity to highlight a complex relationship between social relations in general, with their distinctive gender character, relations at the workplace, technology, wage relations and the forms of resistance. This is done with a preciseness and concreteness which is rarely attainable in studies of large urban-based industry which recruit labour from a wide area. The freshness perhaps also comes from the fact that most workers are women. Established ideology and history have less to say about what resistance is to be expected from unorganized female workers. Consequently there are probably also fewer preconceptions and rationalizations among the workers themselves, as well as among direct or indirect observers.

SPECIFICITIES OF RECENT INDUSTRIALIZATION

Third-world industrial production still represents a small share of the global total. The relative increase of its share during the 1960s and 1970s fostered a great number of studies on industrialization among researchers concerned with development issues. The results of this research constitute a necessary foundation for the study of third-world labour. But undue generalizations on the basis of knowledge about labour in one type of industry, which for a moment seemed to dominate third-world countries, have also seriously limited the debates and the understanding of third-world industrial labour. It is clear, for instance, that the debate concerning industrial wage-labour as a 'labour aristocracy' referred mainly to import-substituting industries with state subsidies and protection, and sometimes to rent-generating extractive industries for export. Similarly, the argument on the over-exploitation of labour referred to export-oriented industrialization within or outside free trade zones. In some cases it may well be reasonable to stress that some layers of industrial workers are relatively privileged as compared to other parts of the population, or that a mostly female workforce employed in free trade zones has a heavy workload. The error came when such cases were understood as a trend, even the decisive trend, in third-world labour generally. As stated by several authors recently, the process of industrialization in the third world is diverse and so cannot be reduced to either the effects of some strategic decision by the transnational corporations or to the effects of the implementation of some political strategy for industrialization (see for example Petras and Engbarth, 1988).

The realization that no one single pattern of industrialization can be deduced either from the development of the world market, or from the inherent structures and needs of economies in transition, has stimulated efforts to develop a more systematic typology of industrialization processes. An ambitious effort to link types of labour market and types of industrialization has been proposed by a group of Danish researchers (Björkman, Lauridsen, Secher-Marcussen, 1988). The distinctions between simple and advanced import-substitution, and between simple and advanced export-oriented industrialization are nothing new. The interest in their typology, however, lies in the description of the labour market as both a constraint on and an effect of the different types of industrialization, an aspect which will be taken into consideration more thoroughly in the next section. Their approach, like the common distinction between import-substituting and export-oriented industrialization, is situated at the level of a national system of accumulation and reproduction.

In contrast, the specificities of recent industrialization are approached from a global perspective in Beverly Silver's concluding contribution to this volume, 'World-scale patterns of labour–capital conflict'. The squeeze on profits, as a result of labour militancy, experienced first by the United States, then by Western European, and finally by Japanese corporate capital, led to an increase of industrial investments in third-world countries, mostly in the 'semi-periphery', to use Silver's concept. The wave of new investments included simple as well as advanced export-oriented industrialization (the former being more labour- and the latter more capital-intensive), and also, although this is not discussed in Silver's chapter, import-substituting industry. The general drive behind those investments lay in the search for cheaper labour, and to this, as we know from other sources, could be added access to protected markets (see e.g. Humphrey, 1982).

To Silver, labour movements cannot be understood if not related to processes in the capitalist world economy as a whole. In this way she proposes a holistic approach, which Björkman, Lauridsen and Secher-Marcussen accuse labour studies in general of lacking. Silver reports on patterns of labour unrest in the world, contrasting the two periods of British and US hegemony, and analysing the reasons for an increasing unrest in the first period, the constant high level of unrest in the second, the high politicization in the first and the often non- or anti-organizational character of the unrest in the second period. Unlike writers concerned with the 'new international division of labour', Silver does not situate the causes of industrial investment in third-world countries in the strategic calculations of transnational management. Instead, she situates them in the social and economic effects of the organization of the industrial labour and production process *and* the constant efforts by the workers to ameliorate their situation in forms given by technical and social conjunctures.

The cases of industrialization treated in this book differ widely in timing and character: the mining industry in which the Basotho workers in Guy and Thabane's chapter are involved does not fit into the fourfold typology mentioned earlier. Within Silver's approach it has its time and its logic in the period of British hegemony when industrial production was still concentrated in central capitalist countries in which, however, the need for raw materials resulted in the bringing forward, mostly by coercion, of a labour force in mining and on plantations in some third-world countries.

The two Nigerian cases, with their mixed foreign and national ownership, would in the above typology be considered to be a relatively simple type of import substitution. This is most clearly so in the case of the cars produced at Steyr, which Yusuf Bangura takes up in Chapter 7: 'Steyr-Nigeria: the recession and workers' struggles in the vehicle assembly plant'. The labour process, however, is relatively mechanized, requiring a certain stability of labour in order to maintain the flow of production so as not to immobilize expensive machinery. This is also the case in respect of the more advanced of the textile plants discussed by Andræ and Beckman in the preceding chapter, 'Textile unions and industrial crisis in Nigeria: labour structure, organization and strategies'. This can be part of the explanation for the relatively institutionalized wage-labour relation existing at the factories under study, which also reflects an earlier history of labour and trade union militancy. The two Nigerian case studies are made at the particular point when industry is hit by a general economic crisis induced by the steep fall of oil prices in the beginning of the 1980s and the country experiences deindustrialization: what is at stake is the extent to which workers protect themselves against the recession, and uphold the institutionalized wage-labour relation.

The two Algerian industries under study in the chapter by Chikhi and El Kenz, just like the Nigerian ones, are in the first place oriented towards the internal market. Both the steel industry and the truck assembly factory must be considered more advanced. In the case of the latter, the local value added is much higher than in the Nigerian plant. Both Algerian factories are highly mechanized, with work on the line, in the case of the truck industry, requiring a certain stability of labour if actual production is to attain potential outputs. During the periods covered by the Algerian study – that is up to the mid-1980s – this was clearly lacking. It must be stressed in this context that the Algerian and the Nigerian economies should be distinguished from the other cases studied in this book because of the formidable impact of oil rent; i.e. the state controlled revenue from oil export. In

Algeria this gave room for ambitious heavy industrialization in the name of national independence and, in Nigeria, wide opportunities to local and foreign investment based on imported raw materials and with a heavy bias in favour of upper middle class consumption goods. In both countries a fall in oil prices and general instability of the oil market have put an end to this form of capital accumulation and reproduction.

The textile workshops in Mexico studied by Fiona Wilson are mostly oriented towards the internal market but, without following up the intricacies of commercialization, this cannot be clearly proved; and they also raise the question of whether this really matters. Some production is directed to the local market but most is sent off for urban consumption, inside or outside Mexico. The question here is whether the two parts of the capital–labour relation – that is production relations (workplace conditions and control of labour) and exchange relations (wage conditions and recruitment) will be any different if production is geared towards the internal or external markets. If, as is probable, the production goes mainly to the former, then will there be definite differences in capital–labour relations as compared to those in Tunisia, Egypt or Southeast Asia or for that matter other Mexican industries where production is sold abroad?

PROLETARIANIZATION AND WORKING CLASS FORMATION

According to the model formalized by Björkman, Lauridsen and Secher-Marcussen (1988: 99), there is a difference between import-substituting and export-oriented industrialization as regards the labour–capital relationship. In the latter, the focus is on the maintenance of very low labour costs as this is the basis for successful competition on the world market. Hence costs per production unit are kept low by extraction of absolute surplus value, long working days and intensification of work. This in turn implies that the labour force can often not sustain the effort for a long period and is regularly replaced with new labour. In the case of advanced export-industrialization, the higher capital-intensity of production can induce a certain scarcity of labour with specific skills and make way for increases in real wage and open up a labour market situation which is 'not basically different from the one which

prevailed in Western countries at an early stage of their industrialization' (p. 77).
When it comes to import-substitution things are much less clear.
Simple import-substitution industrialization produces 'a high degree
of variability' (p 75) in capital–labour relations, while in the case of
advanced import-substitution it is clear that relative surplus-value
production is considered dominant and consequently a continuous
running of the production process is necessary. But 'it is not possible
to specify actual mechanisms introduced to adapt labour to the
production line, for these rather reflect the actual stage of class
struggle and its historical origin'. In any type of industrialization,
however, they argue that 'international capital will have a disproportionate influence on the formation of the labour market in the
sense that it shapes the technological conditions of production in
decisive and important branches, thus influencing the capital–labour
relation which obtains in locally owned enterprises' (p. 69). This is
even more so when integrated production processes are transplanted
to the third world, as the technological adaptation in this case is
minimal.

The assumption of this approach is clearly that state and capital
(national and/or international) have strategies that aim at ensuring
the further reproduction of capital and the social system, strategies
which have as their framework a national mode of accumulation and
as their condition the state of the world market and the competition
which takes place within it. Those strategies are at the same time the
condition for and the complement to labour strategies, which, as the
authors stress, can lead to the break-down of the process of
industrialization.

The cases treated in this book raise serious questions about the
usefulness of the distinctions between the national and international
as units of analysis and about the assumed oneness of strategies.
Nowhere is this more clear than in Chapter 7, by Bangura, showing
how, from the very beginning, international lobbies with commercial
interests and national bourgeois groups with consumptionist interests,
behind a weak pretension of national development and industrialization, managed to push the military in power in Nigeria at that time
into a series of dubious vehicle assembly projects. The fall in the oil
prices, which is the immediate background for the acute crisis of the
industry, should not be allowed to conceal the weak and contradictory position taken by both capital owners and the state. In the case
of the textile industry, studied by Andræ and Beckman, Nigerian

production could not compete with textiles produced in Asia on an open market; but state authorities were incapable of stopping smuggling and thereby endangered the local market. Neither did they provide sufficient incentives for local production of raw materials which would have made the industry less dependent on availability of foreign exchange from highly unpredictable oil incomes to pay for such imports (see also Andræ and Beckman, 1987).

This is not to say that the Nigerian state or bourgeoisie, or for that matter the Algerian one, is merely inefficient or short-sighted, but rather to suggest in Balibar's words (1988: 230) that: 'there is no "capitalist class" *strictu senso*, only different types of capitalists'. He continues by claiming that those different types of capitalists form a class 'only at the condition that they tend to unite with other social groups seemingly exterior to the "fundamental social relation": intellectuals, civil servants, land owners etc.' The issue of the unification of a capitalist class and of its conditions clearly goes beyond the scope of this chapter. What matters here is that proletarianization presupposes the intervention of both capitalists and the state, but it cannot be assumed that there is any unified strategy underlying their intervention. We cannot even assume that there is on the side of capital and the state any pressure for unification and elaboration of a unified strategy. Historically it would seem, on the contrary, as if unification of the labour market and the labour relation is hardly the result of a dominating international production process with its concomitant strategy being introduced, but predominantly of two processes on the side of labour; one being trade union pressure for homogenization, the other being labour's own pressure in periods of labour shortage.

State intervention *can* also have a unifying effect whether pushed by labour demands or not. No hasty conclusions can, however, be drawn as to the role of labour unification in the state's policy. In Chapter 8 by Bosco Parra, 'Trade unions and democracy – Chile in the 1980s' – which has at its prime problematic the obstacles for unity among the labouring and the poor in general, and the elaboration of a materially based strategy to defeat dictatorship and uphold democracy – there is an illustration of this.

In Chile, in a period when liberal economics dominated at the level of state policy, a contrary principle having its origin in the social consensus surrounding the very existense of the Chilean nation state gave the state some responsibility to relieve 'extreme poverty'. Together with the wish to control unemployed youth, this made the

Pinochet regime launch local labour programmes for the unemployed. These programmes had as an (unintended) result that for the first time since the 1920s it became possible for unemployed to join the trade unions, which had been prohibited by law. While employment under the labour programme was only temporary it was still considered by the authorities to be a sufficient foundation for membership of trade unions.

Although the Chilean case shows a paradoxical push for unification, it cannot, as already stated, be taken for granted that there exists any capitalist or state strategy with this goal. As Michael Burawoy has convincingly shown in his book, *The Politics of Production* (1985), different relations in production and different forms for recruitment – that is, labour market conditions – can coexist in the same country, even in the same region, and even in a single industrial branch. This is also clearly shown in the comparison made by Andræ and Beckman of the two Nigerian towns of Kano and Kaduna, the first having a textile industry controlled by local capital and the second one dominated by state ownership and transnationals. In the older town of Kano, with a long tradition of handicraft textile production, recruitment of labour and relations in production tends to keep some of their pre-industrial characteristics, while the industry in the colonial town of Kaduna tends to recruit in more modern forms and to implement a more formal labour relation to their often recently urbanized labour force. This has left more space for trade unions in Kaduna than in Kano, which, as the authors suggest, is also an effect of the greater number of workers employed in each factory in Kaduna and the pattern of ownership.

At the level of capital and state there are thus several strategies concerning the forms of exploiting, dominating and keeping up the competition and insecurity within the labour force. The strategies not only compete but sometimes contradict each other. They can only be explained when confronted with the *strategies, elements of strategies or practices developed by the people undergoing proletarianization.* And this is what all the contributions to this book are about, from the individual Mexican woman who goes to court to get what she considers that her employer owes her; to the young automobile workers in Rouiba who constantly go slow, frustrated as they are by the lack of prospects offered by the work on the line as compared to the experience of the first generation of Algerian industrial workers and who do not have any alternative; from the anger expressed by Bauchi automobile workers when they feel cheated and walk the director of the company out of the factory; to the textile workers who choose to go back or not to go back to agriculture when employment opportunities get scarce in Kaduna and who choose to participate or not to participate in street fighting at a time when the company wants to pay only half salaries. The role of the trade unions in the broadening and deepening Chilean opposition to dictatorship, and the migrating Basotho mine workers' pressure for better pay, as well as the world-wide search for the best possible employment possibilities by the Calabrian peasants, all constitute not only pieces of knowledge but also part of this contradictory process.

Without tapping further the richness of the individual accounts in this respect, one aspect – which is present in all but one chapter and at the centre of the analysis by Giovanni Arrighi and Fortunata Piselli on 'Feuds, class struggles and labour migration in Calabria' – warrants special mention, this aspect being labour migration.

Not just any urbanization or rural exodus, but *labour migration* is in fact a background factor in the whole book. This may be at the point of emigration, as in the Mexican case, where male migrants have left women behind with the economic necessity and the social possibility to earn some cash and where some of the workshops have been set up by returning migrants. It may also be at the point of immigration, where a large part of the workers have recently arrived. In the case of El Hadjar we meet former peasants who once emigrated to France and now return, although not back to their original village or town. Even in the case of Kano, with its long urban and textile tradition, part of the workers come from other places in the country, having left farming to which they will only return as a last resort. Migrating, long-term, short-term, long distance, short distance, as a last resort or as a real alternative; returning 'home' as something normal and planned or as a final option when employment opportunities dry up or are too badly paid, seasonal migration as a permanent solution . . . Labour migration cannot be reduced to the one aspect stressed by Meillassoux; that is the exploitation of the domestic and agricultural work done by the women and old folks left behind in order to allow for the payment of wages to migrant labour below the costs of reproduction. While this has certainly been an important feature of some migration experiences – for example in colonial Africa – this was not a stable model in most cases (see Brandell, 1987). Families have followed migrants and migration has been used to accumulate in order to invest in agriculture or other activities at the point of origin.

Thanks to the comparative approach chosen and to the long time-span of their study, Arrighi and Piselli in Chapter 5 offer an analysis of labour migration understood as a series of different strategies depending on the potentials of the social group of origin. This in turn depends on the whole social outcome of the struggle over rural and agrarian structures, the use of possibilities offered by demand for industrial labour in regions far away (USA and Latin America) and, at a later point, by the demand for unskilled and semi-skilled labour in the rapid industrialization of northern Italy after the Second World War. The whole process has led to the formation of a wage-labour force in a peripheral environment, over decades of depeasantization and proletarianization, where migration not only was a 'substitute for and a complement of social conflict in shaping the developmental processes' (p. 138) but also 'provided the individuals who were clever enough or lucky enough or generationally fortunate to migrate at the right time with a way out of peripheralization. In addition, it changed the scale and the terrain of social conflict, thereby creating the conditions for successful redistributive struggles' (p. 139).

The big struggles at the end of the 1960s in the factories in northern Italy were dominated by the immigrant workers on the line. At the same time, upheavals in Calabria itself precipitated heavy transfers of financial means to the 'underdeveloped' southern regions. As stressed by the two authors the Italian situation is peculiar in that the south is a periphery of the 'world economy', but not the north. Latin American, Asian and African migrants have to cross borders to come to the center. The element of migration in the other studies of this book relates also to migration from one periphery to another perhaps somewhat less peripheral region. Migration however stands out as a central feature in the formation of a wage-labour force and as a strategy which both substitutes for and complements social conflict in most third-world countries.

THE CENTRALITY OF LABOUR

It remains to justify the importance given to industrial labour in this book, taking up the challenge evoked in the opening paragraphs. There I argued that it is unlikely that the industrial labour force, with some exceptions, will ever comprise the same relative share of the active population as it once did in the now highly industrialized countries. Several authors have gone further, stressing that the social movements which exist and have an impact in the South are rarely labour movements, but more often movements among youth and slum dwellers. In the African context, for instance, René Galissot (1983) and Michaela von Freyhold (1987) have insisted on theoretical and political grounds that any transformation of the *status quo* is likely to come from broader movements, not from the working class *per se*. Some proponents of the new international labour studies point in the same direction by broadening the concept of labour into that of the labouring poor and by stressing the importance of domination in terms of ethnicity and gender as distinct from the classical Marxist concept of exploitation. The long series of urban riots in the 1980s, protesting against austerity measures and sometimes expressing demands for democratization, cannot but support this view.

The contributors to this book certainly do not all take the same stand on the issue of the centrality of labour, although most have chosen it as the focus of their research. Nor do the members of the research group, AKUT, which organized the seminars where the chapters were initially presented, have any unified theoretical or political positions on this issue. All that will be done here is to advance some arguments for further debate in favour of the centrality of a perspective with a focus on industrial wage labour.

The questioning of the centrality of labour in general and industrial labour in particular often has as its explicit or implicit point of departure a rejection of a certain brand of marxist orthodoxy, which everywhere, always, and despite everything is waiting for a class-conscious proletariat to finally arrive at the centre of the scene and fulfil its historical mission. Our own point of departure is quite different.

Let us remind ourselves again that not only Marxism but also social science in general have given labour, and most commonly industrial wage labour, this central role in theories of modern society. In 1963, the now well-known French sociologist Pierre Bourdieu (1963: 312) wrote in the context of his great sociological study of labour and workers in colonial Algeria: 'With permanent employment and a regular wage a rational time-conscious mind can be formed and evaluations and ambitions be organized in function of a life plan. It is then, and only then, that a revolutionary attitude will replace the evasion into dreams or fatalist resignation'. 'Revolutionary' in this context should be understood as contrary to tradition; that is, a modern rational mind open to change, a prerequisite for development and progress. Such a blunt statement, for what it says and what it implies, would hardly be made now, especially not after the insistence in the 1970s on wage workers' alienation and the insistence in the 1980s on values and cultural categories as an explanation for resistance as well as for openness to change.

So what are today's more prudent arguments for 'bringing the workers back in' (Burawoy, 1985)? Roger Southall, in his introduction to the anthology, *Trade Unions and the New Industrialization of the Third World*, suggests that 'Because so many states [in third-world countries] lack legitimacy and stability, unions commonly supersede the political parties and represent the most significant bloc of social forces after the military. Precisely because workers are concentrated in a few industrial sectors and are conscious of their potential, they can have much greater impact than did similar groups in industrial countries during the period of early industrialization' (Southall, 1988b: 29). Here, what other authors consider to be a weakness, is turned into a force in a society where few other cohesive groups are found. For Björkman, Lauridsen and Secher-Marcussen (1988: 69) the idea that even small segments of society can have great importance is linked to the international domination of capital: 'the internationalisation of capital, regardless of its specific form, whether via complex or fragmented plants, makes a disproportionate impact upon the local labour market structure . . . in the sense that it shapes the technological conditions of production in decisive and important branches, thus influencing the capital–labour relation which obtains in locally owned enterprises'.

The reach and implications of such defence of the labour centrality thesis remain to be explored. It could be argued, for instance, that those who question the centrality of labour do not deny that it can form the basis for an interest group or for corporate resistance against other social forces and the state. What they may suggest, however, is that labour lacks the capacity to supersede other divisions that characterize third-world societies, including those based on regional, ethnic, cultural, gender and religious cleavages in a general context of heavy underemployment. This is precisely what Ronaldo Munck (1988) tries to clarify in his recent introduction to international labour studies.

Munck (1988: 212), although wanting to give due space to other elements of oppression, makes a strong case in favour of the centrality of labour: 'While rejecting "a proletarian messianism" which invests the industrial working class with an impossible duty, we need not reject the centrality of social class'. He recognizes the importance of the orientation in radical social analysis in recent years towards other forms of oppression, but '[E]conomic, racial, sexual and national oppression are all seen as equivalent in this new radical pluralism. An exploitation-centred concept of class need not neglect other forms of domination. It must, however, retain explanatory priority in our social and historical analysis if we are not to slip into subjectivism'. And he continues 'The working class, subject to capitalist exploitation, remains at the centre of the capitalist mode of production and thus forms the core of any resistance to it and the only agent which bears an alternative mode of social organization based on cooperation within it'.

Despite Munck's otherwise incisive and open-minded review his defence of labour on this point remains problematic. What is subjectivism in this context and what is its problem? The allegation that to abandon the priority of exploitation implies a slip into subjectivism is no argument outside an internal debate, as long as it has not been made clear why and how subjectivism implies the end of social and historical analysis. Also the second assertion is more of a statement than an argument: it is simply not clear why the kind of relations to which workers are submitted in the capitalist labour process forebodes an alternative social organization based on cooperation. Munck seeks to bolster his position by quoting Erik Olin Wright who notes: '. . . the shift to a domination-centred concept of class weakens the link between the analysis of class location and the analysis of objective interests . . . domination-centred concepts of class tend to slide into the "multiple oppressions" approach to understanding societies'. But the problem remains: the fact that new radical analysis is moving away from some orthodox Marxist positions does not mean that it is wrong.

Exploitation exists of course; if not there would be no accumulation. But does exploitation and its forms constitute organizing principles in societies all over the world? Common economic interests among groups can be articulated but are they necessarily decisive when compared to other types of interests? Should status and ideology, dear to Max Weber, necessarily be subordinated to class?

In an important contribution addressing this very debate, Etienne Balibar (1988) has put his finger on a couple of weaknesses in current class analysis, weaknesses which have their origin in Marx's own writing. Proletarianization, which is the process at the basis of the very idea of the creation of a working class at the level of economics and of a proletariat at the level of politics, has in fact three different aspects, or *moments*, in Balibar's French. First, there is the aspect of *exploitation*, in its commercial form; that is, the creation and the appropriation of surplus, the difference between 'necessary work' (according to historically given conditions for the reproduction of labour force) and surplus work. This aspect requires at the same time a stable legal form (a 'contract') *and* a permanent balance of forces involving technological constraints, coalitions and state interventions. The second aspect is *domination*; that is, the social relation established in the very process of production, going from formal to real subordination of labour through the processes of mechanization, fragmentation, division of labour and the social institutions 'adapting' labour or resisting (the family, the school system and so on). And third, the final aspect is the *insecurity* or the *competition* among workers: unemployment, underemployment, a tendency countered by trade union organization and by employers' need for a stable labour force but never fully eradicated. Balibar argues convincingly that these three aspects have been united by Marx and by marxists in a kind of an 'ideal-type' process of proletarianization, in theory a necessary counterpart to the unity of the valorization of capital. But the price for this has been quite questionable and speculative assumptions about history.

Instead, says Balibar, the empirically observed divergences (*décalages*) and sometimes contradictions between the different aspects of proletarianization should be understood not as temporary but as part of the concrete conditions of historical capitalism. These conclusions can be corroborated by the astonishing diversity of what Michael Burawoy (1985) calls 'factory regimes' in his already quoted broad historical comparison of social relations in relatively similar industries. So what we are witnessing in history, according to Balibar (1988: 225), is not any predetermined sequences of forms, but a combination (*un jeu* – a play) of *antagonistic strategies*, strategies of exploitation and domination and strategies of resistance, departing all the time from a new point as an effect of their previous impact, notably at the institutional level. At this point 'the concepts of class and of class struggle denote . . . a process of transformation without preestablished end, which would in other words correspond primarily to a permanent transformation of the identity of social classes'.

Leaving aside the issue of bourgeois and/or capitalist strategies, the points which need to be clarified here are, first, the issue of resistance, second the question of the centrality of exploitation as compared to diverse forms of domination, which is Munck's problem, and third the issue of the constitution of a working class.

Resistance is in fact a problematic concept: once we leave behind the idea that proletarian resistance necessarily prefigures the classless socialist society we have no simple yardstick for measuring the significance of a particular expression of resistance. The Mexican textile workers studied by Fiona Wilson developed a resistance which aimed at the establishment of a clear contract regulating the exploitation of their work, and extending the regulating intervention of the state in the industry. In the passage from the domestic to the capitalized workshop this implies that resistance in this case calls into question a form of domination based on the institution of the patriarchal family. The Basotho miners, interviewed by Guy and Thabane, resisted insecurity and competition among workers by their use of ethnic cohesion, which at the same time was part of the pattern of domination in the South African mines. The Algerian workers in state-owned enterprises, in a context where exploitation as well as competition/insecurity are heavily state-regulated – at least until the 1980s' decentralization of Algerian industry – resisted so as to assert their autonomy *vis-à-vis* the efforts by the state to establish domination in a context which up to 1989 was described as 'socialist development'. Both the Algerian and Italian cases demonstrate the deep cleavages between workers and workers' organizations, highlighting an issue to which we will come back; that is, the constant reconstitution of the working class. The resistance of the Nigerian car and textile workers is predominantly oriented to limit their insecurity and sustain the provisions of the labour contract in spite of the recession and the serious doubts cast on the long-term viability of the industries, as discussed in Bangura's contribution. The comparison between the two cities of Kano and Kaduna, undertaken by Andræ and Beckman, hints at a higher degree of autonomy towards the whole process of proletarianization among the workers in Kano, which does not mean that they were not exploited and dominated in non-wage forms outside the factory as well.

Each in their own way, these studies throw light on both the 'reactive' and productive aspects of resistance, or in other words their conserving and transgressing dimensions. It is then possible for analytic purposes to relate the specific case of resistance quite firmly to one of the three aspects (exploitation, domination, insecurity) which constitute proletarianization, and subsequently point at its more general socio-economic and political impact by putting it into the framework of other strategies evolving in the whole process of proletarianization.

Now, what about the relationship between the three aspects as they evolve in the process of proletarianization and other forms of domination and oppression, gender, race, cultural or generational? What about these 'other contradictions' and the risk of 'sliding into a "multiple oppression" approach to understanding societies', as Erik Olin Wright put it? There is no reason to pretend that racism or in some cultures oppression of 'the other gender' are less universal than exploitation and domination in the form taken by the process of proletarianization. There is probably no reason either to maintain as an axiom that work is the 'essence' of human beings and of social relations, the fundamental ground for social antagonisms. But, as is shown with particular relevance in the contribution by Fiona Wilson for gender oppression, and by Guy and Thabane for ethnic oppression, proletarianization and the division of labour are constantly interfering with and influencing other forms of oppression and antagonism without making them less universal.

This would not mean much if proletarianization, wage work and the division of labour were limited phenomena in society. This is not the case, however, not even in third-world societies subjected to the limits set by the international economy on the development of coherent capitalist strategies and state functions. Although 'islands in seas of petty commodity production' as Andræ and Beckman put it, factories in third-world countries constitute the dynamic factor if not in the economy then in the constitution of society and state: the focal point of antagonisms. This is because industry and industrial production represent the yardstick for the whole idea of economic growth, modernity and welfare which during the last decades has constituted the dominant frame of reference and nurtured the rhetorics of social and political forces and the state. Here we have the one sector in the productive system which in principle links the international system and its norms (inputs in machinery, capital and devices for management, export markets) with the formation of economic and social actors inside the national frame. Here it is possible to compare efficiency and success among different national contexts regardless of weather and environmental conditions and regardless of history and tradition, as industry at a superficial level is the same all over the world. Here is the meeting point of the 'traditional' and the 'modern', the projects of the future and the possible scapegoats for shortcomings, not only for individual enterprise but for the whole national economy and project.

The example of Algeria is illustrative here even in a longer historical perspective than that covered by Chikhi and El Kenz. At independence, a limited and short-lived experience of workers' self-management in industries was turned at the ideological level into the very novelty of Algerian socialism. Some 25 years later workers' refusal of lay-offs in the context of the restructuring of an inefficient industry have been described as backward, reactionary and throwing into question the very survival of the national economy. Although of limited economic importance in the short run, state regulation of self-management in 1963 and the violent establishment in 1989 of insecurity in employment become central issues in an ongoing constitution of social forces, strategies, ideologies, and their canalization at the level of the state into legitimate representation of the nation and its future. Over and over again even limited cases of resistance against one or another aspect of proletarianization evoke the fundamental issues of the linkage between economic growth and social organization, between the very basis of the nation-state and the political forces evolving within its frontiers.

But this precludes any determinism when it comes to the constitution of working classes. On the contrary these are made up of a multitude of individuals living under different and contradictory constraints and having mutually irreducible interests. Working class, labour movement, and workers' organization are not equivalents. They unify, mobilize, and institutionalize on the basis of one or more, but not all, aspects of workers' interests. They regroup and reconstitute themselves; new divisions occur and new organizations are created, without ever achieving complete representativity. This is why it is so important to observe what sometimes in this book is called *workers' practices*; this is where the 'new international labour studies' offer an important contribution. Some of those practices are abandoned while others provide an input into a labour movement, to strategies of organization which necessarily evolve in confrontation and coalition with other social movements or organizations and with the state.

To analyse unification and division, constitution and reconstitution presupposes knowledge of the parts as well as about the whole. Most of the chapters in this book focus on one factory or one branch of industry. The issues of the unification of a working class, the relationship between this unification and the state, and a possible 'reconstruction' of the state are explicitly addressed by Bangura and are at the centre of Parra's contribution. The latter argues that for specific historical reasons the trade union movement in Chile has a clear and recognized interest in democracy: parliamentary democracy has meant in the Chilean case defence of trade union rights and improvements of workers' conditions (labour legislation, minimum wage and so on). This pro-democratic bias is not necessarily shared by bourgeois groups whose interests have sometimes been better served by dictatorship, or by other popular forces which have received few benefits from democracy and are consequently predisposed in favour of a counter-dictatorship. The problematics of Parra's chapter revolve around the strategy to follow at the level of organization so as to unify large strata in a non-hegemonic way and how to reorganize state and society in order to make dictatorship impossible.

When Beverly Silver in this book places the contradiction between capital and labour at the level of the world economy – and does so in a very forceful and convincing manner – labour manifests itself in this context in workers' militancy, not as working classes with workers' organizations. The latter evolve only in the national context. Or, as Balibar (1988: 238) puts it, 'in spite of the fact that the world economy is the real "*champ de forces*" of class struggle, there is no world proletariat (except "in ideas"), even less than a world bourgeoisie'. What Silver shows is in fact a model of how successive strategies of corporate capital to counter the squeeze on profit lead to decreases and increases in workers' bargaining power in different parts of the world; all in the context of different types of production processes and depending on the relative importance of wage-labour in a specific society. Her alternative future scenarios point to an explosive mix of demands in the semi-peripheral countries ('from South Africa and Brazil to South Korea and Poland') where the bargaining power of industrial workers has increased with the extension of more mechanized industrial production and where industrial conflict 'is taking place in the context of demands for fundamental economic and political democratization' (p. 229).

So the *centrality of labour* as a category for the analysis of society and as a fundamental dividing and integrating factor in reality can still be claimed. At the international level it provides the key to the movement of productive capital and patterns of unrest. At the local level it cuts across and influences other social and cultural forms of organization and domination. And at the intermediate level of nation-states it is the central target in the ongoing constitution of social and political forces and strategies, while it is fundamental to the representation of the state as a nation-state being something else and more than national. And with this we are back to the beginning, the issue of practice and strategy.

Workers' social practices take place in a factory, in a town, but their strategies for survival and for social mobility do not necessarily stop there, or at national borders. National and even international mobility is one way to 'supplement for and complement social conflict'. At the same time, by crossing the border or moving to another town, workers' practices become an input in another labour process, another social conflict. Capital becomes transnational, trade, finance, and even production are moving and organized on a world-wide scale.

The national bourgeoisie, unified by a national state, and the national proletariats, unified by a labour movement – products of local institutions and of an identity built on self-representation of social practices – are now inescapably parts of history. In highly developed countries those classes are dissolving for a series of reasons, not least the effects of their own actions.

In third-world countries for another series of reasons these classes do not form in the way we expect from history: one reason for the bleak prospect for the development of national bourgeoisies and national proletariats in third-world countries lies in the apparent weakness of the national state because of the general penetration of international capital and not least international institutions. Another reason is the use and abuse of socialist ideology, which hints at some difficulties in presenting it as a unifying, progressive workers' ideology, even in third-world countries less touched by the criticism of Soviet-type development. Furthermore, socialism, in its initial communist or social-democratic versions, was an internationalist, anti-national ideology, while nationalism in most third-world countries is the ideology of the oppressed and as such not challenged, except perhaps in the context of a muslim community, the *umma*.

Still, the nation-state is there as an unavoidable centre for the regulation of proletarianization, unification of strategies, and bargaining on the basis of social antagonisms: the principal 'reducer of complexity' in modern history. The challenge to social science in this situation – but not only to social science – is not to reduce practices and strategies to those that can be easily recognized and have a clear impact on national or international structures, but rather to acknowledge that there are other contexts, while still not avoiding the ambiguous unity and identity of nation and class.

REFERENCES

G. Andræ and B. Beckman, *The Nigerian Raw Material Crisis and the Case of Textiles and Cotton.* Research report no. 80 (Uppsala: The Scandinavian Institute of African Studies, 1987).

G. Arrighi, 'Labour Supplies in Historical Perspective: a study of the proletarianization of the African peasantry in Rhodesia', in G. Arrighi and J. Saul, *Essays on the Political Economy of Africa* (New York: Monthly Review, 1973).

—— 'Fascism to Democratic Socialism: logic and limits of a transition', in G. Arrighi (ed.), *Semiperipheral Development. The Politics of Southern Europe in the Twentieth Century*˜ (Beverly Hills: Sage, 1985).

G. Arrighi and B. Silver, 'Labour Movements and Capital Migration: the United States and Western Europe in world-historical perspective', in C. Bergquist (ed.), *Labour in the Capitalist World-economy* (Beverly Hills: Sage, 1984).

E. Balibar, De la lutte des classes à la lutte sans classes?, in E. Balibar and I. Wallerstein, *Race, nation, classe. Les identités ambiguës* (Paris: Editions La Découverte, 1988).

M. Björkman, L. S. Lauridsen, and H. Secher Marcussen, 'Types of Industrialisation and the Capital–Labour Relation', in R. Southall (ed.), *Trade Unions and the New Industrialisation of the Third World* (London: Zed Books, 1988).

S. Bologna, 'Composizione di classe e teoria del partito alle origini del movimento consiliare', in S. Bologna, and A. Negri (eds), *Operai e stato, lotte operaie e riforme dello stato capitalistico tra rivoluzione d'Ottobre e New Deal* (Milano: Feltrinelli, 1972).

P. Bourdieu, *Travail et travailleurs en Algérie* (La Haye: Mouton, 1963).

I. Brandell, 'America Manna: femmes et migrations dans une perspective globale', *Studi Emigrazione/Etudes Migrations*, n. 85, March (1987).

——, *Tankar kring arbetarklassens framväxt i tredje världen* (Thoughts about the emergence of the working class in the third world), Akut series no. 22 (Uppsala: AKUT, 1982).

H. Braverman, *Labor and Monopoly Capital* (New York and London: Monthly Review, 1974).

M. Burawoy, *The Politics of Production. Factory Regimes under Capitalism and Socialism* (London: Verso, 1985).

S. Chikhi, 'Question ouvrière et rapports sociaux en Algérie'. Thesis in Sociology (Paris VII,1986, unpublished).

B. Coriat, *Science, Technique et Capital* (Paris: Seuil, 1976).

——, *L'atelier et le chronomètre* (Paris: Christian Bourgois, 1979).

A. El-Kenz, *Le complexe sidérurgique d'El Hadjar – une expérience industrielle en Algérie* (Paris: CNRS, 1987).

B. Feuer, 'Betweeen Dictatorship and Democracy – Bolivia 1966–69 and Peru 1978–80: a comparative study of mining unionism and national politics'. Working paper, the AKUT Seminar on Workers' strategies in Third World industrialization (Uppsala, October, 1987).

B. Freund, 'Labor and Labor History in Africa', *African Studies Review*, vol. 27, no. 2, June, 1984.

M. v. Freyhold, 'Labour Movements or Popular Struggles in Africa', *Review of African Political Economy* (1987) no. 39, September.

R. Galissot, 'Interrogation critique sur la centralité du mouvement ouvrier au Maghreb', in N. Sraïeb, (ed.) *Le Mouvement ouvier maghrebin* (Paris: CNRS, 1985).

A. Henni, *Etat, surplus et société en Algérie avant 1830* (Algers, 1984).

J. Humphrey, *Capitalist Control and Workers' Struggle in the Brazilian Auto Industry* (Princeton: Princeton University Press, 1982).

C. Meillassoux, *Maidens, Meal and Money – Capitalism and the Domestic Community* (Cambridge: Cambridge University Press, 1981, origin. in French).

R. Munck, *The New International Labour Studies: an Introduction* (London and New Jersey: Zed Books, 1988).

C. Offe, 'Le travail comme catégorie de la sociologie', in *Les temps modernes*, 41e année, no. 466, mai (1985).

C. Palloix, and P. Zaffarian, *De la socialisation* (Paris: Maspéro, 1981).

J. Petras and D. Engbarth, 'Third World Industrialisation and Trade Union Struggles', in R. Southall (ed.), *Trade Unions and the New Industrialisation of the Third World* (London: Zed Books, 1988).

M. Piore, *Birds of Passage. Migrant Labor and Industrial Society* (New York: Cambridge University Press, 1980).

Quaderni Rossi, periodical, Istituto Rodolfo Morandi, Milano 1961–5.

K.-H. Roth, *Die 'andere' Arbeiterbewegung und die Entwicklung der kapitalistischen Repression von 1880 bis zur Gegenwart* (München: Trikont, 1974).

R. Southall, 'Introduction', in R. Southall (ed.), *Labour and Unions in Asia and Africa'* (London: Macmillan, 1988a).

—— 'Introduction', in R. Southall (ed.), *Trade Unions and the New Industrialisation of the Third World* (London: Zed Books, 1988).

G. Therborn, 'The Travail of Latin American Democracy', *New Left Review* (1979), n. 113–14, Jan–April.

E. P. Thompson, *The Making of the English Working Class* (London: Harmondsworth, 1968).

Map 1   Northern Algeria: Major Industrial Towns

30

2 Workers' Perceptions and Practices in Algeria: The Cases of the El Hadjar Iron and Steel Works and the Rouiba Industrial Motor Car Plant*

Said Chikhi and Ali El Kenz

The concept of *strategy* from which the focus of this volume emanates (and of which it occupies a central part), seems to us to be problematic enough to justify some preliminary epistemological and methodological reflections.

This concept, borrowed from military art and from mathematical game theory, has had a considerable success in sociology, particularly the sociology of organization and *ethno-méthodologie*. Today, in Algiers, as probably at other universities around the world, small circles of social science researchers often use the term 'strategy'. The state, the parties, but also groups, individuals, classes, all who can be identified as subjects of determined action, are said to have a strategy; the peasants, but also smaller groups within the class, like small or large peasants. The same goes for the workers, the middle class and so on. Even family strategies, women's strategies are mentioned. The sociologists, having lately discovered military art, have begun to see society as soldiers, a battlefield, where 'actors', tactics, means and ends are facing one another.

---

* This study summarizes a series of results of surveys carried out by us in the two industrial plants. In the study we used the method of participant observation as well as interviews and documentation – statistical and other – on the work collectives (cf. references).

In this use of military science, sometimes legitimate but often exaggerated, for our part we tend to see an epistemological acquisition by sociology, which can be partly explained by the theoretical weakness of the sociological scientific foundation, and in particular by the still very limited empirical understanding of its object.

The concept of strategy is certainly pertinent when referring to a battlefield, where armies, provided with staffs and troops, perform movements according to a plan, set up in advance; it is pertinent because it is used about equivalent historical subjects or social actors.

It is still justified when referring to the commercial or technological action plans of large enterprises, electoral projects of organized parties, or the social and economic struggles of powerful unions, with an organic social base of their own, solidly structured and carrying on stable activities.

Occasionally it is justified when referring to collective units (groups, classes, social entities) characterized by a strong sense of common identity, resulting from a common history. It is also a prerequisite for collective action of a strategic kind; that is, with a collective consciousness of means and ends, capable of elaborating and carrying out a *social calculus*.

These conditions are more or less present among the working classes in western societies today. As Gramsci has noted, this leads to a 'war of positions', where well defined social adversaries, who recognize themselves as such, face each other.

But there is nothing of the kind in third-world countries, certainly not in Algeria, where the working class, as we will show in more detail has hardly been constituted, and where it is still immature, with a weak sense of identity. Among other things, it is characterized by a weak 'identification with industrial work', by the frequent subordination of class solidarity to regional, ethnic and other inter-class solidarity, and by cultural fragmentation in society as a whole.

All these things certainly do not prevent actions, but they do prevent strategically and collectively conceived actions by workers, with a common *social calculus* where means, ends and reactions of adversaries and other protagonists are taken into consideration.

To call their actions a strategy seems to us to transfer a western matrix onto societies and classes which do not yet, or perhaps never will, fit into such a matrix. It would prevent us from understanding other practices, other forms of action and other social movements which are specific to the social structures of the third world.

These could, in Gramsci's words, be captured by the concept 'war of movement', in contrast to the 'war of positions', which characterizes social struggle in the capitalist societies of the west. Beyond the epistemological criticism of the concept of strategy, then, the whole problem area of social struggle and social movements in the third world emerges. More specifically, should workers' actions be understood through the western framework of analysis? Or would this involve the risk of transplanting preconceived ideas, perfectly valid there but not elsewhere? There is, for instance, the idea that working classes are 'social actors', which should be analysed as such, and think of themselves as such; and the idea that collective consciousness is determined principally by the relations of production. These issues, along with others in this collection, should be dealt with, as a precondition for comparative analysis of social struggles, or at least as theoretical reflections along with empirical field research.

THE GENERAL CONTEXT OF ALGERIA

The period 1970–83 was a very special one for the Algerian working class, its numbers were increasing from about 240 000 to almost 1 100 000 during the period. This spectacular increase of the labour force can also be illustrated by its share of the total employed population: from 13 per cent in 1969 to over 29 per cent in 1983.

These increasing numbers are concentrated mostly in heavy industry. The fundamental objective of the state in the 1970s was to teach Algerian workers how to mould, forge, enchase and work complex parts. Thus the steel industry saw its numbers grow from 13 800 in 1973 to 38 000 ten years later. Sonacome (*Société Nationale de Constructions Mécaniques*) tripled its numbers in only seven years (1973–80), while the motor car industry doubled its numbers between 1976 and 1986, from 4415 to 9830.

Economic and social changes in Algerian society are grafted onto a backcloth of considerable development of the nation's workers. Urbanization and rural exodus, the generalization of schooling, the growth of wage labour, the emigration and the 'western' pattern of consumption of the elites, provoked an inexorable loss of symbolic values of the traditional universe and doomed local patterns and the 'village' hierarchy of values to gradual extinction.

The traditional universe was shaken furthermore by the rapid turnover of labour, evident from the second half of the 1970s and onwards. The motor car plant at Rouiba lost between 1200 and 1500 people every year and was forced, between 1976 and 1986, to recruit over 17 200 workers, to keep only 5400 in the end. Between 1974 and 1983 this plant trained 6100 qualified workers, or three times the needs of the company, but still, these were not satisfied (cf. Chikhi, 1986b).

Again, the rapid turnover of personnel tends to disrupt the traditional universe. It facilitates exchange and mixing, at the same time modernizing the workers' behaviour (through confronting experiences, systems of remuneration and know-how). This immense turnover occurs against the background of incessant and rapid creation of new factories and extension of old ones. A continuous and considerable demand for new workers follows. This veritable turbulence in manpower also creates favourable conditions for the promotion of older workers to white-collar jobs, as a result of the rapid growth of the industrial workforce.

But the very marked increase of turnover implies also a profound destabilization of the workforce. It is perpetually making and unmaking itself, thus making very difficult the crystallization of know-how and accumulation of technical knowledge necessary for production. In fact, this turnover has prevented any experienced and qualified manual labour force from taking root, and hampers the formation of a modern working class for large-scale industry.

This is because the turnover touches not only the qualified, older and experienced workers, but to a growing extent also the great mass of rather young workers who lack experience of factory work. Data given by 21 firms in June 1984, in the course of an inquiry made by the Ministry of Heavy Industry, throw some light on this phenomenon: workers under 30 years of age make up nearly 70 per cent of those leaving; and over 87 per cent of those who have worked for less than five years belong to this mobile labour.

In the light of these figures, the question of the 'durability' of the working class status is raised. This means that a large part of Algeria's workers are only waiting for an opportunity to leave their original position. It means also that their identification with factory work is half-hearted and relative, and that the succession of generations of workers, which is already lacking in Algerian industry, will be difficult to achieve (Chikhi, 1987).

In view of all this, it does not seem as if the history of Algerian society and industry has led to the formation of a working class with an organic character. The strong presence of an unstable population, who are workers yet refuse to belong totally to the factory and to identify themselves with the values strictly linked to the industrial world, seems in fact to be a symptom of heterogeneity and absence of collective identity. Thus our task seems to be almost the opposite of an analysis of a working class identity with a proper, consistent and well-defined social strategy. On the contrary, our task is to see whether the Algerian workers with their behaviour and their perceptions of the productive sphere, of their own position in the technological and social division of labour, and of their social possibilities, all extremely fragmented and diverse, can be integrated into a world of labour or not.

THE CASE OF THE IRON AND STEEL WORKS

It took 20 years to complete the iron and steel works of El Hadjar (1964–84), today the largest industrial plant of Algeria with a staff of 18 000, including 15 000 workers, 2500 shop-stewards and their equivalents, and 500 managerial staff. Situated in the eastern part of the country, 15 kilometres south of the port city of Annaba, the fourth city of the country, the El Hadjar plant consists of several technological networks, built with the participation of some 12 countries.

The cokery and the two blast-furnaces are Soviet, the two oxygen steel-works (pig-iron and pellets) are a combination of Soviet (continuous flow of pig-iron), German (continuous flow of pellets) and Japanese (converters and regulation) technology. The hot rolling-mill is principally Italian, the cold rolling-mill principally Japanese, the electrical steel-mill and the weld-free pipe-mill are principally French, the spiral pipe-mill principally Austrian.

This diversity has had not only technological but also organizational consequences. Every participating country has influenced the organization according to its relative weight: the relationship between maintenance services and production, the organization of recruitment and selective tests; the relationship between training and production, the definition of hierarchical functions, the elaboration of the pay classification schemes, and so on. All the same, it is possible to maintain that the French organizational pattern, particularly strong in the complex as a whole, in the management, training, and selection of personnel, is dominant.

On the regional level, the plant has had an important impact in several ways. It has increased the geographical mobility of individuals by attracting large numbers of the labour force within a radius of 200 kilometres and turning them into industrial wage workers. Around 50 000 workers have passed through the plant during the two phases (construction and operation). These individuals have permanently left work on the land and ceased to be peasants. For the most part they have settled in Annaba or on the outskirts of smaller towns or at gathering points for the transport services. El Hadjar has changed both the occupational structure and the settlement structure of the population from a rural peasant into an urban workers' pattern.

It is possible to distinguish, roughly, three stages in this rapid social transformation, the process of putting to industrial work a population, which at independence in 1962 was still largely underemployed or employed in services or in small and middle-sized agro-based industries.

The first stage started shortly after independence, in 1964. This was the period of construction and, from 1966 on, the starting up of the first workshops (pipe-mill, first blast-furnace, the hot rolling-mill). Elsewhere (El Kenz, 1987) we have called this the *euphoric phase*, in the sense that it occurred at a moment of total confusion of a people who had naively believed that independence would resolve all problems and instead found itself facing growing unemployment: an economy in slow motion, made worse by the failures of self-management in agriculture and the political instability that eventually led to the *coup d'état* of 19 June 1965. The construction of the plant was received with joy by the population of Annaba, which had in the meantime swelled through the return of emigrants from France, refugees from the Tunisian border, and the 'displaced' from the closed French army camps.

The starting-up was done in a mood of 'general mobilization', and of involvement in an extraordinary task. The young unqualified workers left their arbitrary and underemployed situations in the villages and were happy to learn a hard but much more interesting trade; the qualified workers and shop-stewards were old steel-workers who had returned from France, happy to work for their country, or young secondary school graduates who had been sent abroad for training and had come back, very proud to manage teams and master complicated technologies. The managerial staff, all very young, considered their work a 'mission' and engaged themselves in it like militants in a party. The problems of this period were important but not dramatic. It was all a matter of training and discipline. There was a need to train everybody in the new technology of steel-making, still unknown in Algeria, and everybody applied themselves to it. The aim was to make El Hadjar an 'educational factory', which was in fact done in certain parts (for example, the spiral pipe-mill, the oxygen steel-mill). Discipline was more difficult to master. Absences reached heights of 30 per cent in the summer seasons as many of the workers returned to their villages to help out with the harvest. The turnover was great, too, over 10 per cent a year. Many of the new workers could not stand the new rules of behaviour, the anonymous role of their functions in work collectives that were too large, compared to what they were used to, the working in shifts of 2×8 or 3×8 hours and so on. But these problems were not overly obvious and were often superseded by more positive aspects: industrial wages were much higher than the payments in other sectors (notably agriculture and administration), there was not yet any crisis of housing, inflation was low, and the chances of promotion through training were very favourable.

The second stage began in the early 1970s with the launching of the extension program (increase of the capacity of the older workshops, construction of new ones). Several thousand new workers were needed for the building and running of the plant (8000 workers in 1973, 16 000 in 1976). Some hundred large and small national and foreign firms were working on the site. Thousands of new families settled around the plant and rapidly created immense shanty towns around Annaba (10 000 inhabitants in Bou-Hamra, for instance). Very rapidly the city was saturated, services became insufficient, housing overcrowded (whole districts were turned into shanty-towns), inflation reached levels well over the national average, shortages appeared with their corollaries of queues, favouring the formation of new social relations founded on patron–client bonds, string-pulling, and regionalism.

The works were taken by surprise by this new social dialectic, which they had helped to launch. The favourable conditions at the opening stage seemed now to be very far away; it was no longer possible to count on a mood of 'general mobilization'; the indicators of the plant administration were all showing red lights; turnover, absence, sanctions, and work accidents increased, while production simultaneously stagnated or diminished.

But these facts had a new bearing: absences were considerable throughout the year and concerned all kinds of workers. They were no longer due to the hardships of working conditions in the factory, they were due to the problems of external living conditions (health, food supplies, and so on). The same goes for the turnover, which rose to 15 per cent, affecting the more qualified workers as well as the shop-stewards, while interest in work was diminishing for everybody, including the managerial staff.

The fact is that the positive difference between the employment at the works and other activities had rapidly disappeared. The wage system, put into practice in 1967, adjusted with wage increases in 1971 and 1975, could not any more compensate the accelerating increase in costs of living. The demands for housing (3000 in 1973) grew to 7000 in 1979. The promotion process, which was rapid in the 60s because of all the holes to fill, became slower. At the same time the training system did not any more correspond to the increasing needs in the work-shops.

The workers did not identify with their work, not because they rejected it as such, but because it no longer allowed them to earn a living. However, they were still able to identify with the plant and paradoxically more so than ever, thanks to the new system of management: the so-called socialist management of enterprises. They were allowed to 'participate' or at least to influence indirectly the major decisions of the plant through an elected Assembly of Unit Workers (ATU). In fact, when compared to other industries in the country, and notably the Rouiba motor car plant, the management participation of El Hadjar workers has been remarkable. Its assembly was very popular with the workers up to 1982, when it was 'taken care of' by the single party, the Front de Libération Nationale (FLN). It presented the most important problems of the workers (hygiene and security, training and employment, social issues) to the board, forcing the company to take care of a large part of them, including even problems normally handled by other authorities, such as health, consumer cooperatives, leisure activities, and so on.

At first the goal was to become an 'educational factory'. Now under the pressure of the workers, El Hadjar was becoming a 'social factory'. We may call this second stage of the social history of El Hadjar, the *participatory stage.* It ended with the domestication of the workers' assembly in 1982 (a national phenomenon), and with the transition to more orthodox forms of management.

From this stage, which coincided with the completion of the works, the national experiment of socialist management was intentionally limited by the FLN. Meanwhile, a new official theory of economic and social development emerged. Industrialization practically came to a halt, the enterprises of the state sector were restructured and their fields of activities were demarcated. At the same time, a national pay classification scheme called SGT (Statut Général du Travailleur) was put into practice in all enterprises. These were accused of being 'too social', of having 'an over-abundant workforce' and of not being profitable. They were therefore called upon to clean up their accounts and their management.

El Hadjar transferred all its extra-economical 'out-growths' to the administrations concerned (health services to the Ministry of Health, consumer cooperatives to the Ministry of Commerce, leisure activities to the Ministry of Youth, and so on). The managers stopped recruiting and prepared a plan to cut down on the workforce. Simultaneously, internal pressure was enhanced by new and more strict procedures for dismissals and punishments for absences. On the regional level, the district authorities evicted all inhabitants of the shanty-towns and transferred them to their areas of origin, while the police force raided the city and arrested workers without mission orders.

In the factory, the immediate results of these new national and local measures soon appeared. Absences diminished to 5 per cent in 1983 while production continually increased: 1 million tons of liquid steel in 1983, 1.4 million tons in 1986. The production enthusiasts of the factory are happy but the more cautious still feel troubled. The mass of workers have closed in on themselves, the hatred of the managers is absolute. Workplace solidarity has found other outlets than the old union, which is useless today, and the old workers' assembly, now silenced. Regionalism, patron–client bonds, the pulling of strings, which had developed mainly outside the factory during the second stage, have today become general inside the factory and the workshops.

With a reference to Sartre, we may call this third stage that of *inert practice* (a concept created by Sartre in *Critique de la raison dialectique*). This stage cut short the development of workers' solidarity starting to form in the different but cumulative experiences of the two earlier stages. The individuals are thrown back on inter-related networks of affinity (ethnic, linguistic, residential, religious), which are all *informal* and all very weakly linked to work in the factory.

THE CASE OF THE INDUSTRIAL MOTOR CAR PLANT

Workers' practices, such as absences, turnover, slow-downs and strikes are quite frequent at the Rouiba motor car plant. The problems we shall investigate here concern the meaning and the special implications of these practices, and the kinds of perceptions they indicate.

Absences have for a long time been one of the principal concerns of all the managerial staffs. They have even been called a 'social scourge' by the government. The available evidence at the motor car plant shows the development in the rate of absence: in 1976 it was 7.9 per cent of all employed, reaching 15.47 per cent by 1981. But these averages are still below the rate of absence of manual workers which are even higher and have a tendency to increase: from 14 per cent in 1977 to 20 per cent in 1981.

One of the principal explanations for these high rates is the fact that the factory is far from the city and its life. This means that the social conditions of reproduction of the workforce are totally incompatible with the exigencies of mobilization for production and with discipline within the factory. The problems of the workers are less with the work than with the essential issues relating to everyday life, which are constant factors of destabilization and 'general demobilization'. In these circumstances, the workers increase and expand their absences, pointing explicitly to the lack of accommodation, the scarcity of transportation, the omnipresent shortages, the administrative burdens and so on, as reasons for their behaviour.

But such social conditions of reproduction of the workforce are not by themselves enough to explain the workers' absences at the motor car plant. In fact, the workers are unanimous in affirming that productive work is not the basis of their value systems or their modes of behaviour in the factory. They even declare that this is not a factory any more: the devaluation of productive work in general and that of manual workers in particular has in the long run led a large part of those in the productive sphere to move into administration and management. It is in fact a very particular feature of the motor car plant that employees not directly taking part in production make up about 70 per cent of the workforce. Even the workshops are not spared from this over-abundance of not directly productive labour. The 'mechanical building' and the center for 'assembly of lorries and buses' each have a ratio of 1.13 and 1.66 respectively of non-productive to productive employees (Chikhi, 1984).

A major consequence arises from this point: if the worker does not appear regularly at work, it means he is conscious of the fact that productive and industrial work does not constitute the pattern of social relations, and that what he actually does in terms of productive work is less significant than his position at the workplace. More profoundly, he is convinced that productive work does not shape his image in terms of social utility.

Being absent is thus a way of contesting the conditions of existence, a way of refuting a social space where productive work does not constitute the matrix for realization of the collective personality. Finally, it is a way of protesting against the lack of means of expression.

The workers stay away because they have a strong feeling of non-existence at the motor car plant, linked to their incapacity to express themselves. Because they find themselves in a system where there is a lack of communication, worker initiative is not aroused, creativity is not evoked, and skill does not count. This situation is due to the very hierarchical model of organization and the 'Taylorized' work structure at the factory. The hierarchy of the factory, inspired by the French Berliet system, functions to a considerably larger extent through command than through participation. The work process does not allow for any flexibility, nor does it allow for variation of tasks. The workers are used for fixed operations, maintenance is provided by specialized staff, and quality is not considered on the assembly lines. Absences thus result from the organizational framework which tends to sharpen the difficulties of expression, integration, and apprenticeship of workers as well as to consolidate the authoritarian character of command.

Going to work in the black market is another reason for staying away from the factory. This is primarily a possibility for those who have a 'universal' trade. The tinsmiths, the welders, the mechanics, the electricians have tremendous opportunities to supplement their monthly pay and often even to provide themselves with two or three times the factory wage. In this case absences constitute the price to be paid for a strategy founded on low wages and deplorable social conditions, since such a strategy is a major obstacle for the stabilization of the trades necessary for large-scale industry. Very often, black market work is transformed from a complementary occupation into the principal occupation. This leads to turnover at the workplace.

In good years as well as bad, turnover is seen as one of the principal obstacles to ensuring continuity in production. The plant has remained a kind of 'railway station': workers come there, others leave in batches, and this instability proves to be highly disruptive in the performance of the different annual production plans of the factory. And yet the Rouiba plant has mobilized ample means (training, internal promotions, social actions) to counteract this loss; but the mobility of the workforce acts as a veritable landslide and constantly entails the vicious circle: 'departure of qualified personnel/recruitment of inexperienced personnel', with its negative impact on the quality of production and the rates of scrapping. People like toolmakers or model builders need five years to master their trade and then leave to work elsewhere, not necessarily in their specialized trade. The need for foreign technical assistance and maintenance work only partly arises from normal requirements; it is just as much a result of the turnover of labour.

To a large extent turnover is caused by the same factors as influence the absences of the workers. The living conditions are inherently unstable, the workers are always on the look-out for a factory which will pay more or offer housing. Since the factory does not consider their productive work, they search for other workplaces where they can be socially more 'recognized'. Having no means of expression at their disposal, they go elsewhere in the search for a more sociable context.

But to analyse turnover solely in terms of working conditions involves, at least in the case of the motor car plant, the risk of losing sight of other aspects. The workers here are very young: in 1981 over 60 per cent were less than 30 years of age. They are for the most part educated: only one fifth of them are illiterate. This also means that the majority are of urban origin. Their socialization in and by factory work is rather problematic and their integration into work collectives is quite difficult. Their aspirations are mixed up with those of other social groups and their life ambitions are not really linked to industrial development. In fact, these youngsters are rather city-dwellers than workers: they want to 'consume' the city but refuse to integrate themselves into a world defined by industrial work. In this way, they develop notions and behaviours, inside the city and the factory, which can hardly be ascribed to their role as workers alone.

From this perspective, the whole distance separating these recently employed young workers from the older generation of workers with their old confidence and hopes is emphasized. The latter are a little suspicious of these new recruits, who are less docile and more restless, less productive in their working hours and more demanding in their consumption habits, less respectful of the hierarchy and more indifferent towards the goals of the factory. The managerial staff complains most about these youngsters, treating them as 'migratory birds' who sow disturbance through their restlessness and their undisciplined behaviour.

Like all the other forms of workers' behaviour mentioned above, the slow-downs are regularly brought up by the managers of the motor car plant. They indicate that the workers have a tendency to slow down their movements and pace, not to go to their workplace when work begins, to prolong the regular breaks, to talk too much, to go off for strolls inside the workshops, to reduce their efforts. What is this strolling and slowness about? What does it signify: the laziness of workers or a contestation of the existing situation? Lack of consciousness or a retreat from the technological and social organization of the work? Indolence or a substitute for other forms of resistance? What is the significance of these go-slows?

Just like the absences and the turnover, the workers are holding back their efforts because they reject the social conditions of the mobilization of their labour power. They 'stroll' because they have to survive the day, which allows them only tiny opportunities to relax. They stop working ahead of time because they tend to adjust their effective labour input to their wages, badly paid as they are.

What is disputed is not so much the work tasks, which are not very demanding in a technical and productive sense (Chikhi, 1984). Rather the workers reject the absurd human and social conditions at the plant. Their low productivity is due to those social conditions and not to industrial work in itself, they clearly say.

The workers also reject the technical irrationalities due to either lack or unsatisfactory organization of work. Sharing a rather 'Taylorist' ideology they blame their low productivity on the organizational system. They 'stroll' because the lack of organization allows them to do so and because their efforts are perpetually wasted in long dead periods and multiple technical stoppages. This feeling about the unsatisfactory technical organization is quite specific to the Rouiba plant and is shared by all the workers. They are confronted with a productive space which in principle requires a continuous flow of supplies without disruptions, and a constant circulation of parts, tools and raw materials. They can easily see that production from this point of view is far from the 'Fordist' ideal and that the factory seems incapable of creating continual production cycles and securing a regular pace of work from the machines.

This technical visibility of 'unrhythmical Taylorism' provokes deep suspiciousness in the workers' collective. If they do not care how they produce, it is because the plant has not managed to function as a factory, neither has the government managed to function as an industrial entrepreneur. It is exactly on this level that the workers' conception of the managerial staff is founded. 'The staff is useless' is a formula which comes back again and again when the workers are talking. In fact this formula signifies two different things. The managerial staff is useless since it is just as incompetent, according to the workers, as they are themselves in mastering the foreign machines. But the formula also signifies that the staff is incapable of ending the current mess in the work organization. And if the managerial staff cannot or will not do anything about it, how can they expect the workers to get to work? This seems to be the crucial question posed by the workers considering the technical irrationalities linked to their go-slow. Furthermore, not only is the managerial staff incapable of 'taking charge of their part of the work' and keeping their part of the contract; that is to assure stability and continuity of production. They also appear among the workers exclusively in order to demand their submission to the rules of the workshop or to permanently remind them of the management's power to take disciplinary measures. Here, the workers in the car plant are pointing at something important: the dichotomous relationship where hierarchy and submission in many aspects dominate over the technical work relationships. The nature of the hierarchical relation can be specified: in 1980, one shop-steward was enough to control about 12 workers; in 1984 the same shop-steward supervises no more than eight workers! And still we would have to add managerial and other supervisory staff.

These technical irrationalities and incapacities of the managerial staff to regulate the management and to end either the technical disruptions or the degradation of the living conditions of the workers cannot stimulate the efforts of the latter. Those will not exert themselves under these conditions, and they refuse to give all since the contract is not fulfilled from the other side.

The slow-downs are, then, a way of adjusting badly organized work to an equally bad life, a way of rejecting technical irrationalities and the incompetence of the staff, and finally a means which is used instead of more open forms of protest. They are resorted to in situations where other forms of struggle have proved unsuccessful. The workers do not respect the modes of operation and thus slow down production because their demands cannot be voiced through a union and because, all too often, nobody takes the time to listen to them.

It is evident that the distance between the workers and the trade union in the Rouiba motor car plant is well-established. The union has proceeded to patron–client practices; it acts on the basis of clan affiliation and has not fulfilled its task of unifying the workers. Centred on its own interests and built up as a service organ it is very much an empty space. It does not incite any social mobilization neither has it been able to homogenize collective action.

So the workers of the Rouiba motor car plant act separately from the union. In the Taylorist organization model of the factory, this entails a lively opposition to the management as well as the union. Sometimes, this opposition will emerge in the form of a wild-cat strike, unauthorized by the union and unorganized. Otherwise it is expressed in a permanent fashion through consolidation of the withdrawal of the workers (absences, turnover, slow-down, and so on).

Furthermore, these withdrawals of the workers can develop into veritable, collective secret evasions. This is the direct consequence of a work organization which strengthens socialization through clan and other affiliations. The social relationships structuring work in the workshops become ever more informal. The center of collective interest in these informal social relations is not production, it is retraction from this production, channelled through personalized relationships, through a system of underground alliances and diverse affinities.

In this situation, the workers seek to cultivate links between themselves and petty agents of the management in order to attain a minimum of security. The workers bring them tokens of fidelity, which is more essential than skill. Suddenly, it is the fraternity of villages, the solidarity of neighbourhoods and the regional links which come to the forefront and structure the majority of social relations. Small communities are formed, carrying on a very strong symbolic opposition to the 'managers', but keeping a distance from the impositions of the labour process and the ethics of the factory.

IN LIEU OF A CONCLUSION

The two cases which we have presented in this chapter are certainly not representative of all workers and workplaces in Algeria. They are in fact the two largest industrial complexes of the country and it is probable that their sheer size has an impact. The behaviour and the perceptions of the workers are in these cases specific rather than marginal. This specificity is also a source of diversity, and distinguishes these two experiences, not only from the rest, but also from each other.

The workers' collectives in the two plants thus behave in perceptibly different ways in regard to their work, the hierarchy, the environment. Although they are generally subject to the same socio-economical constraints, they react differently on the level of involvements and refusals. So we conclude with the initial question underlying this whole essay: Is it possible then to speak about 'strategies' at this level?

REFERENCES

S. Chikhi, 'Le travail en usine', *Les Cahiers du CREAD*, no. 4 (1984).
—— *Non identité au travail et société en Algérie* (Alger: CREAD, 1986a).
—— *Question ouvrière et rapports sociaux en Algérie* (Paris VII, thesis, 1986b).
—— 'Les ouvriers face au travail au CVI', *Les Cahiers du CREAD*, no. 9 (1987).
A. El Kenz, *Le complexe sidérurgique d'El Hadjar - une expérience industrielle en Algérie* (Paris: CNRS, 1987).
J.-P. Sartre, *Critique de la raison dialectique* (Paris: Gallimard, 1960).

Map 2 Central Western Mexico: Regions of Small-Scale Industry

3 Day-to-day Struggles in Mexican Workshop Production

Fiona Wilson

In the 1980s a handful of Mexican researchers discovered evidence of a major growth in small-scale industry and sub-contracting in rural western central Mexico. Their findings were intriguing. They suggest not only the onset of a new period of industrial deconcentration and diffusion but also that significant changes are taking place in patterns of capital accumulation and forms of production in the Mexican countryside. Characteristically these are 'non-traditional' industries employing a predominantly female labour force, producing consumer goods in new ways for distant markets. Though the situation is still far from clear, it appears that processes are at work which to some extent contradict the assumptions generally made about rural social and economic relations.

These phenomena demand greater attention, especially in light of the number of localities involved (at least 50 industrializing small towns in western central Mexico alone) and size of area (large parts of the states of Jalisco, Guanajuato, Aguascalientes and Michoacan). In this region a wide variety of goods are produced (principally in the clothing, footwear and food sectors) and one can find many different forms of production (ranging from production put out to industrial home workers, domestic enterprises using family labour, workshops employing small labour forces, to factories with over 100 workers).

Since 1986 I have been engaged in a research project investigating the emergence of industrial specialization in a single locality in the state of Michoacan and have tried to pay particular attention to its historical and geographical context. Here within what was a relatively impoverished, depressed small town the production of knitwear was introduced some 30 years ago (in 1960) and since then the industry has flourished. From the start production was organized within small workshops which both make knitted cloth from purchased yarn and sew the garments – sweaters, sport shirts and occasionally trousers.

49

Most workshops have engaged home workers to accomplish particular parts of the labour process (especially the adornment phase).

During the research I have explored how workshop-based production originated in such a poor locality; the patterns of workshop
growth associated with industrial development; and changes in labour
relations as a result of pressures from both workers and owners
(Wilson, 1991). This chapter focuses on the last of these topics and
aims to describe and contextualize certain aspects of contemporary
labour relations in the workshops. I want to present selected case
histories of workers' strategies and struggles as these throw light on
the way workers are viewing their relationship with capital.

Before presenting the detailed empirical material I want to point to
three broader discussions which are necessary in order to situate the
labour–capital relationship, first in its geographical context (that is, in
contemporary rural Mexico); secondly in the locality's historical
context; and thirdly in relation to a specific form of production
(that is, workshop production under which knitwear is 'characteristically' produced). I shall begin with a few remarks about two
different interpretations of the decentralizing industry in western
central Mexico, and then sketch in some salient points about class
and gender relations prevailing in small towns prior to industrialization. Finally, I shall address the problem of defining the production
form I am calling 'capitalized' workshop production.

THE DEVELOPMENT OF A RURAL INDUSTRIAL REGION IN MEXICO: TWO MACRO PERSPECTIVES

The growth of certain types of industries in the Mexican countryside
is still gathering momentum. The industries are not spreading
everywhere; clearly some prior investments have been required to
develop infrastructure and communications in the small rural towns.
But while the new era of industrial diffusion got underway during a
period of economic prosperity (beginning in the 1960s and expanding
greatly in the late 1970s), the recession of the 1980s does not seem to
have slowed down the rate of growth markedly or the tendencies
towards increasing decentralization.

The recession that hit the larger, registered industrial sector hard
does not appear to have had the same effect on the many small
enterprises found in western central Mexico. On the contrary, one can
point to important instances during the recession of capital's 'flight'

from urban areas to the countryside and interpret these as being part of a strategy to lower production costs through the 'informalization' of production. Hidden in the countryside, small enterprises stand a better chance of evading taxation and legislation protecting labour. Scattered small rural enterprises can easily escape detection by inspectors and are not brought to account. For example, after the earthquake in September 1985 devastated certain industrial quarters of Mexico City and exposed the 'illegality' of many large garment making factories in the capital, owners have tended to rebuild their enterprises in a new location, away from public scrutiny. And this has tended to strengthen even further the decentralization of the garment industry.

But the issue of legality/illegality is complex and needs to be explored from another perspective. One can suggest that in many cases compliance with the law is not seen as relevant or appropriate for small towns previously suffering great poverty, deprivation and enforced out-migration. Thus, very significantly, the 'social will' prevailing in many small towns of central western Mexico has meant that both struggling small scale capitalists and their workers have been prepared to make sacrifices in the short run as a way of trying to ensure the future viability of their industrial specialization. In this way, the 'pacts' which capital could make with labour especially during the early phases have been extremely beneficial for capital accumulation.

The diffusion of manufacturing activity can be discussed from the point of view of processes of informalization (as noted above). But on its own this does not satisfactorily capture what appears to be going on. As has been pointed out by Arias (1986), the industries now found in western central Mexico have tended to become increasingly specialized and diversified while production units remain small and labour intensive. To take the case of the garment industry, some 75 per cent of registered firms employed five or less workers (according to 1975 figures) while the sector as a whole was thought to occupy some 15 per cent of the total national labour force. The sector is present in all states, but there are marked concentrations of activity in particular regions of the country: especially in and around Mexico City and in the western central region. Garment manufacture is less technologically advanced and more dependent on the labour input than other branches of manufacturing industry; as a proportion of total production costs, labour ranks high in garment production (20.8 per cent), compared with manufacturing activity as a whole (16.6 per cent). But these characteristics of small size and labour intensive production do not necessarily denote a backward or static form of productive organization.

Mexico's garment industry has been creating and responding to a highly volatile market situation. Increasingly, the sector is producing 'fashion' clothing for a mass market in which styles, materials, colours, decorations alter at specific times of the year (often in line with 'spring' and 'autumn' collections). In addition the demand for clothing is often subject to seasonal variations so that sales exhibit sharp peaks and troughs. Markets are differentiated in terms of price range and quality and there has been a tendency for the demand for 'middle' quality goods to grow relatively fast especially where the youth have had access to cash incomes. To respond to the demand for higher quality and to fashion and seasonal change, labour needs to be skilled while production needs to remain flexible. Enterprises must respond quickly to market changes; be able to call on fast, skilled workers and be able to alter the intensity of production. Small-scale manufacturing is not necessarily a disadvantage in such circumstances as there are limitations as to how much capital intensive technology can replace labour.

In this context, there are strong incentives to engage in subcontracting at various levels within the garment sector. A division may emerge at the management level in which large city commercial houses take decisions concerning style, raw materials and markets and then subcontract production out to a myriad of small enterprises able to undertake production. And at the local level, too, producers selling under contract may well develop their own subcontracting links putting work out to dependent smaller firms and industrial home workers so as to achieve greater flexibility. As the small-scale garment industry proliferates it often becomes hard to discover who in reality are the 'owners' and main beneficiaries especially when subcontracting is closely interwoven with clandestinity.

In summary, this brief account of the garment industry has tried to show the imposition of two sets of characteristics within these decentralizing industries. They are not necessarily contradictory or in opposition, but relate to rather different view points taken up in recent literature. One set is consistent with observed processes of *informalization* and capital's search for lowered production costs, achieved especially through lowering the cost of labour by shifting from an urban to a rural location. The other set is consistent with a version of '*post-Fordist*' industrialization: specialized production geared to meet highly differentiated volatile markets in conditions where geographical distance no longer imposes real 'costs'. This double optic has had implications for the way that the production units themselves have been perceived. But, before looking in greater detail at some of the characteristics of 'modern' workshop production, I want to introduce some remarks about the social relations that form a background to rural industrialization in western central Mexico.

CLASS AND GENDER RELATIONS PRIOR TO THE EMERGENCE OF RURAL INDUSTRY

The rural regions of Mexico have suffered a long history of violence and disruption. Older people recount in an intense and dramatic way how they felt themselves thrown around by currents of history which offered them limited choice or negotiating space. The Revolution of the 1910s led into a period of banditry, violent struggles over land, and finally to the Cristero Wars, 1926–9, fought particularly savagely in western central Mexico. The agrarian reforms instigated in the 1930s proved to be a false dawn of hope for the majority of the peasantry. Haciendas and large private holdings were expropriated and their lands distributed but the chief beneficiaries were most likely to come from social strata already possessing some resources (often small town traders or craftsmen) who could afford initially to invest in agriculture and stock raising and who in time were able to drive out the poor peasants forcing them into more precarious livelihoods as sharecroppers or landless workers.

Instead of 'solving' the land question by bestowing property rights on those working the land, then, agrarian reform in fact opened the way for a more intensive capitalization of the agrarian sector which threatened to exacerbate social unrest and enhance population mobility and dislocation. As households lost land, so they had to compete to rent plots on which to grow their staples of maize and beans. Rents even for marginal lands rose and sharecroppers were forced to accept ever-worsening deals, paying back at least two-thirds of the maize harvest in return for use of the land. Furthermore, many of the new rural elite were intent on expanding their use and control over water which robbed many 'ranchos' of their water supply. Diets deteriorated and people remember periods of acute hunger and thirst especially in the early 1940s. Many were forced to move from the 'ranchos' of their birth; families might decide to resettle in local small towns or they might spend several years wandering about.

The break with the old agrarian system and the undermining of household production of subsistence goods carried different implications for the lives of men and women. Men from impoverished households tended to travel further afield to find occasional wage work, usually in the richer agricultural regions, and combined migration with limited work in food production at home. Women staying at home had to restructure their activities and take on an increased work burden. The time taken up by domestic tasks needed to be compressed so that some women could maintain the household's production of subsistence goods when men were absent and others could work to earn money locally.

Traditional branches of 'women's work' in domestic services (especially washing and cleaning) and domestic manufacturing (especially sewing and preparing food) became increasingly bought and sold; not only were poorer women 'helping out' richer women and reimbursed with a little cash, but the pressures to restructure domestic tasks in small town settings were tending to lead to greater levels of task specialization and the growth of networks of exchange that used money to make the transactions. But as cash was used primarily to facilitate exchange amongst impoverished women (for example, one might 'sell' the extra tortillas she made to another who 'took in' washing), the amounts of money changing hands in these transaction were very small. Seen from the perspective of being a return to women's labour their work was being barely remunerated.

In western central Mexico, the longer-run effects of land reform, greater capitalization of agriculture and re-organization of rural class structure and gender divisions of labour might have fueled a return to social violence, had it not been for a new 'opportunity' which suddenly was brought within reach of peasant men: contract labour in the US. Before 1940, men migrating to the US or to distant Mexican cities had largely been drawn from the more prosperous social strata. But the character of the migration streams changed abruptly when, to compensate for labour shortages during wartime, the US government signed an agreement with the Mexican government to massively contract Mexican workers for farm work.

A flood of poor peasant men left to take advantage of the Bracero Programme (as the scheme became known) which lasted until 1964. And once men had gained some experience of *el norte* and knew the ropes, many preferred to cross the border 'illegally', so saving the expense of 'buying' a contract. Cynically, the new local political elites representing the interests of the capitalizing farmers 'sold' labour contracts to those whom they were intent on 'robbing' of their land. For them it was a very convenient solution and undoubtedly the Bracero Programme acted as a safety valve, diffusing and confusing social protest and unrest.

Many men spent years away returning home for only a few weeks each year. As before, women and children remained behind eking out an existence while waiting for remittances from their menfolk. Prolonged male migration generated many additional tensions and changes at the household level. The life experiences of those leaving diverged increasingly from those staying behind, meaning that the worlds of men and women became ever more insulated, contained and each unknown to the other. A shared international migration experience tended to consolidate bonds based on gender that even partially overrode division rooted in class. Many men, regardless of their social position back home, suffered humiliating employment conditions in the US and experienced racial discrimination. Though men were given better access to wage work in the US than in Mexico, the dangers they faced of 'losing' the money earned (through theft, trickery, gambling, and alcoholism) or of injuring themselves were infinitely greater. Men's new power to earn higher cash incomes tended to become associated with their adoption of more aggressive images of masculine identity – alcoholism and domestic (and public) violence became rife and many challenged the rights of their wives to the money earned under such dangers and refused to accept 'responsibility' for their families. Not only were traditional gender identities being undermined, the differential cash earning power of men and women was creating new conditions for the emergence of more forceful expressions of male dominance and female subordination.

Women living in the small towns might find themselves in an even worse position during the Bracero Programme than before. Men disappeared for longer and the 'rights' of the family back in Mexico to the cash a man had earned in the US were often in dispute. Women continued to scrape cash and goods together in order that their large numbers of children could survive. Exchanges of domestic goods and services among households continued and within households relations between the older and younger generations of women intensified as work burdens increased further and new patterns of work allocation were sought. But, as in the case of the men, long-term male migration also had the effect of generating certain solidarity amongst women that could cross social and class boundaries. Sharing a common experience as 'abandoned' and 'needy' wives, links might be fostered to 'help out' and 'lend' cash especially during emergencies and times of particular adversity.

In sum, one can point to a period of intense hardship following the destruction of the old agrarian system and the onset of capital's greater intervention in agriculture during which class and gender relations were undergoing rapid and profound changes. Rural class relations were being restructured. A minority was able to secure access to available resources while the majority was forced to adopt new 'strategies' for household survival. By and large men were forced to look for wage work at the end of a migration channel, while women struggled to manage increasing work burdens at home so as to combine work in subsistence production with remunerated and unremunerated domestic labour. These tendencies could open up both new areas of solidarity (as demonstrated by the reinforcement of men's 'machista' culture or women's networks of emergency assistance) and new areas of tension and domination–subordination (as shown in the conflicts over the intra-household distribution of cash and older women's control of younger women in the household).

Though this discussion has drawn on the example of Mexico, the general tendencies outlined would appear to be of much wider relevance. But what is of particular interest in the case of Mexico is that matters did not rest there. Instead, at a specific historical juncture, local people in a plethora of small towns in a comparatively accessible region were able to grasp the opportunity to introduce industry into their impoverished communities. While building on and concretizing the deep ambiguities that had appeared in class and gender relations, at the same time the new industries opened up perspectives for local people of a quite different order.

LABOUR RELATIONS WITHIN 'CAPITALIZED' WORKSHOPS

The *workshop* as a form of production has not yet received the theoretical attention that it deserves. It has been generally seen as some intermediary way of organizing production, which has departed from household based petty commodity production (in that wage workers are employed) but which has not yet reached a fully capitalist 'stage' of production. In a Latin American context, industrial workshops are usually assumed to be small unregistered units of production flouting labour and tax legislation and possibly also engaging in criminal activities (such as using smuggled inputs or supplying illegal export markets). This clandestine identity has meant that analyses have often lumped workshop production together with other 'backward' forms including petty commodity production (where households hold the property and provide the necessary labour) and industrial home work, and defined as constituting the contemporary 'informal' sector (see the discussion by Portes, 1983).

This simplistic positioning of the workshop in a continuum of production forms – labelling it as a type of 'backward', 'informal' production – does not seem to get us very far. A more thorough analysis of the workshop as a distinct form of production with its own characteristics and trajectory in the contemporary world lies outside the scope of this chapter for there are many important aspects one should touch on. Here, I limit my remarks to one aspect only: *the evolution of labour relations as seen in certain rural industrial workshops.* I shall argue that one can distinguish two main phases in this evolution. During an earlier phase labour is heavily exploited and labour relations are often modeled on those of the household. During later phases both workers and workshop owners press for changes in the content and terms of the labour relationship and must find a new *modus vivendi.*

An appreciation of this temporal division is fundamental in understanding the trajectory of the workshop form of production. In many situations, highly coercive labour recruitment and bonding typically underpin the start of workshop production, giving rise to servile relations where workers are definitely not 'free' to sell or withdraw their labour. Such servile labour relations may be disguised or obscured; and a convenient way of doing this has been through recourse to 'natural' household social relations and divisions of labour. But reliance on force or 'disguise' cannot be sustained over longer periods of time, where an industry expands and greater capital investment occurs. In time, the household no longer appears to either workers or owners as such an appropriate model on which to base labour relations. And where force is applied at the same time that labour is put to work with more sophisticated, expensive machinery then heavy penalties may be imposed through industrial sabotage or a serious slowing down of the pace of work. The heavy exploitation of labour characteristic of the earlier phase will at some point in time come under attack. At this juncture, one might say that the workshop faces a crisis which can be resolved through an acceptance of less personalized, more formalized relations between labour and capital. And at this juncture workshops may be forced to alter their status in relation to the law, being compelled through threats of 'exposure' by discontented workers to comply with some of the legal codes.

One can argue that, unlike other 'backward' forms of production, workshops usually come to rely on the employment of a 'free' wage labour force which cannot be indefinitely subjected to 'extra-economic coercion'. Thus there is reason to believe that workshop workers will increasingly see their own interests as divergent from capital's, will develop a clearer understanding of their class situation, and will come to struggle in a more open and direct way with the aim of improving the quality of their lives. Such an evolution of labour struggle is virtually precluded under petty commodity production on account of the overlapping identities (of property ownership with labour as well as of household with industrial activities). It is also generally precluded in the case of industrial home work due to the extreme fragmentation of the production process and isolation of the workers. It has been the changing nature of labour struggle which has particularly fascinated me, seen from the perspective of knitwear producing workshops in Michoacan over a period of 25 years.

THE FORMATION OF WORKSHOPS AND THE EARLY PHASE OF LABOUR RELATIONS IN WESTERN CENTRAL MEXICO

At particular historical moments, available technology can permit the decentralization and diffusion of industrial production and for various reasons this became a possibility in Mexico in the early 1960s. Families pioneering industrial workshops in the countryside often originated from the more privileged social strata of local populations who had earlier faced temporary set-backs or even eclipse as a result of the changes taking place within agriculture. Some who had migrated to work in Mexico's large cities were able to learn a new trade, acquire the necessary machinery and inputs to begin production, and come back home as small industrial producers. While the existence of a class of potential industrial capitalists is necessary, it is not sufficient to guarantee the spread of industry. A local source of 'cheap' workers needs to be available. Also, what is very often forgotten in analyses of industrial diffusion, local society needs to have already developed resilient, adaptable strategies of social reproduction that can allow households to re-allocate and deploy their labour resources so that some can take on highly time-consuming poorly-reimbursed wage work.

In situations of massive male out-migration, men's labour is relatively expensive but their wives and children, not previously employed through capitalist labour markets whose labour is not yet 'valorized', are a much needier group and also one especially attractive to local capitalists. Yet the constitution of an appropriate labour force for workshop industry is not merely an economic matter. Workshop production has thrived in communities and regions where social groups have already been defined as 'inferior bearers' of labour. This does not only mean that they are 'cheaper'. It also follows that there is wide local acceptance that the law does not apply to these workers or to the work they perform. Instead, officialdom has no 'right' to intervene. Typically in Mexico as in many other places, the labour of women, children and 'ethnic minorities' has been seen as falling within the orbit of 'private' as opposed to state protection.

In the initial phase of workshop based industrialization, capital invades and makes use of prevailing social relations marked by dominance–subordination as between genders, generations and/or ethnic groups but which (unlike class relations) have as yet only indirect connections with capitalist labour relations. The mechanisms 'subordinating' young female labour in particular can be recreated in the workshops when the 'household model' is adapted so that gender and generational hierarchies are carried over from the domestic domain. The successful adaptation of the domestic model demands that certain continuities are maintained; for example, it demands that owning wives play an active role as workshop managers taking charge of the parts of the labour process performed by women; the workshop produces goods that conform to local ideas concerning what is appropriately 'women's work'; and in physical terms, the workshop continues to form part of domestic space located within the household of the owners.

The transference of a domestic model suggests that labour relations in the early phase of workshop development reflect the contradictory nature of household relations. On the one hand, wage workers can be depicted as 'helping out' and contributing, just as household members are expected to do. But, on the other hand, hierarchies of control and authority based on gender and generation are assumed as 'natural' in the workshops as in the households from where the workers are drawn. In such a household, labour processes are segregated according to gender and age. And the expectations of the young men and women employed have differed and diverged. To some extent, the few young men employed have been treated as apprentices or surrogate sons who sooner or later are expected to start their own independent business. Young women enter the workshop as 'helpers' of the owning wife giving loyalty, hard work and discipline in return for 'protection' and occasional financial 'help' in times of emergency. Marriage spells the end of women's workshop work, in the same way that it entails moving away from the parental household.

As workshops accumulate capital and further capitalize production so owners press to reach a different kind of 'contract' with labour, taking greater control over the worker's labour time, effort and person, in an effort to reach higher levels and/or higher quality of output. With this comes some preparedness to reimburse labour with higher cash wages and to re-structure older forms of labour organization and hierarchy (defined by gender and seniority). Workers on the other hand feel growing pressures to explore and demystify their relations to capital which no longer are disguised under a household model. Only after a separation has been made as between the social relations of household and workshop can workers hope to articulate their opposition and take up a more active struggle as workers.

LABOUR STRUGGLE IN KNITWEAR PRODUCING WORKSHOPS OF SANTIAGO, MICHOACAN

The knitwear industry of Santiago Tangamandapio (population c. 9000) began in 1960, grew rapidly in the late 1970s and is surviving. By 1986 there were some 50 workshops employing from between three to 37 workers. A handful of men (in some cases all family members) work the looms knitting cloth while all other stages in the labour process are performed by women.

Examples of labour negotiation in the early period

The earliest generation of workers described their employment situation as 'helping out'. The money was necessary for them, but they insisted they were never wage slaves. Several instances of this view can be gleaned from the personal accounts. Owning wives remember the struggle they had with older women, of their own generation, not that they did not work hard or well but because they refused to perform the precise task that the workshop demanded. The out-working embroiderers were especially undisciplined, wanting to create their own designs and disputing the workshops' chosen patterns. Reimbursement was small, but owners had to accept that women workers in particular had other demands on their time; they had to be released for family and religious duties. The early workers also believed that part of their reimbursement lay in their rights to relatively large cash loans from workshop owners. The pioneering owners saw themselves as being put on trial by the out-workers who did not repay the first large loan contracted although they would repay all subsequent loans. Workers spoke of good employers as being those who tore up an IOU half way through the repayment time.

This labour situation was not conducive to giving workers the sack. If a workshop enterprise was to adhere to the household model of social relations, workers could not be dismissed outright unless proved guilty of a serious misdemeanour, such as stealing. Two main strategies were used to bring about the resignation of unsuitable workers: they were paid wages lower than all other workers until they left of their own accord, or the workshop closed down for a period and only a selected group of workers were given their jobs back. This policy worked quite well until the late 1970s.

The eruption of labour protest in 1978

By the late 1970s, owners of the largest workshops were being pressed into a further capitalization of production and into improving the quality of their product so as to reach higher priced markets. This had differential perspectives for the men and women employed. The most expensive capital item which owners could now acquire was the Carrousel loom; on this vastly more productive machine, one operator could produce ten times more cloth in a working day than could the old motor-powered loom (one male worker had looked after two such motor looms). The capitalization of knitted cloth production therefore spelled redundancy for many men.

Investment in more specialized sewing machines was mechanizing parts of the women's labour process that had formerly been undertaken by hand or by less efficient equipment. Some women might be laid off, but in general there was a growing need for female machine operators and a declining demand for hand-workers. The pressures put on women were twofold. First, the concepts of 'work' and of working relations were being changed so that owners demanded more rights over women's labour time than formerly. The assumption was growing that women should sell their time as well as their skills and dedication. Second, owners were starting to rethink the form of remuneration given workers. Until the late 1970s all workshops paid piece rates, but piece rates and quality improvement did not necessarily go well together.

Though mechanization of production only began around 1978, (when the first Carrousel was introduced in Santiago), the climate surrounding labour's contract with capital had been changing; no longer could an ideology of household relationships manage to obscure the nature of capitalist production. The expansion of production during the 1970s had meant that many more loom operators were employed; and they were seeing themselves increasingly as workers, rather than as aspiring workshop owners. The growing pressures placed on the workshop sewers to speed up output and improve quality were also difficult to fit with a household model. Several women workers of that period recalled their growing sense of alienation and their determination to find time during the day to escape the owners' notice, stop sewing, relax and talk for a time. As the workshops were located in rooms in the owner's house, not all the sewing rooms could be effectively supervised. Women demanded greater control over their labour time still as a right.

The national labour unions had become aware of the growth of clandestine industry in the towns of western central Mexico and of the labour displacement provoked by technological change in certain industrial sectors. Organizers of the officially recognized unions were keen to help the loom operators start a union in Santiago and offered assistance. A major initiative was launched in 1978 and lasted until 1980; it came mainly from men employed in the largest workshops, those most threatened by labour redundancy once owners invested in Carrousels. The external support from the unions meant that the owners and municipal councils had to treat the activity with some caution. But, in the end, the local President was able to frighten off the bulk of the male labour force, threatening retribution should men get involved with the unions. The attempt petered out and the ringleaders were dismissed.

Women employed by the workshops had never been part of the union initiative; no effort had been made to attract them to join. Women's protests were spontaneous, happening without the support of any outside body. The first attempt by women to seek justice against wrongful dismissal came in 1978 from workers formerly employed in the workshop of José Martínez. The four Sánchez sisters had been employed for between four and eight years and they had no previous problems with their employer. On the occasion of their brother's wedding, they had requested and thought José had consented to their taking four days off unpaid in order to prepare for the celebration. When they returned to work José locked the doors against them, told them not to return and handed them a joint separation pay of 20 000 pesos. They sought legal advice in Zamora at the office of the Council for Arbitration and Conciliation, and secured a lawyer willing to take up their case against wrongful dismissal. He later refused to bring their case. The sisters assumed he had been bought off by José, and considered it hopeless to continue their stand. They were now unemployable in the workshops, blacklisted for being trouble-makers. But, as their family had some property and cash, they were able to establish an independent enterprise, as dressmakers employed largely by the young workshop workers.

During the same year, the frustrations felt by women workers at the workshop of Lola and Juan erupted into an attempted strike. Two sisters tried to rally the ten women in the sewing room to campaign for higher rates for piece work to compensate for the extra time needed in sewing if the quality improvement demanded by the owners was to be met. Collectively they went to the owners to demand a rise. The owners said little in front of the group but that evening visited the homes of the younger workers to intimidate them and also visited the two sisters to try and buy them off with separate deals. The sisters refused, saying they would not return to work unless the rates were increased. The owners agreed to look into the matter, but the rates were not raised. The workers were unable to follow up with another protest action.

The following year, the sisters tried once again to provoke collective action for an improvement in labour's contract with capital. This time the struggle centered on workers' rights to hold national holidays; the chosen date for protest being May Day. The workers agreed to stay away from work, but the owners once again went around to workers' homes and in front of their parents accused them of disloyalty and dishonesty. Workers were worried by the reaction of their parents and feared dismissal. In the end only the two sisters stayed away from work, and they gave up the attempt to provoke more collective action.

Workers' strategies and protest in the mid-1980s

After the eruption of collective protest there followed a period when individualized protests grew once again. But individualized forms of protest could become more harmful to owners in the mid-1980s than earlier. Once workshops were stressing quality rather than quantity, and expecting workers to handle more complex, expensive machinery then a policy leading to dismissals and resignations was certain to rebound on workshops through a drop in labour productivity and by the need to constantly train new recruits. While motor loom operators were expendable, the men trained to work Carrousel looms were not; and while the loss of one or two experienced sewers brought little problem, a walkout by several could be serious, especially when they took their skills to a rival workshop (and did not leave only to marry). The pressures forcing owners to improve employment conditions were coming from just such examples of more individualized protest; no longer did workers need to come out on strike in order to get owners to respond to their demands.

Two instances of this kind of individualized labour struggle with far-reaching consequences will be explored in detail. One concerns the question of industrial health in José's workshop, always in the forefront in terms of the capitalization of production and subsequent alterations in labour relations. In the earlier period, most owners had been willing to assist workers with medical bills and sometimes even transported them to Zamora for treatment. This 'benevolence' was also a strategy to keep workers from demanding social security. But where labour relations were being restructured, responsibility for health was passed over to the workers. The second instance centres on women's struggle in the largest workshop in town which had developed a particularly bad reputation.

Labour and health

After José had bought a Carrousel loom in 1978, he kept it running for 24 hours a day, in three shifts. Pedro, a young loom operator was given the chance to learn the new machine and was put on the night shift, from 10 p.m. to 5 a.m., though paid at the same rate as the day workers. On occasions he was obliged to work two shifts running, a total of 16 hours. Pedro worked the night shift for four and a half years until his health seriously deteriorated. He suffered increasing problems with his eyes and began spitting blood. José refused to take Pedro off the night shift but gave him 5000 pesos to consult a specialist. Pedro was advised to take a month's rest, work fewer hours and give up night work for good. But José was adamant: if Pedro was not back on the night shift by the end of the week, then he was dismissed. José did offer, however, to give Pedro social security. He was not fit enough to return to work, so was sacked receiving a small sum by way of separation money.

Pedro decided to fight his dismissal and talked first with the Office of the Council for Arbitration and Conciliation in Zamora, but it was not willing to intervene. He was then counselled to get in touch with a left-wing lawyer in Morelia. This lawyer agreed there was a case to answer and drafted a petition of protest which described the workshop's illegality. José was summoned by the Council to appear before a session in Morelia.

After receiving the summons, José called on Pedro at home offering him 40 000 pesos to drop the labour petition, but he refused. At the hearing, the Council took note of the conditions and ordered José to pay 80 000 pesos in compensation to Pedro. The success of Pedro's demand forced José to take two decisions in the workshop. First, he began to pay all his workers wages at or above the legal minimum. Now that his workshop was known to the Morelia authorities, he could expect much greater harassment by inspectors in future if he remained 'illegal'. José recognized that the workers had 'put a noose around his neck'. The other decision he took was to purchase a second Carrousel so as to avoid night work. But he did not offer work to Pedro; indeed he will not even acknowledge him should they pass in the street.

For Pedro, the loss of his job at José's workshop was not so damaging. As a competent Carrousel operator, he did not suffer the same fate as loom operators who worked the motorized looms. His skills were in demand and despite his known left-wing politics he soon found work.

Once José began paying minimum wages, he had hoped that his workshop would be free from labour protest. Many skilled workers now sought employment there and he could select only the best workers. But the question of responsibility for health costs had not been solved. José rewarded the male loom operators with social security, but gave it to only three women workers.

Labour dismissal in the Hernández workshop

In 1986, the Hernández workshop was employing 26 women and nine men. Of the women, 24 were unmarried and aged between 14 and 22 years; and two were married in their 30s. (A 12-year-old had been employed but was sacked for lack of discipline). Two main groups could be discerned from the wages paid out: the 14 machine sewers received some 7000 to 7800 pesos per week (in early 1986, when the legal minimum was nearly 10 000 pesos per week) and the others performing more menial work got between 4000 and 6500 pesos per week. Though there were two main categories amongst the women workers, the Hernández brothers followed a highly personalistic policy so that the precise wage level was open to negotiation. Workers were pressed to compete with each other, trying to find favour in the employers' eyes. As a result the same job might be reimbursed with markedly different wages; this was also the case with other sums, such as separation money. Workers generally were suspicious of each other and unwilling to risk collective action

Physical conditions in the workshop were particularly bad. In converting an old house on the main square, interior walls had been torn out and windows boarded up. There was no natural light; neither was there sufficient ventilation and the whole building stank with fumes from the motorized looms. Acrylic dust hung in the air. In the hot months the workshop heated up like an oven. The workers were shut up in the workshop from 6 a.m. until 3 p.m. with a half-hour break at midday.

The workers were frightened of the health risks they ran and angry that the owners did nothing to improve working conditions. Until the end of 1986, no worker had social security. This negligence was seen to contradict the religious atmosphere which the owners' mother tried to bring to the workshop, with shrines to the Virgin of Guadalupe and occasionally prayer meetings. The owners shared labour supervision with a male overseer, one of them usually walking about the workshop urging the women workers to work faster. Workers recorded how much they hated the men 'breathing down their necks'. The owners had adopted different management styles: the younger owner was apparently 'sweet' and 'considerate' though also extremely flirtatious; the older owner and the overseer were thought to be rude and abusive, swearing and speaking harshly to the workers. The expression of labour control most deeply resented by the women was the verbal abuse of the older owner and overseer. This was equated with a gross lack of respect. They tried to humiliate the women, screaming at them or treating them with icy disdain. Many workers said wistfully how they longed for some words of praise. Some of the workers refused to meekly accept the abuse and learnt to stand up for themselves. Lupita, for example, recalled saying to the older owner: 'Why are you shouting at us? You have no right to. You are not my father. You should treat us with respect. I am a worker and I demand that you treat me with respect as a worker.' The owner referred to her and others who 'answered back' as 'niñas malcriadas' or naughty little girls.

Lupita and Silvia had been employed in the Hernández workshop since it had first opened in 1982. Lupita, 22 years old, had the reputation of being able to work every type of sewing machine; she had first entered a workshop at the age of 15 years. Silvia, 19 years, had worked in agriculture before entering the Hernández workshop. On various occasions they had discussed the working conditions with other workers in the sewing room, but the first concerted effort to take action came in March 1985. The sewing room workers appealed for the right to have Mother's Day free from work, partly so as to celebrate their own mothers, and partly so as to bring their cause to public notice since the celebration of Mother's Day fitted in well with the Church's attitude towards 'Marianism'. A sewing room 'spy' informed the owners of the plans and the owners threatened to dismiss any worker who stayed away. Only four were sufficiently brave not to appear, Lupita and Silvia being publicly reprimanded for their disloyalty at a chance encounter with the owners in the main square. The four workers lost a day's pay but not their jobs.

Lupita left the workshop in November 1985 when she married but Silvia decided to try again to channel the women's grievances into demanding the right to hold national public holidays free from work. This time the date was set for 5 February 1986, Constitution Day. The workers pressed for their legal right: a day off or double pay. Once again a spy kept the owners informed. On 4 February, the owners confronted Silvia at her sewing machine and in front of her 'compañeras' threatened her with dismissal. She spoke up bravely, but looking round for support, found herself now alone in the workshop for the other women had fled. Only Silvia stayed away from work the following day.

The older Hernández brother summoned Silvia to his office on 1 March, ostensibly to complain about her slow pace of work. He also upbraided her for being a trouble maker and after a torrent of abuse, shouted that if she did not like the conditions of work, she could 'get the hell out'. Silvia replied that she knew that conditions in the workshop were bad and illegal. Since she did not accept them, she considered herself dismissed. She was handed her week's wages and in an already prepared envelope 20 000 pesos 'separation' money. The latter amount Silvia refused, saying it was far too little to compensate for the number of years of employment. Silvia intimated that the Hernández would hear from her again to which the brother replied: 'You can ask the help of whatever lawyer you like, but you'll never get one centavo more from us'.

On 12 April the younger Hernández brother came to Silvia's house and offered her back her job and a sum of money to buy 'a new dress'. By this time the Hernández knew that Silvia had taken advice from her brother-in-law (a well-known left-wing activist). She refused their offer. Silvia was trying to find a lawyer in Morelia. On 15 April the lawyer came to Santiago to gather details about her case. Together they prepared a 'demanda' or petition listing the many ways in which the workshop transgressed the law and claiming larger compensation for loss of job. The 'demanda' specified the following points: the workshop did not pay minimum wages, or give Social Security provisions; workers did not receive the statutory two weeks' paid vacation, neither did they receive national holidays; the women workers had to work extra hours to clean up the workshop each day; only one lavatory was provided for both men's and women's use and the owners abused the labour force, as in the case of Silvia's dismissal.

By coincidence, the candidate for the ruling party (Partido Revolucionario Institucional, PRI) in the elections for the post of State Governor visited Santiago on 11 May. At a rally a young PRI doctor stood up to inform Martínez Villacana of the abuses in the town. Here, the workshops employed minors of 12 years, did not pay minimum wages or Social Security; there were no paid holidays and no distribution of profits. The candidate was seen to take notes.

The petition arrived at the Hernández workshop on 13 May summoning the owners to attend a hearing of the Council for Labour Conciliation and Arbitration in Morelia on 22 May. The brothers were furious, and telephoned the news around other workshop owners. But both owners came to Silvia's house on 18 May to try to charm her out of the fight. They offered her 70 000 pesos and her job back if she would give up 'the joke'. They also told her that the worry of the pending case had made their mother ill.

Silvia replied that she was not in such desperate need of money, that, for her, the case was no 'joke'.

On 22 May, Silvia, her mother and brother-in-law went to Morelia to the hearing of the Council of Labour Conciliation and Arbitration. In a closed session (Silvia's family sitting outside the court) the owners claimed that Silvia had said a week before 1 March that her mother wanted her to stop working; there had been no dispute like the one she claimed. They were prepared to offer Silvia her job back with the same conditions of work. She refused on account of their misrepresentation of her dismissal and because working conditions were so bad. The owners then offered her 100 000 pesos by way of compensation, to which Silvia replied that the money did not interest her. She didn't want them to go on making a fool of her, she was prepared to go on with the fight. A document was prepared by the Council summarizing the proceedings and noting that the hearing would continue on 12, 13 and 16 June. To this meeting, Silvia would need to bring witnesses in support of her claims of illegality while the owners were charged with finding documentary proof as to how they complied with the law. Silvia told the court she would bring Lupita and another worker (who had resigned in June 1985) as witnesses. The owners said their witnesses would be the overseer and two workers.

On returning to Santiago the owners spread word around the town that Silvia had behaved so badly that even her own lawyer had been forced to tell her off. Her mother they claimed had spent the time weeping outside. The mother was incensed by their allegations, especially that she had ordered Silvia to quit her job. As she put it: 'As her mother I am responsible for safeguarding her honour, her health and her person, but as she is now nearly 20 years old, her work is her own affair'.

By chance on 30 May the younger owner met Lupita in the plaza. He said how surprised he had been that she had been taken in by Silvia's lies; did she not realize that she would perjure herself if she testified about the dismissal? That was why he himself could not be a witness. If she went on with her silliness, she risked being sent to gaol. Didn't she realize she would get a sentence of at least two years for perjury? Silvia was only out for herself, that was why she was claiming the ridiculous sum of 1 000 000 pesos (sic) from them. Neither of Silvia's friends were in any position to act as witnesses for neither had even been employed in the workshop at the time of Silvia's leaving. She had not been sacked so why was she complaining. Lupita broke in constantly to challenge these remarks. What about their own witnesses then, she asked. They had not been present at the dismissal either. They were not ordinary workers like her and Silvia; everybody knew they were better paid because they informed against their fellow workers. She knew she too would have been sacked sooner or later, and that it was accidental she had left before this happened. If she did go to gaol, it would be his job (as a former lawyer) to get her out; would he really like the town to know that he had put away a pregnant woman? (Lupita was by then three months pregnant). The owners were not going to make a fool out of her either.

The owners circulated a letter around the workers on 31 May, asking them to sign it. The letter stated that workers received regular wage increases, extra payment at Christmas-time and paid holidays. The owners explained to some workers that Silvia was holding them to ransom; but to her friends, they said nothing. The latter did not realize the letter was connected with the pending case. All the workers signed.

Lupita was then threatened by her uncle, also a workshop owner who depended on the Hernández for access to thread. He visited her and her mother at home. He repeated what the younger owner had said and added the following points: the owners had already bribed Silvia's lawyer; the younger owner still had good connections in the legal field and was determined to win the case. If there was more trouble in the town, owners like himself would close their workshops since they could easily live off their investments in the bank. But the workers would lose everything; Lupita's mother became extremely nervous.

These allegations appeared to carry weight when Silvia's lawyer failed to appear at a meeting arranged for 5 June and sent no message. He was to come to talk over the case with Silvia's witnesses. There was much speculation as to whether he might really have been bought off by the owners; Silvia and Lupita felt worried and less decisive. They talked over the possibility of organizing a second letter and collecting signatures from former workers who were more prepared to speak out about the illegal conditions, and they asked Silvia's brother-in-law to draft it, but he was busy. By 10 June, nothing had been heard from the lawyer so Silvia's brother-in-law set out to look for him, taking a day off from school teaching. The lawyer was found on 11 June in Los Reyes where he had been trying to get peasant clients out of gaol. He was furious about the story that he had been bought off, but he was no longer in a position to represent Silvia the following day. He rang a colleague to take Silvia's case and it was agreed that they would meet in the Morelia bus station at 9 a.m.

They left Santiago in the early morning but at the appointed time there was no sign of the lawyer in the bus station. He finally arrived there five minutes before the hearing was due to start. He briefly explained to Silvia what the Council would wish to ask her about. By the time they arrived at the Council's offices the Hernández brothers and their lawyer were already waiting. Immediately they offered her a new settlement; this time 250 000 pesos (of which 50 000 pesos would go on her lawyers' fees). There followed some confused negotiations with the lawyers running back and forth to their clients. After some minutes' hesitation Silvia decided to drop the petition and accept the settlement. So with a certain air of festivity the two sides entered the Council offices and signed an agreeement; and Silvia was congratulated on her 'victory'.

For Silvia the victory felt hollow. Many reasons could be given in retrospect as to why it had been a good decision to settle. Clearly the case would have gone on for months and have posed heavy financial and emotional costs for her and her family. The cost of getting to Morelia by bus for a day had been heavy for a family where nobody had a regular income. Silvia felt constrained by her mother's request the night before that she settle if offered a decent amount by way of compensation. Furthermore, Lupita might well have been unable to act as chief witness and supporter at a more advanced stage of pregnancy or after her child was born. For Silvia, the moment she relished most was when the workshop owners had been forced to await her decision as to whether to continue or drop the case. The compensation Silvia received was the largest amount awarded to date to any Santiago worker, and it was particularly remarkable that she, a woman, had won it. Her brother-in-law was of the opinion that the time was not ripe for a prolonged struggle but that her example might inspire others to fight for their rights. It was subsequently discovered that the Hernández' case had been seriously weakened by the last minute refusal on the part of two of their witnesses to appear (the overseer and one of the workers).

Two days after the Morelia meeting, the Hernández announced their intention to raise wages in the workshop. Now the top overlock machine sewers who had been longest in the workshop would receive wages pegged to the official minimum level, and the rest could hope for higher reimbursement once profits had increased. This decision to increase wages had partly been provoked by Silvia's action, but it also reflected the workshop's loss of experienced machine sewers who left to work in the better paying workshops. Labour productivity was falling alarmingly as the less experienced sewers could not work as fast as women like Lupita and Silvia. By early 1987, the brothers were making public appeals through the loud-speaker system on the church tower for experienced sewers promising them official minimum wages and the future possibility of social security.

REFERENCES

P. Arias, *Nuevas modalidades de la industria de la ropa en el medio rural: pueblos naquilleros, pequena industria y trabajo a domicilio en los Altos de Talisco* (MS, El Colegio de Michoacan, 1986).

A. Portes, 'The Informal Sector: definition, controversy and relation to national development', *Review*, 1,VII (1983).

F. Wilson, *Sweaters: Gender, Class and Workshop-based Industry in Mexico* (London: Macmillan, 1991).

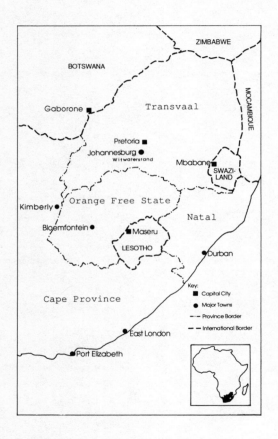

Map 3   South Africa and Lesotho: Area of Basotho Labour Migration

4 Basotho Miners, Ethnicity and Workers' Strategies

Jeff Guy and Motlatsi Thabane

THE ORAL HISTORY PROJECT

The October 1987 AKUT seminar on 'Workers' strategies and third world industrialization' encouraged us to return to a body of material collected between 1982 and 1985 by the Oral History Project of the National University of Lesotho from a group of 'third-world' workers; in this case men from the Kingdom of Lesotho who spent much of their working lives as migrant labourers in South Africa, predominantly in gold and diamond mines, but also in industry.

The Oral History Project was supervised by Jeff Guy, and the life histories were collected and translated by Motlatsi Thabane. The Project was set up as a result of our conviction that the National University, established in a country which for over a century has been a major supplier of African labour to neighbouring South Africa, should (i) give priority to labour studies while (ii) the Department of History could usefully draw on the skills being developed internationally in oral history. We were both dissatisfied at the general, liberal, approach to migrant labour studies in Southern Africa which tended to depict the migrant purely as victim, and which saw the oppressor in migrancy itself; with the implication that exploitation could be ended by the introduction of stabilized wage labour. We had also some experience of orthodox research projects in Lesotho which sought to extract perceptions and attitudes by means of the prepared questionnaire, and we felt that there was a strong tendency for researchers using this method to create evidence which confirmed their own views of labour migrancy.

We felt that the world of the migrant labourer was still a closed world. The Southern African migrant labour force has generally been characterized as 'cheap, unskilled, with a rapid rate of turnover' –

that is just the sort of workforce which leaves little behind in the way of historical record. Oral history, it seemed to us, was a way of gaining some access to this world and making a start in creating a social history of labour migrancy based on the worker's own perceptions of his world.

In the first phase of the Project, Thabane collected 20 interviews. The general approach was to initiate as free an interview as possible, allowing the informant to reminisce on his personal history, concentrating on his childhood, his first contract and then life at work in South Africa. Thabane did have a standard set of questions and these were introduced after the free interview had ended, although not necessarily in a structured way, and they were often interspersed with questions which sought to clarify earlier parts of the testimony.

The interviews are of course as varied as the personalities of the informants themselves – but they include some of great depth, interest and insight into the lives of Southern African workers. For this paper we have used 12 of these interviews, which make up over 900 pages of typed transcript. All but two of them were from men who took their initial contracts after 1925 and before 1939.[1] We examined them with the object of seeing how they reflect on the subject of 'workers' strategies'; and it was immediately clear that the term itself raised a number of issues some of which have been at the centre of some of the most significant historiographical debates in recent years.

THE HISTORY OF CLASS

One of the major questions was raised at and about the AKUT seminar itself. As indicated earlier, Ali El Kenz and Said Chikhi questioned assumptions in the title of the seminar (see Chapter 2). The concept of 'strategy' they felt implied the existence of well-organized, consolidated, powerful social groups, locked in struggle with other groups, and devising methods of combat. We cannot assume, they argued, the existence of 'workers' without worker consciousness – the subjective awareness of the objective conditions. Moreover in the third world class awareness is subordinated to ethnic, religious and other non-class forms. There is activity but not strategy. In particular, the concept 'workers' strategy' cannot be applied to the early stages of industrialization when capitalist and pre-capitalist forces clash in chaos, the one incompletely formed and the other still a force, and individuals move from one social formation to another. It is possible to discuss workers' strategies in the industrialized world, but in the industrializing world we cannot assume the existence of workers' consciousness and organization and therefore a notion of strategy. The concept, it was argued, prejudged the topic under consideration and ran the risk of imposing categories derived from the industrialized onto the industrializing world. The position taken by these Algerian authors is understandable. The word 'strategy' does have military implications and suggestions of large-scale, well-organized planning. However there are dangers of restricting the idea of 'workers' strategies' to just this meaning. It forces workers' history towards the study of the history of workers' leadership, of working-class institutions and organizations, and major public confrontations with capital. It also runs the danger of ignoring the personal struggles, private defeats and the victories of small groups, and the continuing attempts of workers to gain control over their lives, thereby giving much of the lived history of the working class only marginal significance.

Moreover, by defining workers' strategy as the conscious product of organized groups one is moving in a different direction to some of the most interesting historiographical trends of recent years. For example, away from trends in social history which concentrate on recreating the lives and activities of people and organizations conventionally ignored as insignificant; away from oral history which has provided a methodological basis for writing more democratic histories; from the greater awareness of the totality of working-class experience.

It is also in danger of moving in a different direction from the very significant trend in modern historiography which has its origins in the works of English historians like E. P. Thompson and Stedman Jones and has been taken up in class history in Finland (Haapala, 1987). Increasingly writers on the subject are stressing the limitations of taking too narrow a view of the history of the working class. The existence of the theoretically pure workers – that is, the free worker under capitalism in the fullest sense, freed from the ties of the past, dependent on the wage, and organized around questions of exploitation under capitalism – is being questioned. It is giving way to analyses of workers who are not only members of a class, but also of communities, located in a specific national past and culture, and who work in an industry which is similarly contextualized. Such an approach stresses the importance of building into the analysis the specific material and ideological links with the pre-capitalist past and a broader social present. This means of course a careful awareness of the specific in the study under consideration and careful contextualization.

Such approaches have been developed to a large extent in opposition to what are seen as workerist or narrowly Marxist approaches which insist upon presenting labour history as the emergence with industrialization under capitalism of a self-conscious working class, free of extra-economic constraints and organized around a self-awareness of its historical role as the conqueror of its exploiter, capitalism – for which of course it has to develop an effective strategy.

However, while both these positions offer important insights and useful correctives, both have dangers if taken to extremes and we have to seek a position between them. In stressing the significance of what is specific to a situation we must not lose the crucial general concept of class. This means contextualizing the problem within a productive system, and defining a group not only in terms of its culture and its consciousness of itself, but also its position within historically defined forces and relations of production.

In the case of the Sotho workers (s. Mosotho, pl. Basotho) we are dealing with migrants who, although they worked long contracts within a capitalist system, also spent much of their lives as peasant farmers. We are therefore dealing with people who are neither free labourers nor totally denied access to the means of production and who express in their lives many of the contradictions of their ambivalent economic situation. But because such variations on classic theoretical positions exist this does not mean that the theory should be excluded. Productive forces, relations of production and class are theoretical landmarks which make it possible for us to locate ourselves historically, to measure change, to make useful comparisons, something especially necessary when we search for the general amongst the specific in the confusing and contradictory world on the periphery of capitalist development.

Similarly, on the question of the meaning of 'strategy', we have to try and find a middle path. To apply the concept only to the self-conscious, stable institutions of organized labour, which confront in their different ways organized capital is too restricting. On the other hand, strategy should not be allowed to apply to all aspects of activity on the part of the working class. In one sense it is possible to see every action taken by a worker as a strategy – given that the social context is to a large degree defined by capitalism. The problem with the term is not unlike that of 'resistance' in that it is so broad that it can disappear in the minutia of everyday life.

Thus too narrow a definition restricts the idea of the 'worker' and ties the strategies adopted to those over working conditions, the wage, and revolution. Too broad a definition loses such indispensable concepts as production and class and their capacity for analysis and comparison, and moves history away from the crucial ideas of labour, conflict, and capital, too far towards the narrowly personal and psychological.

This chapter attempts to deal with these problems of definition and conceptionalization not so much by defining them beforehand as by providing a context and looking at aspects of lives as process.

THE BASOTHO MIGRANT WORKER

The workers who form the subject of this chapter were migrant labourers, dependent to a large degree, although not entirely, on the wage. They made up a significant part of the huge migrant workforce which has built the gold mining industry of South Africa, and with it the most powerful regional economy in Africa. The South African mining industry has dominated the political economy of Southern Africa and has been built upon a large, African workforce drawn, until the 1970s, to a significant degree from beyond South Africa's borders. It is a formally unskilled labour force, working on contract, whose members return to their place of origin between contracts.

Lesotho is a politically independent state completely surrounded by South Africa. It was annexed by the British in 1868 and regained its independence in 1966. For a century its people have played a major role in the industrialization of Southern Africa. At the end of the Second World War about a quarter of a million men were working on the South African mines – perhaps one-fifth of the total population.

Lesotho has always been seen as home by the majority of workers, and the family land and livestock have far greater value than any price they might raise on the market. However, rural production is dependent upon the wages earned by the migrant workers. Consequently, despite the strong social attraction created by this rural base which families continued to farm, under traditional forms of land tenure, chiefly rule and customary law, the significant presence in other words of pre-capitalist forces of one kind or another, these men should be considered 'workers'.

Labour migrancy, together with organizational cooperation between the mining houses, made it possible for mining capital to keep African wages low. Moreover, it was a controlled workforce, the mine workers being housed and fed in large strictly controlled compounds attached to each mine. Work was racially defined. Most African miners were kept by law in unskilled positions with limited movement into supervisory roles. White miners supervised and managed the African labour force. Labour in the South African mining industry has always been migrant, cheap, formally unskilled and racially organized. The mines are deep and the ore-body narrow. Working conditions are therefore uncomfortable and dangerous.

The context, then, of this chapter is that of an extremely repressive working environment: of badly-paid labour, harsh working conditions, and the continual threat of racial violence where workers' rights were minimal. Living conditions were regimented and controlled, in huge single-sex compounds. Those workers who lived in towns escaped some of these aspects, but their lives were generally deprived and insecure. This case study concerns attempts which were made to ameliorate such conditions – attempts which, we would argue, can be seen as strategy.

We use the word 'strategy' to mean not just resistance to these repressive conditions, but attemps which indicate that workers have projected their predicament into the future as a means of gaining some control over it. We have been selective in the topics presented here and tried to isolate aspects which seem from the testimony collected to have a wide significance, choosing the social rather than the intensely personal. Most important, we have chosen to ignore one large area in which workers are deeply involved – the strategies whereby wages are invested in the developmental cycle in the rural area.

Any discussion of workers' strategy has to be firmly situated chronologically. Most of the men whose personal histories form the basis of this chapter were born about the time of the First World War. They herded their fathers' cattle in the 1920s and took their first contracts in the 1930s. Thus a formative event in their lives was the great depression which was associated not only with the collapse of agricultural commodity prices and the closure of a number of the diamond mines which employed large numbers of Basotho workers, but also a serious drought and famine in 1932–3. This formed the background to a great increase not only in migrant labour but also in more permanent moves to the cities of South Africa. It became possible in the period of industrial expansion after the depression and during the Second World War for the determined Basotho worker to find more permanent employment in industry which paid better than the mining.

The opening of the Free State gold fields in the post-war period meant that Basutoland was the closest labour source. From the start Basotho mineworkers dominated the Free State mines and it was here that they consolidated their reputation as a group with specific mining skills. In 1963 the Aliens Controls Act made it more difficult to follow the by now usual path of gaining entry to the South African labour market by taking a contract on a mine and then moving into the better-paid work in industry.

These miners whose working lives straddled the Second World War also experienced important changes in the technology and the labour process in mining especially in the moving of rock underground. Our informants were therefore aware that aspects of underground work had become easier. But there had been little possibility of changing the technology of mining the ore-body and thus the rock-breaking process in the stopes remained substantially unaltered.

In 1966 Lesotho gained its independence from Britain, an event which caused little economic change for the Basotho worker – unlike the rise in the gold price in the 1970s, which was for a time reflected in the first substantial increase in real wages on the mines since the beginning of the century, and the emergence of unemployment. But while our informants were keenly aware of these developments few had experienced them personally as they had already completed their last contracts and moved back to permanent residence in the rural areas of Lesotho.

ETHNICITY AS A STRATEGY

Reading through these workers' life histories one overwhelming 'strategy' emerges. It is based on the sense of ethnic commonality – of being a Mosotho amongst other Basotho, and the need to guard and draw on this for support and protection – of being a worker amongst other workers from the same background, with a shared history and language; of coming from a country which resisted the attacks of the Boers and which had not been incorporated into the

Union of South Africa; of coming from a British colony, and therefore with a history very different from that of black South Africans.

This sense of being a Mosotho is to be found at all points in the workers' lives; it is in the initial decision to take a contract often with advice from an experienced relative and using his contacts on the mines; it is to be found in the planning of the shared journey to the recruiting station; on the train; in the vast, controlled, single sex compounds where workers were housed according to ethnic groups. It was also to be found in those districts in the townships and slums which became Basotho enclaves, and in the urban gangs of Basotho who guarded the community from similar ethnically defined groups, and attacks by criminals or police.

It is, however, hard to document in the sense that it is of such obvious significance that it is assumed rather than articulated. But in the personal histories collected in the Oral History Project it is to be found most urgently and dramatically in the cry of the isolated individual suddenly in danger as he calls out for help: 'Banna ba heso! [My countrymen . . .!]'[2]

This sense of ethnic identity and the ethnic support it could mobilize in times of need in a hostile and dangerous environment provided the basis for the most important of the strategies developed by Basotho (and other workers from different backgrounds) during this period in South African mining history. However, we must stress from the outset that we do not consider this sense of ethnicity to be an objective manifestation of links with a clearly-defined ethnic past. It is also, to an important degree, an 'invented' tradition with a dynamic, socially-created content. Secondly, this content has been created not only by the people themselves as a strategy in a changing and threatening world but also by those who seek to control them – specifically by the South African state and the mining industry, and its benefactors and beneficiaries.

Thus the nineteenth-century conquest of the peoples of Southern Africa reinforced the divisions between them as a prerequisite for effective rule. The attack on rural agricultural self-sufficiency and the resultant creation of the South African workforce was associated with policies based on ethnic compartmentalization and racial segregation, in which perceived ethnic differences were stressed and ethnic rivalry encouraged. One strategy of mine management to divide the work-force and the compounds lay in the control of the *induna* in a system which was supposed to imitate 'traditional', 'tribal' political structures. This was capped by the policy of apartheid which promoted ethnic difference to the rank of state ideology.

Alternative strategies were present – the broad-based nationalism of the African National Congress, the call for political equality of the liberals, and the call to class of the trade unionists and communists. At certain times these alternative ideologies have been influential. But ethnic identity has remained a powerful force coming time and again to the fore during crisis and struggle. And the men whose life histories form the basis of this chapter fall back on their sense of local identity, shared histories and experience as protection in the struggle during their working lives.

However, ethnicity in this situation is also a negative force from the workers' point of view. It can be manipulated by management and the state as a form of control. It is particularly destructive when what the authorities see as 'tribalism' manifests itself in violent physical clashes between miners. But a sense of ethnicity is also a means whereby the individual finds security and safety as a member of a wider group which can protect him in the violent and dangerous world of wage labour in South Africa, and, as such, must be seen as a 'worker's strategy'.

ETHNICITY AS STRATEGY – SHAFT SINKING ON THE MINES

We have already published two papers in which ethnicity is a major theme and which can be re-examined in the context of workers' strategies. One considered the identification of ethnicity with specific work skills – in this case the widespread belief that Basotho mine workers had unchallengeable skills as manual rock loaders. This was especially true in the organized rock loading process during the particularly dangerous stage in mining – shaft sinking (Guy and Thabane, 1987 and 1988). It is widely held by mine management that Basotho abilities in shaft sinking are unique. This point of view was also held by our informants:

There are no people apart from Basotho who know how to dig shaft sinking. Other peoples arrive when the shaft sinking is over. Every shaft is dug by Basotho. When they have dug it, and it is completely finished, then other kinds of people arrive.[3]

and

> *The Basotho are very strong people at work . . . When they sink a*
> *shaft you'll not find any other people there – you'll always find that*
> *the only people there are Basotho . . . Other black people only go to*
> *work when it is a mine down which people go – they don't go to the*
> *mine when it is just red top-soil.*[4]

This opinion has been extended and one often hears the view amongst people in Lesotho that it was Basotho miners who 'opened the mines' of South Africa, and therefore have, or at least should have, precedence amongst miners.

By placing such statements in a broader context we were able to suggest something of their social and economic origins. In the period after the Second World War a vast new gold field was opened in the Orange Free State – a province of South Africa adjacent to the Colony of Basutoland whose people therefore formed the most obvious source of labour for the new gold field. And the initial task was to sink the shafts which would give access to the gold-bearing reef hundreds of metres below the surface.

Shaft sinking is an intrinsically dangerous mining operation because of the presence of large numbers of men blasting and moving rock vertically in a confined space. Moreover, there is an urgency in shaft sinking because until the mine becomes operational the vast amounts of capital invested in the venture are dormant. And there was a particular urgency in the opening of the Free State Fields. The state of the international money market in the post-war period had made it especially hard to raise the capital. Moreover the gold-bearing reef in the Free State did not outcrop and had been assessed by surface investigation only. It was therefore not until the shafts had reached the reef that the economic viability of the Free State fields could be known with confidence.

It is within this context of intrinsically hard and dangerous work, made even more intense by the specific context in which the shafts were being sunk, that the identification of the Basotho with special skills as shaft sinkers developed. It was held by management that the strength of the Basotho and their ability to accept discipline and to work as a team was a particular attribute of their ethnic background. It enabled them to work with enormous productivity in the noisy and dangerous world of shafts; in particular it enabled them to shovel huge quantities of broken rock in an ordered sequence out of the shaft bottoms with great speed thereby allowing the rapid re-entry of the blasting shift and the repetition of the process.

The advantages to management of promoting and encouraging this view is clear. It provided a means of motivating and organizing a workforce in order that it might drive a shaft through rock at record speeds. But the point is that this linking of specific shaft-sinking skills with ethnicity was promoted not only by management but by the Basotho as well and forms, in our opinion, part of their strategy as workers.

Members of shaft sinking crews enjoyed higher wages. The earning capacity of conventional mine workers was low and an increase was restricted by a maximum average scheme whereby the mining houses kept wages at an agreed level. Shaft sinking, however, was a category exempted from this and workers were paid productivity bonuses.

A shaft pays well. If I was to start on the mines at another job and then discovered that there was a lot of money at the shaft then a person would contact me and say, 'Hey, come here my brother, there is money here'. And sure enough when you got there you'd discover there was a lot of money although you'd also discover that there was much more work . . .[5]

Furthermore management was particularly concerned about shaft sinkers' health and strength. They therefore had access to the mine kitchens, and extra rations.

The evidence also suggests that the creation of ethnically defined work skills was not just the result of a drive for greater material benefits. Shaft sinking, with its emphasis on teamwork, physical prowess and feats of strength in the pursuit of record speeds did something to ameliorate the loneliness and the degradation associated with mine work and mine life.

The identification of certain skills with ethnicity in order to obtain better pay was clearly a strategy adopted by Basotho mine workers. But it was of course a contradictory strategy. The physically exciting team work took place in a particularly dangerous environment. The emphasis on ethnic superiority helped create an atmosphere of ethnic rivalry and thus divisions within the labour force. Management was therefore confronted with a divided workforce and therefore one which was easier to control – except for those occasions when, in the tense atmosphere of the compound, these rivalries were manifested as ethnic violence which swept through the mine and disrupted production.

Ethnic violence of this kind was known as faction fighting and was seen by management as part of the 'tribalism' inherent in African life. Such racial interpretations can be dismissed with ease. Nonetheless this does not mean we can accept the views of those who see the explanation for ethnic division solely in the strategies devised by mining capital. For the personal testimonies we collected suggest strongly (i) that ethnicity is a strategy used by not just management but also by labour and (ii) that while a sense of ethnicity is created, nurtured and manipulated by management in particular contexts, it also rests on deeply felt ethnic consciousness which, in this context, is part of worker consciousness and has to be analysed as such.

ETHNICITY AS STRATEGY – GANGS IN THE TOWN

The other paper referred to above introduces the question of ethnicity in a different context. Shaft sinking is associated with the mines and the compounds – the 'classic' Basotho worker environment. But it has to be remembered that for much of their history – and especially in the three decades which bracket the Second World War – many Basotho workers took a contract on the mines as a way of entering South Africa. Once the contract was completed they left the mine to find work in industry, exchanging the discipline and deprivation of the mine compound for the freer more varied life in the African townships or locations which had sprung up near the places of work.

The townships, with their shacks, shebeens and squalor were places of poverty and violence, but offered a degree of freedom and contrast to the regimented violence of the compounds. A feature of the township was criminal violence and the urban gang. There were the juvenile bands of *tsotsis* on the lookout for the lone worker with his pay packet – and the more organized criminal gangs like the Berliners or the Gestapo. There were also ethnic gangs – and the best known of these was the gang of urban-dwelling Basotho called Ma-Rashea – the Russians.

The Russians seem to have originated in the Basotho enclave to the west of Johannesburg in the township of Newclare in the 1930s. It was a gang made up specifically of men from Basutoland. They were identified by their black trousers, white shoes, covered by the 'traditional' Basotho blanket in the folds of which they hid their weapons, in particular the *melamu*, the fighting stick. Their declared intention was to provide safety and security to Basotho in the working class areas. To do this they sought out the *tsotsis*, and the ethnically organized gangs, and attempted to destroy them. By the 1940s and 1950s these inter-gang struggles had gained a momentum of their own and there were epic clashes as members of one gang travelled across the Witwatersrand to confront their enemies, or to defend their own territories.

The Oral History Project's knowledge of the Russians comes from an informant who was a member and who we called Rantao (Informant 11). From his evidence it is clear that the Ma-Rashea was a Basotho gang, an urban gang and a gang of workers and its origins lay in the need for protection in a lawless environment. But Rantao's evidence goes further than this. It enables us to see that the violence was not just to protect and to plunder. Participation in the gang and gang warfare took on a wider social role in the deprived environment of the townships. The intellectual demands in the planning of the fight, the physical demands in its execution, the celebration of victory, the outwitting of the police, all provided stimulation and excitement for the participants. Indeed Rantao made it clear that the Russians spent much of their time fighting amongst themselves and they were divided into two factions which reflected two regions in Lesotho whose rivalry had its foundations in factions around the king in pre-conquest days.

Once again Basotho ethnicity was expressed as a form of workers' strategy. In this case a strategy primarily for physical protection but one which also had the effect of enlivening the sterile, deprived environment of the urban slum. And, as in the case of the shaft sinkers it is a deeply contradictory strategy. The violence necessary for self-defence could also be turned upon the members themselves. More than this, in the South African situation, it is obviously a serious miscalculation to define the enemy as another African ethnic group. Both then and now the Russians were unable to discriminate effectively betweeen their friends and their enemies. Thus in the 1950s it is clear that the Russians were being used by the most reactionary elements to break boycotts, used strong-arm tactics against other Africans to raise funds, and, it was believed at the time, were perhaps even assisting the state in the destruction of other African communities.

INDIVIDUALIST STRATEGIES

The security and the advantages to be gained by staying within the ethnically-defined group and accepting the limitations of communal responsibility in return for certain monetary benefits and privileges provided the general framework of the strategy adopted by the miners who were interviewed. Nonetheless, there were some men whose strategy included attempts, if not to leave the ethnically-defined group, then at least to find the means to become dominant within it and move up the organizational structure to positions of responsibility – that is as team leader, foreman or 'boss boy' underground, or as *induna* or tribal representative in the compound. Moreover, in the case of some informants, promotion was obtained not just by convincing management that they had the abilities needed to take positions of responsibility – it was also necessary to obtain supernatural assistance from traditional doctors and their medicines.

Traditional medicine and promotion

The visit to the traditional doctor for medicine to assist in work on the mines seems to have been widespread. It could take place to ensure safety during the contract, or to assist in gaining the favour of white supervisors in the hope of getting fair treatment and possibly promotion.

Rantao describes his visit to a famous doctor in some detail (OHP, Informant 11, p. 15). In 1937, at the age of 15, before taking his first contract he consulted a woman doctor with a reputation for being especially skilled in safeguarding miners. Payment was three pounds, a portion on delivery and the balance on completion of the contract. Rantao told her of his wish for promotion. She gave him two different types of medicine, one of which was mixed with water and applied when washing and the other taken orally. She also gave him a warning:

> *My countryman, there are Motselekatse* [the labour centre in Johannesburg] *when you get there, you remove your clothes. You are searched in every article in your clothes and the medicines are thrown away there. But if you are clever you can pass with them.*

Experienced miners taught Rantao how to hide these medicines by crushing them inside his shoes against the toecap so that they remained in place when the shoes were searched. On arrival at the mine Rantao immediately discovered the harshness of mine labour and began his plans for less onerous work. He decided that he should become a *picannin* – that is the personal servant of a white miner underground. The next day Rantao woke early and went to the wash house to apply one of the medicines. He then went to the mine supervisor's office, placed the other medicine in his mouth and approached a white supervisor directly in his office asking for work. To the amazement of the other senior black workers (Shangaans from Mozambique, who accused him of bribery) he was made *picannin* to a ventilation engineer.

It was then that I saw for the first time that traditional medicines are important things, my man. Yes truly a person who says they do not work [does not know]. *I have tried them at different places. I can tell you the history of them and they work.* (OHP, Informant 11, p. 20)

Traditional medicine was not just for promotion – it was also used to ensure general well-being and to provide safety in the dangerous working conditions. One of our informants experienced a terrifying accident during shaft sinking which, although he escaped injury, killed men at the bottom of the shaft, including his cousin. However the conclusion he drew from this experience was the opposite of Rantao's – it persuaded him that traditional medicine was not effective. Consequently he turned to another form of supernatural assistance – Christianity.

We worked under such terror. I learnt faith when I was there. It was there that I learnt that faith – that I had to pray because traditional medicines did not work. It was at the shaft that I became certain of this . . .[6]

An important use to which magic was put by workers was to gain the favour of white supervisors. One informant spoke of the part it played in the rivalry between miners as they tried to gain the favour of white overseers and discredit their rivals.

. . . they use medicine. It is a matter of medicine. They do not speak with their mouths, instead they speak with these medicines. They eat medicines in such a way that a European is disgusted just by looking

at you, and then wants to fight you. Now if you have not protected yourself, you suddenly realise that even though he once trusted you this European now cannot even look at you . . .
These people work with things [medicines] *that are dug from the ground. They are very dangerous.*[7]

The desire for promotion and the benefits it brought clearly conflicted with the desire to belong to a wider social group. A number of our informants expressed a disinclination to accept positions of responsibility despite the increase in earnings:

No, I did not want to be a foreman. I hate pushing a person. A foreman has no compassion. He does not appreciate that people are not equal in strength. That is, he pushes each and every one in the same way. When he sees that one is strong, he thinks that the other one is deliberately shirking at work. Now this shows a lack of understanding because people are not equal in strength . . . (OHP, Informant 9, p. 51)

And as the implications of individual strategies came into conflict with the desire for commonality they created severe social tension, which could manifest itself in the use of witchcraft. Another informant (no. 13) explicitly linked his refusal to assume responsibility with a fear of the magic that could be used against him as a result:

I do not like being a foreman. There is a lot of witchcraft there. These foremen bewitch each other. They bewitch each other.[8]

It seems likely that the tension surrounding the African supervisor in the mines was a result in part of the fact that promotion in some ways contradicted the major premise upon which Basotho mining strategy was based – the support to be gained from being a member of a larger ethnically-defined group. Thus while medicine helped to gain promotion it also broke the communal ties of ethnically-organized labour, thereby exposing the promoted individual to danger both from rivals and from the consequences of exercising discipline over erstwhile comrades.

One of our informants gave a detailed account of this. He had gained the position of senior *induna* – a man responsible for order amongst a group of miners in the compound on the Free State mines in 1956. He took his job seriously and was proud of the way he resolved conflict between management and labour in a manner, as he saw it, which served the interests of both sides. He acted strongly against white miners who abused or assaulted African workers – and did what he could to end work stoppages and indiscipline on the part of the black miners. 'I knew how to talk to people . . . especially Basotho because I am Mosotho.' (OHP, Informant 8, p. 18)

His account of his downfall through magic has an epic quality. The actors are the major figures on the mine. It was his very reliability and efficiency as senior *induna* which brought him to the attention of the general manager of the mine, thereby incurring the resentment of the white compound manager.

Jealous of our informant's access to the general manager, the compound manager corrupted his best friend. He sent him to Lesotho to obtain medicine from a traditional doctor. A number of attempts were made to trick our informant into taking the medicine, and eventually he was persuaded to smoke a treated cigarette. He collapsed, but before being taken to hospital managed to make contact with a Zulu doctor and to work a counter-medicine. He hovered at death's door until his own medicine worked – the man who had given him the bewitched cigarette was killed in a car accident.

Our informant recovered his health but never his position on the mine – this had been destroyed by the jealousy of a white rival, the duplicity of a black friend, and their use of traditional medicine. This association of medicine and magic with promotion and status, and with failure and disgrace, seems to be a consequence, in part, of the inherent tension in the process of leaving the wider ethnically defined group in the search for better working conditions, and also with the insecurity and isolation that promotion and responsibility imply (OHP, Informant 8, pp. 19–25).

Violence and the 'strike'

Most of our informants had experienced some form of communal violence on the mines. The threat of violence was always there, and had to be avoided by management. At the same time they did not see violence towards the authorities as strategy in the consciously planned sense. It took place against a specific grievance or to end a particular abuse, but with the realization that such action was likely to provoke greater violence in return from management or the state.

A complicating feature of the accounts of violence, as in the one that follows, is the tendency for them to assume an ethnic character. It also reveals that the word 'strike' was used very broadly and could stand for any form of generalized violence against the mine.

Yes, I think it was in 'nineteen' what . . . when was it now? . . . 'thirty-six', in 'thirty-six' . . . a compound was burnt, people went on strike . . . right at the compound, right there where I was. I did not know the reason because I was still young. I did not know what the older ones were fighting for . . . suddenly realized that there was a fight there because when people go on strike they beat the cooks [laughter] *that is the first thing they do when they are on strike. The cooks, they give us so little food there at the kitchen and we therefore start at the kitchen and they spill all the food and we eat the meat there and – they start fighting with Shangaans. It was such a big fight, and the Basotho beat the Shangaans. And we threw so many stones – we used coal as well, because we had no fighting sticks.*

One Shangaan, he was beaten up by a man who still lives here. He was passing by our 'change house' and he beat him and he fell down. As it turned he was finished. There was such a big fight. It did not have an owner [ringleader] *and it was confined* [to the compound]. *When the people fight the compound police run to the outside and they close the door so no one can get out and they kill another there in the compound. And then they called in the police from the town . . . Shangaans can fight even though they are ignorant. They know how to fight, but they got beaten. We beat them so that they should know. I do not know how many died, perhaps it was four but I don't know. And those soldiers came . . . These one who wear dresses. When they got there they said 'Come nearer here all of you'. And they told us that no one was going down the mine. We had to stay above ground. And they started talking:*

'We want the Basotho to come nearer here . . . Basotho should come nearer here . . .' and the same for the Xhosa, and the Mpondo and all the people who were fighting there.

'Basotho should come nearer here'.

And when we got there he talked to us. They were armed with guns and they were terrifying. They were the ones who wear dresses, the Scotch. We thought, 'They are going to shoot us with those guns'. Those guns were fitted with bayonets at the front there. 'Lek' if he pierces you with it it will come out the other side. And then they talked to us and the trouble came to an end.

(But then it started again that evening when the police came from the nearby town and began to beat the people in the compounds.)

'Khelek!' they found a man sewing with a machine there and they did not even ask. They started beating him with sticks and they injured him. He knew exactly what to do. He crept into bed, and he covered himself with his blanket.
The compound fell completely silent. And the police beat people so much:
'You are refusing to work here. Have you come to strike here?'
And then the matter came to an end. Tomorrow the bells rang 'Kekere. ke-kere, ke-kere, ke-kere' and they got up even though they were not happy. People can easily fight there. On the way to work on the mine – it is as far from the compound as about to where that village is over there. While going to the mine you can feel that people could easily fight on the way. But we pass each other walking. But as it happened there was no fighting. Even down the mine people are afraid of each other. But you work [with people from other ethnic groups]. *Perhaps you work with these other people and you are the only Mosotho among them and they could easily do something to you. But then as it turned out nothing happened and the people just worked and that fight came to an end . . .*
I did not know what was being fought for. The ringleaders were arrested. I don't know what happened to them. They came from my home area . . . (OHP, Informant 9, pp.20-1).

None of our informants had planned a strike. As in the case above the word 'strike' easily blended into generalized violence with strong ethnic overtones rather than organized workers' strategy for defined objectives. The term 'workers' organization' was usually identified by our informants with a 'burial society' – that is, an organization which collected funds to pay for, in the case of a fatal accident, the return of the body home for burial (for example, informant 9, pp. 25 ff).

There were of course strikes during the period that these men worked – including the historic 1946 mine workers strike. One of our informants was involved in what seems to have been the 1946 strike but was a somewhat reluctant participant with little awareness of the issues involved (OHP, Informant 7).

None had much faith in the strike as workers' strategy. One believed that they were usually planned by the ambitious and the self-seekers. They were generally aware of the very serious consequences, of the vulnerability of the worker at the hands of management which could starve them out, leave them stranded underground without air or water, or, as some knew to their cost, call in the army.

> *'Ai' strikes are things that are just caused by people with their own plans because, they go on strikes for money, sometimes they go on strike for a very minor things, or just to fight, because people sometimes just quarrel like that.*[9]

Others disagreed with striking as a means of dealing with dissatisfaction and felt that negotiation with management was in the hope 'that they smear us with some jam and throw a little money our way'.[10] Informant 13 put it this way:

> *They were wrong because, the reason why I am saying that they were wrong is that they were supposed to talk nicely. Instead what they did was to fight. What they were supposed to do was to talk to – to the government:*
> *'You should know that we are not happy with this and that thing'.*
> *And then it would respond to them.*
> *We are complaining about money. The money is too little. Let it be that we are given more money, our money should be increased.* (OHP, Informant 13, p. 28)

The 'good boy'

Some of our informants were convinced that cooperation and conciliation were in fact the best strategies. They had taken contracts to earn money, and there was no point in jeopardizing that all-important goal by forcing a confrontation with management. The best strategy was to recognize the existing distribution of power and authority, and work hard to ensure maximum earnings. Shaft sinking was an example of this, as discussed above.

But cooperation could move a stage further and pass over into collaboration with management. Informant 9 stated that the whites liked him because they found him 'straight'. He was proud of the fact that, when Xhosa workers met to discuss how to organize work stoppages as a means of bringing about the dismissal of a white overseer, he and his Sotho workmates exposed their plan. Then the meeting would break up and

*they would all disperse like that and the European would laugh . . .
that was my life, immediately they tried get a meeting together I
would destroy it.* (OHP, Informant 9, pp. 13–14)

Informant 13 gave a full account of the advantages of cooperating
with white management. He spoke of how, when he got older his
white supervisor tried to ease his work load:

*He wanted me to be a foreman. I refused.
'Ao', he said, 'If you do not want to be a foreman now I will put you
at the top of the mine here. Your job will be just to sit at the top of the
mine here, and you should write these tickets of these people, as they
go down to the mine. Your job will be just to write out their tickets.'
Truly, I had really worked. The white man just refused to let me go on
working.
He said, 'You have been working here for too long. You have been my
man for a long time. We have worked together. We've been to many
places together. I don't want you to have to do hard work any more.'
He wanted to make me a foreman.
He said, what don't you like about being a foreman?'
I said 'I do not like being a foreman. There is a lot of witchcraft.
These foremen bewitch each other there. They bewitch each other.
Now I am happy with this job you have given me. It is enough.'
And he just kept on writing a lot of money for me. It was high. I was
getting two tens and five units of pounds. That was my job. I was
getting more than the foremen* [laughter]. *The winch-boy used to get
two tens. The foremen got two tens and two units . . . and as for me I
was getting two tens and five units. I was higher than them. I was
'good boy'* [laughter]. *Yes, I worked there, truly.* (OHP, Informant
13, pp. 4–5)

The 'bad boy'

Against the 'good boy' we can set the 'bad boy'. We collected little
evidence of theft or sabotage as a strategy against mine management.
There are suggestions of the way in which records of work could be
falsified in order to receive higher pay (OHP, Informant 4) and one
informant took his revenge on an aggressive and violent white
supervisor on the railways by quietly re-arranging the documentation
of the goods carriages – sending the carriages to destination
thousands of kilometres from where they were supposed to go.[11]

But there are also examples of sustained rebelliousness, and the determination to defend one's position if threatened – with violence if necessary. Moreover this could gain advantages. Informant 4 saw himself as such a man, a fighter: someone who '. . . ever since I was born I have never run away from another man'.[12] He fought the older boys when herding, he fought to guard the homes of his relatives when they were away on the mines. He stood up for himself physically when mistreated at work in South Africa.

As a result his life story also includes some horrific accounts of the inside of the colonial gaol, its mortuary and the gallows. But his account of his life is filled with spirit and vigour. He captures with ironic humour the predicament of the African mine worker. If you are passive or docile the white man exploits you, extending the work hours and tampering with your work record to reduce you wages:

> *The point of Europeans is that when he realises that he has little to worry about from you, then he comes and eats your money if he has seen that you are sleepy.*

However,

> *When he sees that you are clever then he says 'Motho enoa o ruta choe lebelo – this person teaches an ostrich how to run'. Then you should know that they have understood you, and that they will not want anything to do with you. You are evil, they do not like that kind of thing. Europeans want you to talk like this. You should say 'Yes old boss' . . .*
> [he will say] *'Good boy'.*
> *Yes indeed you are good 'boy' when you do not cause problems. But if you are like . . . if he sees you are like this – jumpy like this, no, then you are evil.* [He'll shout] *'Bloody Hothead', 'You are no good'* [laughter]. *'You do not become tame, mm? It is a monkey this thing; it does not become tame'.* (OHP, Informant 4, p. 51)

And the predicament is repeated: be passive and you will be exploited; stand up for yourself and you are assaulted or dismissed. But the latter course was not only the brave and honourable one, but could also succeed. It could in fact be a successful strategy to counteract exploitation by white management. Thus he told, more than once, the story of how, when he was working on a diamond mine, the white supervisor attempted to extend the gang's work time without pay. His account vividly recreates the verbal violence of this sort of confrontation. Unable to get a satisfactory explanation for this extension of working hours our informant threw down his shovel, picked up his coat, and walked off the job. His workmates – who were Xhosa, and, in contrast to the attitude of most of our informants, admired for their spirit – warned of what was going to happen. Our informant however replied: 'No, a white man cannot do harmful things to me – not when I am surrounded by so many stones'.

The other workers followed me off the job. When we were about to go through the gate the white man arrived, we bumped into him and he opened the gate and he said immediately,
'Hey Mosotho, where are you going?'
'I am going to the compound.'
'Hai, fuck-off man, who told you it is time up? Fuck off! fuck off! go – go and work!'
I said 'Ayikhona' [Never].
He – he rolled up his sleeves – he rolled up his sleeves like he was used to. I hung up my jacket. I stood and looked at him. I held my lamp properly [?].
He said: 'Do you want to fight, Mosotho?'
I said: 'If you want to fight I also want to fight.'
He said: 'What's the matter? What did you say?' and then he said 'Hey bossboy! Come here!'
The bossboy came running, and said 'Mosotho, what's the matter man?'
I said: 'You, I do not want even to see you come near me.'
Then this white man turned, went to the other side, and then went away . . . . . When he saw that I intended to fight, he turned around and he went. I went into the compound and then he went into the compound. They put us on one side. When the shift ended they said 'Men what is the matter.'
I said: 'Now, we go to work at seven and we knock off at seven. Now they make us knock off at eight without overtime. I knocked off at seven and now we are being accused of stopping work without permission.'
He just said: 'Fuck off, go you men!'
And we just left and went into the compound.
You know from that day on, the compound became all right. Immediately at seven the whistle blew. And the compound was all right. It is like it is always said that the compound is not necessarily

put right by a lot of people. It can be put right by just one person. And that was the way it was. (OHP, Informant 4, pp. 44 ff)

But the most sustained example of the rebellious came in Rantao's evidence and the account of his life as a member of the Basotho gang, the Russians. Indeed, Rantao's testimony is interesting because it is structured around a central theme – and that theme is the strategy he developed in order to survive in a harsh and dangerous world.

A WORKER'S STRATEGY

Rantao was born in 1922, herded his father's stock, and took his first contract on the gold mines in 1937. In 1942 he left the mines for industry and the Basotho district in Newclare. He was imprisoned for assault and then murder, released in 1947 and joined the Russians, playing an active part in their defence of their areas and attacks on their enemies, before returning home to Lesotho in 1959. When he was out of prison and fighting for the Russians, Rantao depended upon wage labour. At times of unemployment he joined a gang and robbed trains – but this was an activity resorted to only in times of great difficulty. His life in Johannesburg was founded on wage labour, and it was while he was employed as a worker that he fought as a member of the Russians.

Rantao is important to this chapter not only as an articulate informant on the Russians. His oral testimony is exceptional and varied. The range of his experiences is vast, as a miner, a worker in industry, or on the run from the police. He has been assaulted by the police and has killed men in fights. He has suffered a whipping in gaols, and experienced digging and dealing in illicit diamonds. At the same time he has retained a great interest in Basotho tradition and culture.

From Rantao's evidence it is clear that he believes himself to be a man of talent and intelligence, because only a man of ability could have survived what he has experienced in the towns and gaols of South Africa. These are perhaps not the abilities that a formally educated person would recognize. He is in fact illiterate – or as he put it 'I leave my letters at the post office not knowing they are mine because I did not study'. His lack of formal education however does not affect this because 'What I have is a natural sense that God gave me – and gifts – as for them they are many' (Guy and Thabane, 1987: 441).

The gifts he has include what can be called a finely developed strategic sense, and this underlies his whole testimony. It is not stated overtly and directly but is present in his descriptions of the conflicts which made up his life. We summed it up in this way:

'his philosophy is not an abstract one, but emerges from concrete situations. He sees life as a struggle, a fight, in which one must always be consolidating one's forces, undermining the opposition, and developing a strategy which avoids the obvious frontal attack, and strikes where it is not expected. To succeed in life one has to be continually wary, calculating, and prepared to attack when necessary'. (Guy and Thabane, 1987: 441)

For Rantao life was a struggle for which one had to have a well-developed sense of strategy. It is

'a battle which makes the correct assessment of the opposing forces imperative, requires one to develop strategies of skill and daring, and makes it essential to ensure that when one delivers the final blow it is a telling one'. (Guy and Thabane, 1987: 445)

This philosophy is expressed in the three great interests of his life – all having to do with different expressions of conflict and the development of successful strategy. Lawyers fascinate Rantao, and their methods epitomize his ideas on successful strategy: the correct assessment of the situation, of your own strength and your enemy's weakness; the aggression used to intimidate the opponent into making an error. Again, this is not just an abstract interest. Lawyers were an essential part of Russian life. They kept the members out of gaol and much of the gang's time was spent in extorting money to be used as lawyer's fees.

Another great interest in Rantao's life is football. For him it was not only a game of strength and skill, but one of strategy. Moreover it can be compared directly with the other activity which absorbed so much of his time – fighting.

A fight is like a football. The strength of a football team is at the quarter, at the flanks. Now, in a fight if your flanks are weak and they slacken because of the pressure from the other side, those that remain in the fight will be hit from behind and can no longer concentrate on their front because of the people who attack them from both sides. Now, because of this, the strength of the fight is at the sides. That is where I used to like it. If it was football I would be called Two, at the quarter. Yes, I liked fighting from the sides. (Guy and Thabane, 1987: 441)

In situations where life is so reduced that physical survival is the dominant element then strategy is virtually an end in itself. Rantao prides himself on the fact that he has survived the most difficult situations. He believes he has survived because he has used his inherent gifts effectively, assessed the forces ranged against him shrewdly, and shown skill in the way he has dealt with them. He is in fact proud of his talents in devising an effective strategy.

It is a deeply ambiguous strategy. It can lead to a vital and exciting life, but one which is also dark and violent. There is bravery without principle, planning and strategy without long-term goals or ideals. It is little wonder, for example, that Rantao dismisses workers' organizations. 'A lawyer is much better than a union – I have been there and I know'.

Nevertheless, it seems to us legitimate to consider such a response a form of 'workers' strategy'. The context created the imperatives. A worker's life was dangerous and restricted. Gang activity of this kind provided protection and stimulation by drawing on the idioms of rural, peasant life and putting them into practice in the urban ghettoes. It was visually encapsulated in the image the Russian consciously projected when he stared with menace at the world from under the felt hat pulled low over one eye, wearing his traditional blanket over black trousers and white shoes, and holding his fighting stick.

POSTSCRIPT

This ambiguity continues to the present day. We haven't interviewed Basotho members of the National Union of Mineworkers (NUM), which in 1988 brought its members out on strike for three weeks in what was clearly to be seen as a work stoppage of unprecedented significance in Southern African history. But there are reports that Basotho miners played a significant part in the strike, both in positions of leadership and in the rank and file.

At the same time, there have been reports that Basotho men were queueing at the recruiting stations in the hope that they could take the place of miners dismissed in the strike. There have also been reports that the Russians have been assembling again – offering to act as strike breakers. We don't know how the 1988 Russians compare with those of 30 years ago, but it must be supposed that the Sotho element remains significant.

On the other hand, there have been suggestions that management, exasperated by the number of Basotho workers active in the NUM, is thinking of playing the ethnic card again, this time threatening to replace Basotho miners with more tractable men drawn from Zululand.

Thus, amongst the old themes of ethnicity, violence and accommodation that were played by previous generations of Basotho mine workers, new ones can be discerned. They are being developed by workers in the struggle against the domination of mining capital, and include trade union organization, the work stoppage, and the strike with defined tactical objectives. But to see this form of struggle as the first indication of a general strategic sense is to dismiss the many years of conflict which have characterized the history of the Basotho mine worker. These struggles, although often ambiguous and inadequate, were also often spirited and courageous. They created and nurtured in the workers a spirit of resistance and an awareness of the need to find more effective ways to confront the mining authorities, and thereby make their own work more profitable and their lives more bearable.

NOTES

1.

Number	Date of birth	First contract	Length of transcript
1	1919		72
2	1918		34
3	1913	1934	30
4			130
6	1909	1928	77
7	1911	1939	59
8	1909	1925	45
9	1914	1934	130
10	1924		13
11	1922	1937	222
13	1918?	1928?	47
15	1927	1948	47

2. Oral History Project (OHP). Informant 11 (pseud. Rantao). Born 1922. First contract 1937. Summary of life history in text. For a discussion of such appeals to 'my countrymen', see Jeff Guy and Motlatsi Thabane (1987: 448).

3. OHP. Informant 8. Interviewed April 1983, Ha Leshoele. Born 1909. First contract 1925. Central Rand gold mines, then labour supervisor in the Free State. Served in North Africa and Italy during the Second World War. Page 28 of transcript.

4. OHP. Informant 7. Interviewed February 1983, Ha Telu-Khunoana. Born 1911. First contract 1939. East and Central Rand gold mines before going to the Free State mines. Page 51.

5. SIP. Informant 8, p. 233. The SIP project was a study of unemployment we undertook in Lesotho in 1983. Our findings were presented to the Second Carnegie Inquiry into Poverty and Development in 1984 in a paper entitled 'Unemployment and casual labour in Maseru: the impact of changing employment strategies on migrant labourers in Lesotho'.

6. Guy and Thabane (1988: 268). Informant 15. Interviewed Ha Mofoka, August 1984. Born 1927. First contract 1948. Diamond mines before moving to the Free State fields.

7. OHP. Informant 9. Interviewed Alwynskop, Quting, April 1983. Born 1914. First contract 1934. Wide experience: Central Rand, Kimberley, ISCOR, and worked in the Cape. Page 40.

8. OHP. Informant 13. Interviewed Thaba-Tseka, April 1984. Chronology confused. Birth 1918? First contract 1928? Central Rand and Free State. Induna 4.

9. OHP. Informant 2. Interviewed Maseru. Born 1918. East Rand gold mines. Pages 24–25.

10. OHP. Informant 1. Born 1919. Interviewed November 1982. Served in Second World War. Worked in the docks at the Cape. Page 70.

11. OHP. Informant 3. Interviewed Mokhokhong 1982. Born 1913. First contract 1934. East Rand gold mines, metal works, South African Railways. Page 17.

12. OHP. Informant 4. Interviewed Tsieng, January 1983. Chronology still obscure. Gold and diamond mining. Construction industry. Page 38.

REFERENCES

S. Chikhi and A. El Kenz, 'Workers' Perceptions and Practices in Algeria: The Cases of the El Hadjar Iron and Steel Works and the Rouiba Industrial Motor Car Plant', Chapter 2 in this book.

J. Guy and M. Thabane, 'Unemployment and casual labour in Maseru: the impact of changing employment strategies on migrant labourers in Lesotho'. The SIP Project, presented to the Second Carnegie Inquiry into Poverty and Development (1984).

—— 'The Ma-Rashea: a Participant's Perspective', in B. Bozzoli (ed.), *Class, Community and Conflict. South African Perspectives* (Johannesburg: Raven Press, 1987)

—— 'Technology, Ethnicity and Ideology: Basotho Miners and Shaft-sinking on the South African Gold Mines', *Journal of Southern African Studies*, XIV (1988).

P. Haapala, 'How Was the Working Class Formed? The Case of Finland 1850–1920', *Scandinavian Journal of History*, XII, 3 (1987).

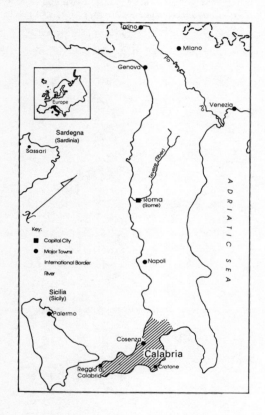

Map 4   Italy: Calabria and Major Northern Industrial Towns

5 Feuds, Class Struggles and Labour Migration in Calabria*

Giovanni Arrighi and Fortunata Piselli

The main purpose of this chapter is to analyse the formation of a wage labour force in a peripheral environment, in this case one of the poorest regions of southern Italy, Calabria.

In the first half of the nineteenth century, a system of land tenure known as the *latifondo contadino* (peasant latifundium) had come to predominate throughout the region. The system was not the same everywhere. Arrangements between peasants and landlords showed great variations from place to place, but all had one characteristic in common: large landed estates were partly farmed by the landowner, predominantly with wage labour, and partly subdivided into plots and farmed by peasants who paid rent in cash or kind. In the second half of the nineteenth century (roughly from the 1860s up to the First World War), the *latifondo contadino* tended to disappear, giving rise not to one but to three distinct social formations.

In the Crotonese (see Map 5), the peasant latifundium was transformed in a way that resembled Lenin's (1936) 'Junker or Prussian road': the landed estates were transformed into large capitalist enterprises (known in the literature on Calabria as *latifondi capitalistici*) run by the landlords (directly or through one of their employees) who employed wage labour, produced for the market, and aimed at a maximum profit. The tenants were evicted and either left the estates for good or continued to reside on them as wage workers.

---

* *Editor's note:* This is an abridged version of a much longer article entitled 'Capitalist Development in Hostile Environments: Feuds, Class Struggles, and Migrations in a Peripheral Region of Southern Italy', published in *Review*, X, 4, Spring 1987, pp. 649–751. In the original article, the divergent patterns of labour-force formation and social conflict analysed here are related to the peripheral position of Calabria in the capitalist world economy.

Map 5   Calabria and the Three Areas Analysed

In the Plain of Gioia Tauro, by contrast, the peasant latifundium evolved in a way that resembled Lenin's 'farmer or American road': the peasants became farmers producing for the market – some turning into small capitalists who employed wage-labour to supplement family labour, and others turning into semi-proletarians who hired out part of the family's labour to supplement the incomes derived from the sale of produce. In this instance, the landlords generally sold part of their land to the more well-to-do peasant-farmers, continued to collect rent on another part, and became medium-sized capitalist entrepreneurs on yet another part.

In the Cosentino, the peasant latifundium evolved in neither of the above two directions. Here, it evolved towards a system of peasant holdings that employed family labour, produced predominantly for direct consumption, and sold in the market both their surplus produce (subsistence produce over and above the consumption requirements of the household) and, above all, their surplus labour.

The key characteristic of this transformation was that a good part of the income, derived from the sale of labour power in distant labour markets, was saved and eventually invested in the purchase of land and other means of production. As a result of this tendency, the burden of rent on the direct producers was progressively reduced (and the landlords were eliminated from the social and economic scene), and the viability of subsistence production was reproduced or even enhanced. We shall label this transformation the 'migrant-peasant or Swiss road' (cf. Casparis, 1982, 1985).

In the first part of this chapter we shall show that, while all three transformations were associated with the further development of a wage-labour force, they generated different social structures. In the Crotonese, the Junker road produced a landed bourgeoisie with a tight monopoly over the means of production and a landless proletariat with access to means of subsistence only through the sale of labour power and the purchase of commodified means of subsistence with the proceeds. In this case, the sale of labour power was the expression of *full proletarianization* of the formerly peasant household. In the Plain of Gioia, the farmer road produced a stratified rather than a polarized structure: the full-bourgeois and the full-proletarian poles were far less important than in the Crotonese, and the weight and number of intermediate strata were far greater. Almost everybody had access to the means of producing an income, but only a minority had access to means sufficient to produce a full-subsistence income, let alone to save and accumulate.

In this case, the sale of labour power for a wage was the expression of *semi-proletarianization*: the condition of petty producers who could eke out a subsistence only by supplementing the sale of produce with the sale of labour power. Finally in the Cosentino, the migrant-peasant road produced neither a stratification nor a polarization, but a levelling of the social structure. Most established households came to have access to means of production sufficient to provide fully for their subsistence (or nearly so). The sale of household labour power, therefore, was only secondarily or not at all the expression of proletarianization or semi-proletarianization. Rather, it was the expression of a process of *petty accumulation*, in the form of an initial fund with which to establish a new household and occasionally in the form of an increase in the productive and unproductive wealth of established households.

These differences in social structure had important implications for the welfare of the peoples involved and for the patterns of social conflict and cohesion that became dominant in the three situations. Thus, in the Crotonese, the extreme polarization of the social structure was associated with an extreme impoverishment of the majority of the population and with an endemic state of class struggle over cultivation and property rights between the landed bourgeoisie and the landless proletariat. In the Plain of Gioia, the stratification of the social structure was associated with less wide-spread poverty and more diffuse wealth than in the Crotonese and with endemic struggles among rival patronage groups that were more akin to feuds than to class struggles. Finally, in the Cosentino, long-distance/long-term migration contributed to the formation and consolidation of relatively prosperous rural communities in which social conflict tended to decline both horizontally (that is, among kinship groups) and vertically (that is, between landlords and peasants).

This tripartite pattern of development poses some interesting questions, which we shall try to answer in the second part of the chapter. Systems of production, often construed as successive stages in the development of capitalism (subsistence production, small-scale commodity production, and large-scale commodity production), developed in Calabria next to each other and at about the same historical time. A first problem, therefore, is to explain how and why in the second half of the nineteenth century a single system of land tenure gave rise, within the same region, to three distinct patterns of social change.

After the Second World War the internal differentiation of Calabria became increasingly blurred as the three roads to wage-labour merged into a system of production in which (i) a large proportion of previously cultivated land was no longer put to agricultural use, and (ii) the land that did remain under cultivation came to be exploited throughout Calabria by a combination of vertically integrated agrobusinesses, full-lifetime farmers using capital- and skill-intensive methods of production, and part-lifetime wage workers who integrated their wage incomes with agricultural production for sale and/or direct consumption. The task of the last part of the chapter is to explain how and why, after a century of divergence, the three roads to wage-labour suddenly (in historical time) began to converge towards a single pattern. A brief concluding section will then sum up the main results of the analysis and point out its theoretical implications.

THE MIGRANT-PEASANT (SWISS) ROAD

The migrant-peasant road as it developed in the Cosentino had three main features.[1] First, it was subsistence-oriented. The direct producers owned or had control over the use of the means of production (land, livestock, tools, and so on). Market exchange played a marginal role in the disposal of the households' products and in the procurement of inputs. Cooperation aimed at self-sufficiency was the organizing principle that dominated social and economic action.

Secondly, the migrant-peasant road was strictly regulated by customary rules. Particularly significant for our present purposes were the customary norms that regulated inheritance and marriage. Various forms of primogeniture prevented the fragmentation of productive units, and, combined with norms that restricted the right to marry, they generated an abundant supply of subordinate domestic labour over and above the requirements of the household. This surplus of labour was not allowed to overburden the household's resources, it came to be mobilized productively through long-distance migration.

This brings us to the third main feature of the migrant-peasant road. As underscored by its very designation, it relied heavily on migration. Three types of migration, each corresponding to a different kind of labour surplus, must be distinguished. The first type was seasonal and short-distance. It consisted of individuals or, more often, groups of kin and neighbours who sold labour power outside their territory within Calabria or neighbouring regions. Through this type of migration, established peasant households transformed the surplus of labour associated with seasonal fluctuations in agriculture activities into command over monetary means.

The second kind of migration was permanent emigration and was largely towards urban rather than rural areas of Calabria and neighbouring regions. In contrast to seasonal migration, it was individual in character, and it involved almost exclusively the lower strata and the deviant members of the peasant community. Through this kind of permanent migration, over-population was drastically reduced, deviance expelled, and the structures and rules of subsistence production correspondingly strengthened.

The third type of migration, and the most important for the development of the migrant-peasant road, was long-term/long-distance migration. It was undertaken by individuals of intermediate social status who fully accepted the rules and obligations of the communities from which they came and to which they intended to return. Being long-term, this kind of migration involved long periods of absence from the community (10–20 years), and, being long-distance, it involved costs and risks that made it a real 'enterprise'. As a consequence, only those who belonged to cohesive and extended kin-groups could mobilize the material and moral resources necessary to undertake the enterprise.

Long-term/long-distance migration from the Cosentino not only reduced demographic pressure and social tensions (as did permanent emigration) while increasing the command of subsistence producers over monetary means (as did seasonal migration). It was also a powerful factor of continuity and generational expansion of the local social networks in which subsistence production was embedded and through which it was carried on (cf. Watson, 1958; Van Velsen, 1960). The wage-labour produced by the migrant-peasant road, therefore, was only in small part that of proletarians selling labour power in order to procure means of subsistence. One of the most important consequences of the development of the peasant-migrant road was the demise of social conflict in all its traditional forms. Historically, the Cosentino had been even less 'peaceful' than the Crotonese or the Plain of Gioia. To be sure, repressive state action played a major role in the determination of this demise. Equally important, however, was the fact that, as landlords were 'bought out' with the proceeds of long-distance migration, the scope for class struggle between peasants and landlords was increasingly narrowed. And as absolute scarcity and social tensions were lessened by all three types of migration, occasions for sustained feuding became fewer. This does not mean that other types of conflict did not arise. Apart from the conflicts that arose in the sites of immigration, to which we shall turn in the part on redistributive struggles, the peasant-migrant road entailed, and continuously reproduced, a highly oppressive and repressive form of patriarchalism.

THE JUNKER (PRUSSIAN) ROAD

Developments in the Crotonese, along what resembles Lenin's 'Junker or Prussian road', offer the sharpest contrast to the migrant-peasant road of the Cosentino.[2] There was little subsistence production by peasants and few socially enforced customary rules and obligations. Massive emigration had accompanied the eviction of the peasantry (that is, so-called primitive accumulation in classic form), and the disintegration of community that this once-and-for-all depopulation of the countryside entailed left the growth of the new institutions unshaped by virtually any of the once customary relational rights or obligations.

The typical and all-encompassing unit of production was the so-called capitalist latifundium (*latifondo capitalistico*), which employed wage-labour and produced for profit by sale in the market. Production switched back and forth between arable and pasturage according to the prices of grain versus those for wool and cheese on the one hand and (given the greater labour intensity of grain production) the availability of cheap labour on the other.

The surplus commanded by the *latifondisti* (a combination of rent and profit) as well as their entrepreneurial energies were mobilized, not to dominate market conditions impersonally and indirectly via revolutions in production functions, but to dominate such conditions personally and directly via political mechanisms. At the national level, the most conspicuous results of this strategy were the protectionist measures taken by Italian governments from the late 1880s up through the Second World War. At the local level, however, the most conspicuous and most consequential measures were in the sphere of labour relations.

The expropriation, through the unilateral elimination of long-term leases, cleared the land of most peasant settlements and transformed the inhabitants of those that remained into rural proletarians who could not piece together even the most meagre of subsistences without selling their labour power to the estates on a continuous basis.[3]

This full proletarianization, however, had two broad negative effects so far as the development of the estates and capitalist enterprises was concerned. First, it curtailed the labour supply because it induced a large wave of once-and-for-all *permanent* emigration, which depopulated the countryside and produced a structural deficiency of labour in the whole area. In addition, the local supply of labour also became 'flatter'; that is, devoid of seasonal and skilled components. As peasants were turned into full proletarians, the seasonal variability of their labour supply was immediately lost, and after a generation or two the wide array of agricultural skills was lost as well. The flexibility gained in the use of land resources by expropriation was lost in the narrowed capacities, and full-time dependence of the labour supply thereby formed.

Secondly, the depeasantization of the latifundium workers transformed the latters' surly compliance in the lord–peasant relation into the straightforward antagonism of the capital–labour relation, with negative effects on disciplined work and respect for land and property. It fed a deep resentment that, whenever the occasion arose, was translated into widespread theft, damage to property, infringement of the rules denying cultivation rights, and pervasively poor work performance.

These contradictions of full proletarianization were never resolved. They were, however, kept in check, from the point of view of capital, by two related developments. One was the development of a symbiotic relation between the capitalist latifundium and the agricultural regimes that were emerging in neighbouring territories such as the Cosentino and the Plain of Gioia. The *latifondisti* of the Crotonese could therefore fill the local deficiency of seasonal and skilled labour by drawing from the labour surplus of the other areas.

The pressure of competition on the local proletariat was particularly intense owing to the fact that the peasants who sold labour power to the capitalist latifundia not only commanded skills that the proletarianized workers of the Crotonese were losing or had lost; they also expected a wage level sufficient only to supplement, or to complement, a subsistence produced or earned elsewhere. As a consequence of this intense competitive pressure, the local rural proletariat was forced to sell its labour power at wages below the level necessary for it to pay even for the foodstuffs needed for subsistence (Inchiesta Parlamentare, 1909: 276, 280; Arlacchi, 1983: 177f).

The strategy of keeping class antagonisms in check through competitive pressure alone was ineffective insofar as non-cooperation and indiscipline were concerned and, moreover, was unpredictable in its capacity to forestall collective action. The symbiotic relation between the capitalist latifundia and the neighbouring peasant communities was paralleled and sustained by the development of an internal repressive apparatus, which made the latifundia assume the twofold character of capitalist enterprises and quasi-military organizations.

Many of the wage workers employed on a stable basis (*salariati fissi*) became armed guards who performed the double role of private police and supervisors of the labour process. They threatened (and when necessary executed) harsh sanctions against transgressors, and they assured the security of persons and property on the estates. The reproduction of the landowners' monopoly over the use of land resources thus went hand in hand with the enforcement of a territorial monopoly over the use of violence.

This double monopoly could of course only be exercised with the connivance and ultimate backing of agencies of the state. Conscious of this dependence, the landowners pursued an active policy of monopolization of local administrative and judicial power either directly or through kin and clients. When state power was disorganized, or the organic links that connected agrarian capital to the state were disrupted, which was the case at the end of the First World War and again at the end of the Second World War, the Crotonese was shaken by sudden explosions of class struggle that had no parallel in other parts of Calabria.

These occasions were accompanied by street demonstrations, seizures of public buildings, violent clashes with both the private police of the landowners and the state's military and police forces. From the point of view of the evolution of social conflict, therefore, the Junker road produced quite different results from the migrant-peasant road.

The difference with the Cosentino is brought out starkly by the fact that the intensification of the class struggle was accompanied by a decline of long-distance migration. At the turn of the century the Crotonese had almost as much experience in long-distance emigration as the Cosentino. But long-distance migration from the Crotonese tended to be *permanent*, rather than long-term (10–20 years) as in the Cosentino. Moreover, in the Crotonese, long-distance migration did not have any of the positive feedbacks on the autonomy and social cohesion of peasant households it had in the Cosentino.

As soon as the process of proletarianization was completed, long-distance migration fell sharply. The rural proletariat of the Crotonese did not command the individual and collective resources necessary to undertake the costs and risks of this type of migration. As a matter of fact, the moral and material impoverishment of the rural proletariat was such that even its ability to compete effectively in the regional labour markets was undermined. And as the scope of 'exit' narrowed, 'voice' became the only option open to the rural proletariat to escape the exploitation and oppression of the landed bourgeoisie and its repressive apparatus.

THE FARMER (AMERICAN) ROAD

The Farmer road, as it developed in the Plain of Gioia, had some traits in common with both the Junker and the migrant-peasant road.[4] As in the Junker road, outputs were sold and inputs were bought in markets, but, as in the migrant-peasant road, the direct producers generally had some control over the use of the means of production. It was regulated neither by the visible hand of the landlords and the state (as was the Junker road) nor by customary rules and obligation (as was the migrant-peasant road), but by a combination of market competition and power struggles among rival patronage groups.

It produced a highly stratified social structure, which included: (i) an upper stratum of landowners turned into medium-sized capitalists, who were also part-rentiers since they leased land to farmers and other capitalists; (ii) an upper-middle stratum of farmers turned into small-to-medium-sized capitalists, who systematically accumulated in excess of what was necessary to reproduce their households' capacity to generate a subsistence income; (iii) a middle stratum of independent farmers, who accumulated more or less what was necessary to reproduce over time their households' capacity to generate a subsistence income; (iv) a lower-middle stratum of semi-proletarianized farmers, who did not accumulate enough to reproduce over time their households' capacity to generate a subsistence income; (v) a lower stratum of fully proletarianized labourers (INEA, 1947).

In addition, the farmer road was characterized by a much greater differentiation of economic activities than the other two roads, since the development of market exchanges gave rise to a whole variety of trading and manufacturing activities. The lower strata of this diversified structure continuously generated a supply of, and the upper strata a demand for, wage-labour. As a consequence, something closer to a competitive labour market than anything that had ever existed in the Cosentino or in the Crotonese came into existence in the Plain of Gioia.

This labour market had important direct and indirect linkages with the economies of neighbouring territories as well as with core regions. The main determinant of conditions in the labour market of the Plain were conditions in the markets of its main crops (olives and citrus fruit). When conditions in the export markets were booming, so was the demand for labour in the Plain.

At the same time, however, the supply of labour from local sources, far from expanding to match demand, would stagnate or even contract because the semi-proletarianized households that were the main source of such supply could meet their subsistence requirements by selling produce as easily as (or more easily than) by selling labour power. An opposite imbalance would occur when export markets were depressed: while profit-oriented production and investment would be cut back both in agricultural and complementary activities, leading to a contraction of labour demand, labour supply would expand owing to the difficulties encountered by semi-proletarianized households in procuring the means of subsistence via the sale of produce. Excess demand would generate inbound flows, and excess supply outbound flows.

This combination of inflows and outflows could also be detected in longer-term migratory movements. In periods of expansion, the Plain of Gioia turned into a site of immigration, not only for the impoverished peasants and outcasts of the interior, but also for a stratum of medium and small entrepreneurs from other Italian regions, who played an important role in the spread of market networks within the Plain, and between the Plain and core markets. In periods of contraction, the immigration from other Italian regions would subside, and long-distance migration from the Plain would experience a sharp upturn.

On average, however, long-distance migration from the Plain of Gioia remained well below the levels attained in the Cosentino. In the former, the looseness of kinship structures and the pervasive influence of market competition generally meant that those who had the means did not have the incentive to emigrate, and those who had the incentive did not have the means. In periods of unfavourable conditions for the activities the middle and upper middle strata were involved in, the incentive to emigrate would however increase, and it was quite common for them to sell land and other assets to finance emigration. However, these departures were always partially or wholly balanced by incoming settlers who bought the land from those leaving.

This account of migration to and from the Plain of Gioia underscores the fact that it was a factor and an expression of market regulation. The pervasiveness of market regulation was indeed the *differentia specifica* of the farmer road as distinct from the migrant-peasant and the Junker road. Market regulation, however, did not take place in a social and political void. On the contrary, it took place and was embedded in a context of struggle/domination among rival patronage groups.

Each round of open struggle ended with the formation of an authority of the mafia type holding a territorial quasi-monopoly over the use of violence. Once established, this authority tended to exercise informal governmental functions: it guaranteed order; mediated conflicts; ensured reciprocity in transactions and the respect of contractual obligations; regulated competition by occupying key nodes in the local ramifications of commodity chains; set limits to profit-making and the exploitation of labour; and protected local interests against the powers of the landlords and the state.

Both phases of the struggle/domination cycle, which continuously reproduced the mafia-type authority, derived their legitimacy from a widely shared 'code of honor'. Whatever the actual origins of this 'code', the social consensus commanded by the mafia-type authority can be traced to the fact that it protected local society from the disruption of unfettered market competition on the one hand and from the abuses of an absentee central state on the other. The mafia-type authority held in check the polarizing tendencies of capitalist production, thereby contributing to the preservation of intermediate social strata.

HISTORICAL CONJUNCTURE AND THE THREE ROADS

We shall now advance some hypotheses concerning the historical development of these three roads to wage-labour: how they came into being, how they unfolded, and how they came to an end. In order to understand this development our focus must shift from the inner dynamics of the three roads to their interrelationships with the dynamics of the world economy and of the nation-state of which they were integral parts. We shall begin by briefly discussing the historical conjuncture that, in the second half of the nineteenth century, sustained their 'take-off'.

The differentiation of Calabria became evident in the particular conjuncture of the 1860s characterized by a boom of agricultural prices on the world market and by the incorporation of Calabria in the newly formed Italian state. The differentiation was consolidated in the subsequent 50 years, which were characterized by a long depression and then recovery of agricultural world prices, and by growing market exchanges within the territory of the new Italian state. Under the impact of the 1860s boom in agricultural prices, capitalist and would-be capitalist producers in Calabria greatly expanded production and sales of traditional staples of regional agriculture, such as grain, olive oil, and wine, as well as of what had previously been marginal crops (citrus fruit and, for a short period, cotton) (Chorley, 1965).

The subsequent long depression, which became acute in the 1880s, did not reverse the trend towards an increased commercialization of Calabria's agriculture. Indigenous entrepreneurs of the most diverse extractions (including many landowners), supplemented by traders from other Italian regions, began to innovate and to rationalize production operations and marketing practices to take advantage of the benefits offered by the creation of new routes and means of transport and by the elimination of other obstacles to exchange within the new national economic space and across its boundaries. In addition, the transformation of relations of production in agriculture was induced and sustained by the greater mobility of labour associated with more secure, faster, and cheaper transports, and by a growing demand for migrant labour within Calabria and immigrant labour overseas (North and South America). When demand for agricultural products in the world markets picked up again in the 1890s and expanded up through the First World War, the differentiation of Calabria into distinct paths of development was well-entrenched, and the new favourable conjuncture simply made the three paths diverge further.

These conjunctures in the development of the world economy and of the Italian state are essential to an explanation of why the three paths of development unfolded when they did. They cannot, however, explain why three locales with roughly the same beginning social structure and geopolitical location should have developed along divergent paths.

On the eve of the transformation of the peasant latifundium along divergent paths, social life in Calabria was dominated by three circumstances: the uninhabitability of many coastal areas in the summer because of malaria; the physical difficulties of travelling in the mountainous interior in the winter owing to the fact that hardly any roads were passable; and the dangers of moving almost anywhere in winter or in summer because of brigandage, which in Calabria took the form of 'an endemic social criminality' (Bevilacqua, 1985: 120). Thus, to take advantage of the new profit opportunities, landowners had to overcome the sociological and ecological obstacles to profit-oriented activities posed by malaria in the coastal areas, a harsh physical environment in the interior, and brigandage everywhere. The Junker road, the farmer road, and the migrant-peasant road represented different outcomes of the struggle of capitalists and would-be capitalists (particularly landowners) to overcome these obstacles.

The prospects of overcoming them were most hopeless in the mountainous areas of the interior, such as the Cosentino, where ecology and sociology militated against any easy solution of the problems of enforcing law and order and of establishing a viable system of transport and communications. Any attempt to reorganize relations of production, exchange, and distribution to the disadvantage of the peasantry was bound to be self-defeating, because it heightened the endemic state of class warfare that was a key component of brigandage. Here, the peasants won. They won informally, to be sure, but they won nonetheless. They retained control over a good share of their labour surplus, organized its sale in nearby and distant markets, increased their command over resources, and further freed themselves from the exploitative hold of absentee landowners.

The situation for the would-be capitalist landlords was more favourable along the coastal areas where transport of commodities could be more easily organized (at first by sea and later by railway) and where the sparse and transitory character of human settlements – owing to piracy earlier and malaria later – made it easier to control land tenure. However, it was not equally favourable everywhere. It was most favourable in the Crotonese where the soil and climate were such that large-scale commodity production could be organized without any major fixed investment in land and infrastructure (Rossi Doria, 1948: 7ff; Bevilacqua, 1980: 191ff).

Rationalization consisted in gearing the production cycle as closely as possible to market fluctuations in prices – an adjustment that generally meant relaxing human constraints on the use of land. It therefore required centralization of control over the activities and resources of the estates in order to prevent the formation of permanent settlements or to eradicate existing ones – an objective that, as we have seen, was attained by creating a powerful repressive apparatus (see 'The Junker (Prussian) Road'). In building this repressive apparatus the landowners did not shun the cooptation of the social bandits of the interior as overseers of the capitalist latifundium in formation. In this way, they killed two birds with one stone: they pacified the countryside and created an instrument of centralized control over production. Here, the landlords *qua* capitalists obviously won, and the road was open for large-scale commodity production.

The situation was not so favourable in other coastal areas such as the Plain of Gioia. Soil and climate were not as conducive to large-scale commodity production on the basis of existing techniques and product mix as in the Crotonese. At the same time, they were conducive to even more profitable production (per unit of land), provided that the techniques of production and the product mix were radically transformed through heavy investment in land and infrastructure (including land reclamation). More specifically, in the case of the Plain of Gioia, a strong competitive advantage could be developed in the production of olive oil (traditionally a marginal non-cash crop). Land reclamation was a prerequisite of all these productions. In addition, they required heavy labour-intensive investment in land improvements and planting of trees, expertise in the selection and improvement of varieties, skilled manual labour in many stages of production, and processing and marketing facilities.

It is immediately obvious that this kind of production process posed far more complex problems of labour control than the relatively simple ones of the Crotonese. In the early stages of development of plantations, large and labour-intensive initial investments meant that relatively permanent settlements had to be induced, rather than discouraged, as was done in the Crotonese. While the supply of labour from the interior on a seasonal basis was relatively abundant, the supply on a year-round basis in the unhealthy environment of the coast was extremely scarce. This meant that extraordinary inducements (such as much higher wages or a piece of land) had to be offered to attract the necessary labour power.

Apart from this, land had to be given to the workforce for two other reasons. In the later stages, the demand for skilled agricultural labour increased. The only way to ensure the reproduction over time of a pool of skills large enough to cover the requirements of the plantations was to make concessions to labour concerning cultivation rights. That is to say, it was necessary to allow petty commodity production to develop side by side with larger-scale commodity production.

In the second place, the far greater value invested in the crops of the Plain made their owners correspondingly more vulnerable to the state of social criminality endemic in Calabria at the time. This meant that agrarian capitalists in the Plain could ill afford the level of class antagonism associated with the full proletarianization of the labour force.

It goes without saying that the stratified social structure of the Plain (and the related pattern of social conflict/cohesion) was not the outcome of some capitalist 'master plan' but the cumulative result of daily confrontations among the various social personifications of labour and capital that populated the Plain of Gioia at different stages of its development. This outcome represented neither a victory of the peasantry (as in the Cosentino), nor a victory of the landlords (as in the Crotonese). It represented, so to speak, a 'draw' that opened the way for the farmer road in its peculiar Calabrian form.

It would appear, therefore, that the emergence within Calabria of three distinct roads of social change in the second half of the nineteenth century was due to the different outcomes of the struggle of landowners and other surplus appropriators or would-be appropriators to establish large-scale commodity production in response to a particular stage of development and to a particular conjuncture of the world economy on the one hand, and to the formation of the Italian nation-state on the other hand. The three outcomes, however, were not independent of each other. It should be clear from our account of the structure and genesis of the three roads that their viability was dependent on the flows of labour that linked them.

These flows are schematically summed up in Figure 5.1, in which the width of the arrows is meant to convey some sense of the size (in terms of numbers involved) of the flows. The most important links are the large seasonal supplies of non-proletarianized labour generated by the migrant-peasant road and absorbed by the Junker road and, to a lesser extent, by the farmer road. The chart also emphasizes the reliance of the Junker road and of the farmer road on 'external' labour supplies, and the reliance of the migrant-peasant road on the other two roads in the procurement of monetary means (through the seasonal sale of labour power) and in the expulsion of over-population and deviance. These interconnections further clarify why three divergent roads to wage-labour and social change developed at about the same time in three neighbouring areas.

THE CONVERGENCE OF THE THREE ROADS

In the world political and economic context determined by the outcome of the Second World War our three roads to wage-labour began to converge towards a common pattern. The path of development that proved to be the least stable in the new situation was the Junker road, which came to an abrupt and complete end.

The capitalist latifundium had reached its highest point of development on the eve of the Second World War. Under fascism, the organic links between the *latifondisti* and the state had been greatly strengthened. The protection and active encouragement of national grain production on the part of the state had attained unprecedented levels. At the same time, the landowners' hand vis-à-vis labour had been strengthened both by the repressive anti-labour stance of the regime and by the restrictions imposed on migration within and across national boundaries. The capitalist latifundia were becoming increasingly dependent on state protection. At the same time, the squeeze on labour incomes tended to accumulate explosive social material ready to detonate at the first favourable conjuncture.

Both tendencies came to a head with the collapse of the fascist regime and the subsequent establishment of new hegemonies at the national and inter-state levels. As soon as the Allied armed forces occupied Calabria in 1943, a wave of acute and widespread social conflict swept the region.[5] In the Crotonese the wave of conflict was more intense and lasted longer than anywhere else. It took its usual

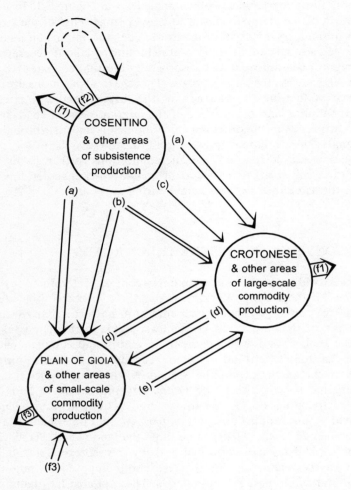

a. Seasonal supply of non-proletarian labour.
b. Permanent supply of fully proletarianized labour (impoverished peasants, *proietti*, deviants).
c. Permanent supply of overseers and other members of the latifundia's repressive apparatus.
d. Seasonal supply of fully proletarianized labour.
e. Seasonal supply of semiproletarianized labour.
f. Long-distance migration: (1) permanent, (2) long-term; (3) cyclical.

Figure 5.1 Short- and long-distance migration flows

form of a confrontation between landowners and rural proletarians over property and cultivation rights. This time, however, the confrontation acquired a new political connotation because it became part and parcel of the post-war struggle for national hegemony between the Communist and Socialist parties on the one side, and the Christian Democratic party and its allies on the other. The Communist and Socialist parties saw in the struggles of the landless peasants an excellent opportunity to make a political and organizational break-through in the traditionally conservative south. They supported from the start the demand for land of the rural proletariat, and through this policy they did in fact succeed in developing close ideological and organizational links with its ranks (Rossi Doria, 1983; Barresi, 1983). Since a powerful movement of protest developed at about the same time in the factories of the north, also under Communist/Socialist hegemony, the Leninist (or for that matter Gramscian) scenario of an alliance between industrial workers and landless peasants mediated by the leadership of the workers' party seemed to materialize in almost ideotypical fashion. This alliance posed a serious threat to the Christian Democratic party and other political forces that were trying to anchor the Italian state firmly within the US sphere of influence. The threat was perceived by these forces to be serious enough to induce them to yield to the pressures for a land reform.

The implementation of the reform began in 1950, and within a few years the redistribution of land broke up the latifundia, largely attaining the political objective of containing and then rolling back Communist influence over the peasantry. The capitalist latifundium disappeared very rapidly and left little trace of its once powerful organizational structures.

The Plain of Gioia, and to a lesser extent the Cosentino, also experienced a wave of social conflict following the downfall of the fascist regime. Far from challenging existing social structures, protest movements in the Plain of Gioia and in the Cosentino were reactions against the hindrances created by the fascist regime to the reproduction of such structures. Implicitly or explicitly they aimed not at subverting but at strengthening existing social structures through a restoration of the *status quo ante*. In the Cosentino, its restoration of the *status quo ante* meant above all the elimination of the restrictions on long-distance migration that had been introduced under the fascist regime; in the Plain of Gioia, the restoration of the *status quo ante* meant the elimination of the restrictions enforced by the fascist regime on the struggles among rival patronage groups and on the exercise of mafia-type authority.

As a consequence, there was no immediate crisis of small-scale commodity production or of subsistence production to match the crisis and disappearance of the capitalist latifundium. On the contrary, in the immediate post-war years small-scale commodity production enjoyed a short period of prosperity as the acute shortages of agricultural supplies on the national markets greatly inflated the prices of some of the Plain's products.

The movements of protest of the 1940s further strengthened the hold of the peasantry on the land and other means of production, and the intensification of competition in the markets for agricultural commodities could not and did not affect producers that sold very little on those markets. At the same time, the reopening of the channels of long-distance migration, which had been closed or narrowly restricted during the war and inter-war years, injected new vitality into the structures of subsistence production. When the crisis came in the middle 1960s, it was the result of the success rather than the failure of migrant-peasants in coping with the new conjuncture at the national and world level.

THE STATE AS SOCIAL ACTOR

The land reform in the Crotonese was carried out by a public institution (*Opera per la Valorizzazione della Sila*, henceforth OVS). Plots of land were granted to most, if not all, the individuals who applied for land, but the majority of the plots could not support a family. Even though the former landowners were left with large quantities of the more fertile land, the loss of the marginal lands prevented them from continuing with the practice of large-scale shifting agriculture based on low fixed investments and a changing combination of grazing and extensive cereal cultivation. For this reason, the land reform dealt a death blow to the economy of the capitalist latifundium. In order to turn a smaller quantity of land to profitable use, the former *latifondisti* had to introduce new product-mixes and new techniques of production that generally required heavy investments in land improvements and means of production.

Faced with this challenge, a few of the former *latifondisti* actually used the generous indemnities received from the OVS for the expropriated lands to turn their estates into modern agrobusinesses.

Others did not stand up to the challenge: they leased or sold the remaining land and placed the rents or the proceeds from the sales, as well as the indemnities, in financial and urban speculative investments. In either case, the *latifondisti* as such disappeared from the social scene, and the social structure of the Crotonese became as stratified as that of the Plain of Gioia.

The top of the new agrarian hierarchy was occupied by the small stratum of landowners who had become full-fledged agricultural capitalists. Next came an upper-middle stratum of small-to-medium-sized capitalist farmers who had obtained from the OVS or had purchased/extorted from the landowners and from the newly-created peasantry more land than was necessary to support their families. After a middle stratum of independent farmers, who had just enough land to support a family, came a large stratum of semi-proletarianized peasants, who had not obtained enough land to support a family. And, at the very bottom, there was a small stratum of full-fledged proletarians, who either had received no land from the reform or had sold or lost what they had received (Pezzino, 1977: 66ff). The state became an increasingly powerful presence engaged (mainly through the OVS) in activities of production, administration, and redistribution. The redistribution of land was only the first step in a process of growing involvement in the restructuring of social and economic relations.

The OVS grew into a huge bureaucratic apparatus with unparalleled power in the everyday life of the Crotonese and neighbouring areas. This growth was chiefly motivated by the need of the political parties in government (first and foremost the Christian Democrats) to break the hegemony that opposition parties had established in the area during the phase of acute class confrontation.

The Christian Democrats followed a three-pronged strategy: they established firm control over the OVS; they transformed the social structure through the redistribution of land; and they resorted to widespread patronage to win votes and legitimacy. Little or no political discrimination occurred in the assignment of the expropriated land, but, as soon as the land had been assigned, the provision of infrastructure, technical assistance, credit, subsidies, marketing facilities, and so on, became conditional on political allegiance to the Christian Democrats.

In building networks of political patronage, the bureaucrats of the OVS came to rely heavily on former members of the repressive apparatuses of the capitalist latifundia. An organic relation thus developed between the OVS and a new class of 'primitive' accumulators whereby the political clienteles of the OVS and the economic clienteles of this new class interlocked in complex configurations of reciprocal instrumentality.

The activities of the OVS also contributed to a *rapprochement* between the ruling party and the former *latifondisti*. As already mentioned, the trauma of expropriation was softened by generous indemnities. In addition, the former *latifondisti* who had turned into full-fledged agricultural capitalists benefited more than anyone else from the heavy investments in infrastructure and from the technical assistance of the OVS.

In sum, the land reform transformed the social structure of the Crotonese into something similar to the social structure of the Plain of Gioia with the important difference that the state rather than the market had the largest influence on social relations. As a consequence, the upper strata of the Crotonese came to include not only capitalists of various kinds but state bureaucrats and party bosses as well.

This all-pervading influence of the state differentiated the social structure of the Crotonese from what had previously existed in the Plain of Gioia. The social structure of the Plain of Gioia, however, was itself evolving towards greater state involvement in everyday life. Yet this all-pervasive influence of the state was established more gradually than in the Crotonese, and through quite different channels.

In the Plain of Gioia it worked its way down from the 'superstructures' of social conflict and redistribution. The first step was the 'politicization' of the feud and the establishment of organic links between national political institutions and mafia-type authorities. When the fascist regime collapsed, many 'scores' had to be settled and the struggle for power and authority among rival patronage groups, partly frozen under fascism, was reactivated. This revival of the competitive use of violence took place in the highly politicized context of the middle 1940s. Partly as a spontaneous tendency, partly as a result of the practice of appointing mafia bosses to public office – a practice inaugurated under US military occupation – rival patronage groups were driven into opposite political factions.

This tendency went hand in hand with the incipient use of mafia power as an instrument of accumulation. Toward the end of the war and in the immediate post-war years, the *mafiosi* began to use their power in the monopolization of activities (such as transport and wholesale trade) that were strategically placed in the struggle for benefits. At first the benefits consisted of the large gains that could be reaped by trading in open and black markets and through smuggling. Later, the benefits came to consist of monopsonistic gains, rents, or outright extortions imposed on the local producers.

In the 1950s, the relationship between national political actors and local patronage groups remained the same as that established in the 1940s; the latter delivered votes to the former, and the former connived with the use of violence and the abuses of power of the latter. This exchange had important indirect effects on the social structure of the Plain of Gioia since the emergent 'entrepreneurial mafia' (Arlacchi, 1986), instead of protecting local society from the disintegrating tendencies of the market and the centralizing tendencies of state and capital, tried to turn these tendencies to its own advantage. As a consequence, the intensification of competitive pressures in the product markets increased the centralization of production and the polarization of the social structure.

In the 1960s, the relationship between local patronage groups and national political actors came to impinge even more directly and radically than in the 1950s on the social structure of the Plain. The number of state agencies operating in the south multiplied and, what is more, the public financial resources earmarked for the modernization and relief of the southern economy increased manifold. Since competitive pressures on the producers of the Plain had become so strong as to threaten the viability of all but the most efficient productive units, accumulation or just survival came to depend on a privileged access to these resources – an access which, in turn, required control over the local articulations of the state and of the political parties.

Two results followed. On the one hand, the struggle for benefits among patronage groups shifted from control over strategic nodes of market networks to control over strategic nodes of political networks. On the other hand, local patronage groups were induced to extend nationally (or even internationally) the scale of their operations in order to ensure the most profitable reinvestment of the capital accumulated in the Plain of Gioia and to establish a more direct influence on the national centres of economic redistribution.

Equally important in this respect were developments in the Cosentino where similar outcomes were produced via a different route. The absence of acute class conflict or of violent struggles among patronage groups meant that there were fewer opportunities and lesser incentives than in the other two areas for the state and political parties to seize upon local social processes in an attempt to secure legitimacy. As a matter of fact, in the Cosentino the reopening of traditional channels of long-distance migration and the opening of new ones were sufficient to create a widespread consensus in favour of the new republican state and the ruling-party coalition.

This 'enclave' of legitimacy and social peace provided the Christian Democrats with a source of reliable cadres to whom they could entrust the performance of state and party functions in the rest of Calabria and beyond.

As the functions of state and parties multiplied, individuals who occupied strategic positions in these networks used them to step into, and establish command over, the state and party bureaucracies. At the local level, party life, governmental functions, and bureaucratic employment came to be completely dominated by patronage based on kinship. On this basis, strong local-power positions were created from which to climb the hierarchies of party and state bureaucracies, both as an end in itself and as a means to securing control or influence over the centers of allocation of public resources.

The same mechanisms that had given the Cosentino a clear advantage over neighbouring areas in long-distance migration were thus activated to create a similar advantage in the occupation of positions of power (Cappelli, 1985: 567ff). Whereas in the other two areas the state and political parties had subverted (Crotonese) or infiltrated (Plain of Gioia) social relations, in the Cosentino social relations were projected into the state and political parties.

MASS MIGRATION

As the state came south, the peoples of Calabria went north. The transformations outlined in the previous section were matched by the development of mass migration. The prelude to this development was a drastic increase in the propensity to emigrate from all over Calabria. In the Crotonese, the land reform changed radically the relationship between the demand for and the supply of labour. On the one hand, the redistribution of land brought about a sharp contraction in the demand for labour. In the short run, this contraction was partly compensated for by the increase in the demand for labour associated with heavy private and public investments in land improvements and in infrastructure. But this increase was transitory and subsided as soon as the switch to the new system of land tenure was completed.

On the other hand, the land reform did not bring about a reduction in the supply of labour commensurate with the contraction of demand. Since most peasants had not received enough land to support/employ a family, they continued to sell part of the household's labour power on the market. They did so, however, from a radically changed condition. Their competitive position vis-à-vis the migrant-peasants of the interior and the semi-proletarianized peasants of the areas of petty commodity production had greatly improved. Since part of the household's subsistence was now covered by production on the plots obtained through the reform, wages were no longer required to cover the full costs of reproduction.

At the same time, the land reform reduced the dependence of the Crotonese labour force on the local labour market. One of the main reasons why the rural proletarians of the Crotonese had been only marginally involved in long-distance migration was that they lacked the material and nonmaterial resources necessary to undertake it (see 'The Junker (Prussian) Road'). The redistribution of land provided them with some of these resources.

The upshot of all these changes was that the Crotonese tended to turn from a net 'importer' into a net 'exporter' of labour power; that is to say, it began to generate a surplus of labour capable and willing to seek remuneration outside Calabria. For quite different reasons, the propensity to engage in extraregional migration increased also in the other two areas. In the Plain of Gioia, the incipient crisis of small-scale commodity production transformed the cyclical alternation of excess supply and excess demand in the local labour market (due to the ebbs and flows of competitive pressures in the product markets) into a structural disequilibrium of cumulating excess supply. Competitive pressure from abroad (Spain, Israel, Greece, Morocco, the United States) on the agricultural activities of the Plain, and from northern Italy on auxiliary activities (sawmills, coopers, basket-makers, and so on), was so strong that it induced capitalist producers either to give up production and emigrate or to undertake radical rationalizations of activities.

This thinning of the capitalist stratum and the rationalization of economic activities further depressed the local economy, leading to new rounds of divestment (particularly in retail and wholesale trade) and of emigration. The semi-proletarianized strata of the Plain of Gioia were thus faced, not only with less remunerative prices for their cash crops, but also with steadily worsening opportunities to sell labour power locally. As a consequence, in the Plain the propensity to emigrate was increasing, not because of an improvement in the living conditions of the labour force (as in the Crotonese), but because of a worsening in their conditions.

As for the Cosentino, the traditional high propensity to engage in long-distance and seasonal migration was further enhanced by two circumstances. In the first place, the previous 20 years had created a 'backlog' of would-be long-distance migrants ready to leave as soon as circumstances allowed. And in the second place, the intensification of competition in nearby labour markets was inducing would-be migrants to seek employment outside the region.

In the first post-war decade, therefore, the propensity to engage in extraregional migration was increasing in all three territories. This greater propensity materialized in three successive waves of migration, each representing a different stage of development of 'mass migration'.[6] During the first wave (that is, from the late 1940s to the late 1950s), extraregional migration remained predominantly long distance. The costs and risks of this type of migration – although considerably lower than half a century before – were still high and generally beyond the reach of the lower social strata.

The second wave began in the late 1950s and lasted until the middle 1960s. It was characterized by a pattern of principally medium-distance (extraregional, intra-European) migration. Moreover, intra-state migration (that is, migration from Calabria to other Italian regions) came to account for a large and growing share of intra-European migration. For the first time, extraregional migration became a mass phenomenon dominated by the lower social strata.

These changes were prompted by the boom of industrial activities in northwestern Europe and northern Italy associated with the formation of the EEC in 1958 and the spread of processes of mass production and capitalist rationalization ('Fordism' and 'Taylorism') pioneered in the US in the first half of the century. It was then not so easy to meet the growing demand for semi-skilled operatives. To some extent it was possible to do so by mobilizing and recycling the surplus of labour that stagnated in low-status/low-paying jobs within the core regions themselves.

In the early stages of development of the new lines and techniques of production, it was therefore quite normal for labour shortages in core regions to be more acute in the slowly expanding unskilled job sector than in quickly expanding semi-skilled job sectors.

In the late 1950s and early 1960s the shortage was nonetheless felt in semi-skilled occupations as well because of the high overall rate of expansion of industrial activities in western Europe. What is more, as soon as the new lines and techniques of production became generalized, the status of semi-skilled jobs declined, and their effort-price tended to increase drastically. As a consequence, shortages in semi-skilled jobs became progressively more acute than in unskilled jobs.

These two kinds of shortages (of semi-skilled operatives and unskilled labourers) prompted and shaped the demand of core European regions for the labour power of peripheral regions. The regional surplus of labour that had grown and stagnated in Calabria during most of the 1950s thus found an outlet that was within reach of the lower social strata, and that could even be exploited on a seasonal basis.

Initially, the impact of mass migration on the social structures of Calabria was limited by the fact that, up to about 1962, the predominant experience of the migrants in northern Italy and abroad was employment in the low-status/low-paying jobs that had been deserted by the indigenous workers. These jobs were a welcome alternative to open or disguised unemployment but not an inducement strong enough to give up self- or wage employment within Calabria. Migration thus absorbed the regional surplus of labour without undermining the viability of existing social structures.

In contrast to this situation, between 1962 and 1966, the predominant experience of the migrants from Calabria became employment in the semi-skilled positions of technologically advanced core industries. The generalization of the new lines and techniques of mass production increased competitive pressures on employers to reduce unit labour costs. As employers attempted to step up the intensity and pace of work in semi-skilled positions (where most of the directly productive work had come to be concentrated), they began to experience labour resistance on the part of the indigenous workers who had come to occupy those positions or labour shortages. The mass substitution of migrant workers for indigenous workers in semi-skilled jobs performed the double function of breaking this resistance and overcoming these shortages. These jobs offered the migrants a higher status and a higher pay than previous occupations, both in the places of immigration and in the places of emigration. To be sure, they also required a far more sustained effort than these other occupations – effort that could hardly be sustained over a full lifetime. However, as long as the migrants perceived the semi-skilled jobs as a stepping stone towards an improved social and economic position, the high effort-price of such jobs was only a minor drawback. Since tenure in semi-skilled jobs was thought to be temporary, the higher the pay per unit of time the better – almost irrespective of the energies expended in their performance.

As we shall see, in the longer run these attitudes and expectations were self-defeating. For a while, however, they endowed migrants from Calabria and other peripheral regions with a strong competitive advantage vis-à-vis indigenous workers, resulting in the almost complete substitution of the former for the latter in semi-skilled jobs. This substitution had 'revolutionary' repercussions on social relations in Calabria. Migration ceased to be a factor of continuity and expansion of subsistence production, as it had been in the Cosentino, or a reflection of labour market disequilibria as it had been in the Plain of Gioia. Instead, migration became a factor of discontinuity in the evolution of subsistence production, and a primary factor in the decline of commodity production.

The two changes which more than anything else have precipitated the disintegration of subsistence production were a change in what Aglietta (1979) has called the 'consumption norm' on one side and a change in the economic relationship between age groups on the other. The main products of the new lines and techniques of mass production (the smaller automobiles, television sets, electrical household appliances, mass produced food and clothing, and so on) required a mass market dependent on the spread of semi-skilled occupations. As these products entered the new consumption norm, the very meaning of 'subsistence' changed. The old concept of subsistence became obsolete, land lost much of its value as a source of status and full-lifetime subsistence, and customary rules and obligations began to break down.

The main agents of the transformation were the younger generations. Apart from being more easily influenced by the change in the consumption norm, the younger generations saw in the new structure of demand for labour in core regions a unique opportunity to switch to the new pattern of consumption and, simultaneously, to liberate themselves from the oppressive patriarchalism that pervaded the structures of subsistence production.

As the younger generations went north or went into higher education, the structures of subsistence production experienced acute labour shortages which could no longer be countered with marginal changes in technical and institutional arrangements. Those peasant households that controlled the best land (in terms of fertility and closeness to the rapidly growing urban markets) and were more entrepreneurially inclined, switched to skill- and capital-intensive techniques of production and transformed their subsistence into market- and profit-oriented activities. The majority, however, either stopped cultivating the land altogether or continued to do so as a side activity from which they did not expect anything more than a subsidy to a subsistence earned elsewhere.'

In the Crotonese and in the Plain of Gioia the competition of core regions for peripheral labour supplies subverted existing social structures in a more direct and immediate way than in the Cosentino. Both areas were characterized by relatively well-developed labour markets in which changes in what labour could earn elsewhere were promptly translated into competitive pressures on workers or employers according to circumstances.

Squeezed between strong competitive pressures in the labour *and* the product markets, small-scale commodity production was plunged into its final crisis. As in the Cosentino, only those households (and enterprises) that controlled the best land and that either had already switched or were quick to switch to skill- and capital-intensive operations were able to survive. All the others either discontinued agricultural activities or were able to pursue them only as side activities.

The recession of 1963–6 marked the end of the second wave of migration. When migration picked up again in 1966 after two years of decline, a third and last wave of migration began. The expectations of the migrants of this third wave were quite different from those of the earlier wave, and in addition they were quite different from what the migrants actually found in the regions of immigration. The main difference was that the migrants of the late 1950s and early 1960s did not expect employment in core regions to provide them with full-lifetime status and subsistence, which in fact they often got, whereas this was precisely what the bulk of the migrants of the late 1960s expected and did not get.

The strength of the migrants of the second wave in competing with indigenous workers of core regions for semi-skilled jobs was that they did not expect to spend the rest of their lives in those jobs and, therefore, were prepared to expend energies at a rate that could not be sustained over a full lifetime. This strong competitive position facilitated the advancement of the early migrants from the low-status/low-pay jobs into the higher-status/higher-pay semi-skilled jobs. This 'unexpected' success shaped the expectations of the migrants of the third wave who went north in search of social and economic advancement. Yet, the more semi-skilled jobs came to be 'monopolized' by migrants, the more they lost status and the more they involved a consumption of energies that could not be sustained for more than a few years.

Thus, the expectations of the migrants of the third wave were bound to be and actually were frustrated. The main effect of the unfulfilled expectations was the outbreak of redistributive struggles of an unprecedented nature.

REDISTRIBUTIVE STRUGGLES

The migrants of Calabria did not accept passively the verdict of the market that decreed (i) the liquidation of their income-earning opportunities in the areas of emigration, and (ii) their confinement in the areas of immigration to dead-end jobs that gave them only temporary access to the means of subsistence of the new consumption norm. Rather, they exploited the social networks in which they were enmeshed to struggle for an improvement in their income-earning opportunities in both areas. In core regions the struggles took the form of industrial conflict aimed principally, although not exclusively, at a reduction in the intensity of work. In Calabria, it took the form of urban rioting aimed principally at a territorial redistribution of state financial resources in general and bureaucratic employment in particular.

With respect to individual conflict, the semi-skilled jobs that migrant workers had come to monopolize in the late 1960s did not provide them with the status and full-lifetime subsistence they expected. But they did provide them with a power they never had before – the power to disrupt production at a low cost to themselves and at a high cost to their employers. Slowing down production or going *often* on *short* strikes cost the migrant worker little or nothing.

Taking advantage of this asymmetry of bargaining power in the workplace, southern migrants initiated in 1968–9 a wave of labour unrest of unprecedented spread, intensity, and length.[7] The main reason why this wave of industrial conflict lasted so long and was so difficult to bring under control was that previous means of undermining workers' bargaining power had been used up, or could no longer be mobilized as effectively as in the past.

Through the introduction of the technological innovations mentioned earlier, the craftworkers were displaced from directly productive roles by semi-skilled workers who were initially recruited among the semi-proletarianized and lower social strata of the core regions themselves. When in 1959–62 the latter gave rise to a new wave of industrial conflict, aimed primarily at obtaining higher wages, they were largely successful in their endeavour, but were quickly displaced from semi-skilled jobs by southern migrants who were willing to expend more energies for the same amount of money. The strong bargaining power of the southern migrants in the late 1960s and early 1970s was rooted in the very processes that had undermined the bargaining power of the protagonists of the earlier waves of conflict. If the power of the migrants had to be undermined, new ways and means had to be found.

As the outbreak of industrial conflict and its successes in winning higher wages and improved working conditions brought into the open the loss of competitiveness of migrant labour, the expansion of mass production levelled off, and the demand for migrant labour declined. The downturn of migration from Calabria, which began in 1970–1 and accelerated after 1973, was partly the result of this reduction in demand. In part, however, it must be traced to the decline in the propensity to emigrate jointly produced by the changed conditions of migration and by the process of growing interpenetration of Calabria's social structures with national political institutions.

The recession of 1963–6 had marked a turning point also in this latter process. It pushed all social strata to seek status, profits, and subsistence in a closer relation with the state in Calabria itself. Pensions, subsidies for agricultural products, contracts for public works, jobs in bureaucratic employment from the lowest to the highest levels – these and other benefits became the object of struggles among individuals and groups of kin and clients whose typical arenas were state institutions rather than the market.

In 1970, a highly visible and dramatic movement of protest broke out in Reggio Calabria and was only held in check by the sustained presence of the police and army for more than a year (Ferraris, 1971; D'Agostini, 1972). Just as the struggles of the migrant workers in the industrial plants of the north were reproducing on a much larger scale the class struggles that had torn apart the capitalist latifundia, so the extensive urban riots in the streets of Reggio Calabria reproduced on an enlarged scale the feuds that had divided and held together the social structures of small-scale commodity production.

The riots broke out as a reaction to the decision of the central government to make Catanzaro rather than Reggio the capital city of

Calabria which, like all other Italian regions, was about to acquire significant legislative and administrative autonomy from the central state. The decision was perceived by the inhabitants of Reggio as an insult to the 'honour' of their city, which had always been regarded (and not only by them) as the *de facto* capital of Calabria. At a more material level, the decision seemed to sanction, and thereby further enhance, the peripheralization of the province of Reggio in relation not only to core regions but also to the other two provinces of Calabria (Cosenza and Catanzaro).

After the Second World War, social and economic decay in the province of Reggio proceeded apace. The crisis of commercial agriculture, which we have outlined with reference to the Plain of Gioia, involved in one form or another the whole province. The recession of 1963–6 was the straw that broke the camel's back. While the lower social strata went north to see their expectations of income and status frustrated, the local bourgeoisie and the middle strata – 'crowded out' from an over-competitive market – found themselves seeking refuge in an over-crowded state apparatus.

The revolt of 1970–1 was a reaction of the people of Reggio to the sense and reality of being left behind. The reaction cemented the highly stratified and segmented social structure of Reggio and its province into a solid bloc impervious to divisive external influences. Feuds among local patronage groups were temporarily set aside in a common struggle aimed at forcing the central government to reverse its decision on the regional capital. As a means to this end the state's legitimacy was challenged through extensive and protracted disruptions of law and order.

Threatened by a general loss of legitimacy, the central government eventually resorted to the compromise of dividing the role of regional capital between Reggio and Catanzaro. The most important effect of the revolt, however, was not this compromise. Far more important was the attempt of the central state to regain legitimacy through a further increase in the economic resources directly and indirectly channelled towards the Mezzogiorno in general and to Calabria in particular. These redistributive measures gave indirect support to the struggles waged by southern migrants in northern industries because they constrained the tendency of northern industries to rationalize production and cut down the employment of migrant labour, while they provided migrants or potential migrants with alternative sources of income in their regions of origin.

These relatively successful redistributive struggles brought to an end the process of transformation of the Calabrian peasantry into a waged and salaried labour force. As mass migration came to an end, no peasantry to speak of was left in Calabria. There still were farmers and agricultural workers, to be sure. But there was no numerically or socially significant group of low-status cultivators that attached importance to land as a source of full-lifetime status and subsistence.

CONCLUSIONS

The experience of Calabria seems to suggest that social conflict is the key intervening variable, to use that language, in the process of social change. It intervened in the determination of the initial differentiation of Calabria along three divergent paths of social change. It intervened in disrupting the viability of the Junker road at the end of the Second World War, and therefore in initiating the convergence of the three paths towards a new single pattern. And it intervened at the very end of our story in bringing to a halt mass migration. These 'interventions' underscore the fact that the peasants of Calabria, and their semi-proletarian and proletarian successors, have not at all been passive pawns in the hands of state and capital. Their history is in fact a history of resistance against all kinds of exploitative tendencies. Sometimes they lost and sometimes they won, and the outcome determined the path of social change for generations to come.

By and large, however, the form, intensity, and outcome of social conflict were shaped by developmental processes that were only in small part, if at all, determined by the present or even past actions of the peoples of Calabria. For example, the conflicts that led to the differentiation of Calabria were sparked by a particular world economic conjuncture (the mid-nineteenth-century boom of agricultural world prices and the formation of the Italian state), and their outcome was largely determined by the social ecology of the terrain on which they were fought. The explosion of class struggle of the late 1940s, which led to the dismemberment of the capitalist latifundia, was an integral part of the Junker road to social change – itself the product of a previous defeat of the peasantry. But the spread and intensity of the explosion were largely determined by the fact that in the Crotonese large-scale commodity production had been associated with peripheralization rather than ascent to core position – a fact that was largely independent of what local actors did or could do.

Moreover, the acute hegemonic struggles that were being fought at the national and world levels when class conflict erupted in the Crotonese, were as essential to the introduction of the land reform that liquidated the latifundia as the rural revolt itself.

Generally speaking, we may therefore say that social conflict is an integral part of developmental processes, and that its role lies not so much in determining the economic regress (progress) of the locale in which it occurs as in determining the distribution of the costs (benefits) of economic regress (progress) among the residents of the locale. Social conflict, however, is not the only weapon available to peasants and proletarians in their struggles against exploitation and peripheralization. The historical experience of Calabria is instructive also because it shows the importance of migration as a substitute for and a complement of social conflict in shaping developmental processes.

In the phase of regional differentiation, short- and long-distance migration played a key role in promoting social change, but along directions largely determined by the outcome of social conflict. In the Cosentino, migration consolidated the informal victory of the peasants over the landlords, while in the Crotonese it consolidated the informal victory of the landlords over the peasants. In the Plain of Gioia, where neither the peasants nor the landlords won, migration facilitated the reproduction of a balanced relationship of forces in the face of destabilizing market influences.

The role of migration was not limited to a consolidation of outcomes already determined by social conflict. After the Second World War, the deepening peripheralization of Calabria on the one hand and the evolution of the labour process in core regions on the other hand created a large supply of would-be migrants in Calabria and a large demand for migrant labour in northern Italian core regions. (See 'The Convergence of the Three Roads'). The mass migration that ensued was a mass response to peripheralization. By going north, the migrants were seeking individually the economic progress that no individual or collective action in Calabria could have brought within their reach. Migration thus began to go beyond the realm of possibilities determined by the outcomes of social conflict.

Many of the migrants actually got what they sought, but their success induced new rounds of migration that undermined the foundation of the initial success. Competitive pressures on migrants in core regions became more intense, while productive structures in Calabria were further disrupted. The two explosions of social conflict of the late 1960s and early 1970s were complementary responses to this simultaneous increase in the exploitation of migrants on the one side and in the peripheralization of Calabria on the other. Mass migration thus played a double role. It provided the individuals who were clever enough or lucky enough or generationally fortunate to migrate at the right time with a way out of peripheralization. In addition, it changed the scale and the terrain of social conflict, thereby creating the condition for successful redistributive struggles.

NOTES

1. Evidence for the account of the migrant-peasant road given in this section can be found in Piselli (1981) and Piselli and Arrighi (1985: 379–92, 424–28).
2. Evidence for the account of the Junker road given in this section can be found in Piselli and Arrighi (1985: 405–14, 420–24).
3. On the process of formation of the capitalist latifundium in the Crotonese, see the important case study analyzed by Petrusewicz (1979).
4. Evidence for the account of the farmer road given in this section can be found in Piselli and Arrighi (1985: 393–404, 415–20).
5. For an overall view of the land occupation struggles in the Crotonese and all of Calabria see Alcaro and Paparazzo (1976), Cinanni (1977), and Bevilacqua (1980). On the activities and role of the Communist party see Tarrow (1972).
6. The quantitative aspects of the three waves are shown in Appendix II, *Review*, X, 4, Spring 1987, 744ff.
7. With ups and downs, and changes in form and substance, the wave of labour unrest lasted for a decade or so. The literature on the subject is vast. Regalia *et al.* (1978), Lange and Vannicelli (1982), and Barkan (1984) are among the best overviews.

REFERENCES

M. Aglietta, *A Theory of Capitalist Regulation* (London: New Left Books, 1979).

M. Alcaro and A. Paparazzo, *Lotte Contadine in Calabria (1943–1950)* (Cosenza: Lerici, 1976).

P. Arlacchi, *Mafia, Peasants, and Great Estates. Society in Traditional Calabria* (Cambridge: Cambridge University Press, 1983).

P. Arlacchi, *Mafia Business: The Mafia Ethic and the Spirit of Capitalism* (London and New York: Verso/Schoeken, 1986).

G. Arrighi and B. Silver, 'Labor Movements and Capital Migration: The United States and Western Europe in World Historical Perspective', in C. Bergquist (ed.), *Labor in the Capitalist World-Economy* (Beverly Hills, CA: Sage, 1984), pp. 183–216.

G. Arrighi and J. Drangel, 'The Stratification of the World-Economy: An Exploration of the Semiperipheral Zone', *Review*, X, 1, Sum (1986), pp. 9–74.

G. Arrighi and F. Piselli, 'Capitalist Development in Hostile Environments', *Review*, X, 4, Spring (1987), pp. 649–751.

M. Aymard, 'From Feudalism to Capitalism in Italy: The Case that Doesn't Fit', *Review*, VI, 2, Fall (1982), pp. 131–208.

J. Barkan, *Visions of Emancipation. The Italian Workers' Movement since 1945* (New York: Praeger,1984).

V. Barresi, *Il Ministro dei Contadini* (Milano: Franco Angeli, 1983).

P. Bevilacqua, *Le Campagne del Mezzogiorno tra Fascismo e Dopoquerra. Il Caso della Calabria* (Torino: Einaudi,1980).

P. Bevilacqua, 'Uomini, terre, economie', in P. Bevilacqua and A. Placanica, (eds), *Storia d'Italia. Le Regioni dall'Unità a Oggi. La Calabria* (Torino: Einaudi, 1985), pp. 115–362.

V. Cappelli, 'Politica e politici', in P. Bevilacqua and A. Placanica (eds), *Storia d'Italia. Le Regioni dall'Unità' a Oggi. La Calabria* (Torino: Einaudi,1985), pp. 493–584.

J. Casparis, 'The Swiss Mercenary System: Labor Emigration from the Semiperiphery', *Review*, V, 4, Spring (1982), pp. 593–642.

J. Casparis, 'Core Demand for labor from Southern Europe: The Case of Switzerland', in G. Arrighi (ed.), *Semiperipheral Development: The Politics of Southern Europe in the Twentieth Century* (Beverly Hills, CA: Sage, 1985), pp. 107–31.

P. Chorley, *Oil, Silk, and Enlightenment. Economic Problems in XVIIIth Century Naples* (Napoli: Istituto Italiano per gli Studi Storici, 1965).

P. Cinanni, *Lotte per la Terra e Comunisti in Calabria: 1943–1953* (Milano: Feltrinelli, 1977).

F. D'Agostini, *Reggio Calabria. I moti del luglio 1970–febbraio 1971* (Milano: Feltrinelli, 1972).

P. Ferraris, 'I cento giorni di Reggio: i presupposti della rivolta e la sua dinamica', *Giovane Critica*, no. 25, Winter (1971), pp. 2–42.

G. Galasso, *Economia e società nella Calabria del cinquecento* (Napoli: L'arte Tipografica, 1967).

INAIL, *Notiziario statistico* (Roma: Poligrafico dello Stato, various years).

Inchiesta Parlamentare, *Inchiesta parlamentare sulle condizioni dei contadini nelle province meridionali e nella Sicilia,* Vol. V, 2, Roma (1909).

INEA, *La distribuzione della proprietà fondiaria in Italia. Lucania e Calabria* (Roma, 1947).

ISTAT, *Popolazione e movimento anagrafico* (Roma: ISTAT, various years).

ISTAT, *Statistica dell'emigrazione italiana* (Roma: ISTAT, 1900 and subsequent years).

P. Lange and M. Vannicelli, 'Strategy under Stress. The Italian Union Movement and the Italian Crisis in Developmental perspective', in P. Lange, G. Ross and M. Vannicelli (eds), *Unions, Change and Crisis: French and Italian Union Strategy and the Political Economy, 1945–1980* (London: Allen & Unwin, 1982), pp. 95–206.

V. I. Lenin, 'The Agrarian Programme of Social-Democracy in the First Russian Revolution', in *Selected Works*, Vol. 3. (London: Lawrence & Wishart, 1936).

E. Malfatti, *Valutazione dei bilanci demografici annuali della popolazione presente nelle regioni e nelle province del Mezzogiorno (1951–75)* (Milano: Giuffrè, 1976).

J. Meyriat (ed.), *La Calabria* (Cosenza: Lerici, 1961).

Ministero del Lavoro, *Bollettino di Statistiche del Lavoro* (Rome, various years).

G. Myrdal, *Economic Theory and Underdeveloped Regions* (London: Duckworth, 1959).

M. Petrusewicz, 'Les sources de l'accumulation primitive dans l'agriculture calabraise au XIXe siècle: le cas des Barracco', in *Etudes rurales*, no. 75, July-Sept. (1979), pp. 17–33.

P. Pezzino, *La riforma agraria in Calabria* (Milano: Feltrinelli, 1977).

F. Piselli, *Parentela ed emigrazione* (Torino: Einaudi, 1981).

F. Piselli and G. Arrighi, 'Parentela, clientela e comunita', in P. Bevilacqua and A. Placanica (eds), *Storia d'Italia, Le Regioni dall Unità a Oggi. La Calabria* (Torino: Einaudi, 1985), pp. 367–492.

K. Polanyi, *The Great Transformation* (Boston: Beacon, 1957).

I. Regalia, M. Regini and E. Reyneri, 'Labor Conflicts and Industrial Relations in Italy', in C. Crouch and A. Pizzorno (eds), *The Resurgence of Class Conflict in Western Europe since 1968*, vol. I (New York: Holmes & Meier, 1978), pp. 101–58.

A. Rossi Doria, *Il ministro e i contadini. Decreti Gullo e lotte nel Mezzogiorno, 1944–1949* (Roma: Bulzoni,1983).

M. Rossi Doria, *Riforma agraria e azione meridionalista* (Bologna: Edizioni Agricole,1948).

J. Schumpeter, *The Theory of Economic Development* (New York: Oxford University Press, 1961).

E. Sereni, *Il capitalismo nelle campagne (1860–1900)* (Torino: Einaudi, 1968).

S. G. Tarrow, *Partito comunista e contadini nel Mezzogiorno* (Torino: Einaudi, 1972).

A. Treves, *Le migrazioni interne nell'Italia fascista* (Torino: Einaudi,1976).

E. Vallini, *Operai del Nord* (Bari: Laterza,1957).

J. Van Velsen, 'Labor Migration as a Positive Factor in the Continuity of Tribal Society', *Economic Development and Cultural Change*, Vol. VIII (1960), pp. 265–78.

W. Watson, *Tribal Cohesion in a Money Economy* (Manchester: Manchester University Press, 1958).

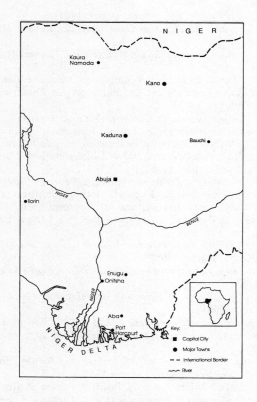

Map 6   Central Nigeria: Major Towns

6 Textile Unions and Industrial Crisis in Nigeria: Labour Structure, Organization and Strategies

Gunilla Andræ and Björn Beckman

INTRODUCTION

The crisis of the Nigerian textile industry

By 1980, Nigeria had developed the third largest textile industry in Africa, surpassed only by Egypt and South Africa, with some 100 factories and some 100 000 workers, not including vast numbers of small garments firms and crafts producers. The industry faced major difficulties, including fierce competition from smuggled Asian products and a fast receding domestic raw material base. Five years later, by 1985, the industry had lost about 40 000 workers and was operating at some 40 per cent of its capacity (Andræ and Beckman, 1984 and 1987).

In 1980 the cause of the crisis was the distortions brought about by the oil boom of the 1970s: a sharp rise in the external value of the Nigerian naira, the erosion of its domestic purchasing power, and sectoral dislocations caused by massive spending of oil revenue and heavy imports (Andræ and Beckman, 1985). In 1985 the cause was a recession following on the steep fall in oil earnings that began in 1981, the full impact of which was only temporarily postponed by borrowing. The domestic market shrank. But the textile industry was unable to meet even this reduced demand. It had become critically dependent on imported raw materials and as the import capacity of the economy collapsed, industrial production fell as well. As part of a wider study on the crisis of the Nigerian textile industry (Andræ and Beckman, 1984) we have discussed elsewhere the

143

response of the industry (Andræ and Beckman, 1987). Here we look at the response of the union.

Workers, unions and crisis: the problem

This chapter, then, is about the way in which the crisis has hit the workers and how they have defended themselves, especially the role played by the textile workers' union. We draw primarily on company and union records and interviews made in 1985 and 1987 with managements, unionists, and workers particularly in eight factories in the northern cities of Kaduna and Kano, two of the three major textile centres in the country. We also use material from the national organizations of both textile workers and employers.

The argument is about workers' and union power and their determinants at the level of production and in society at large, including the level of state and politics. We want to show how determinants in the organization of the individual firm and its labour process interact with those at the level of the industry as a whole and the wider political economy, including the system whereby labour is produced and reproduced in the non-wage economy.

How far has the union succeeded in protecting workers' interests and what are the factors that account for its failures and achievements? The union has been subjected to intense regulation and intervention by the state. We look at the way this has affected its way of responding to the crisis and its ability to represent the interests of the workers.

An overview

We begin by outlining the way the crisis hits the workers, including the fall in employment and income and the intensification of work and managerial control. The formidable dimensions of the crisis may suggest that workers and unions are virtually helpless. We discuss how they have attempted, and in some measure succeeded, to protect themselves against the full impact of the crisis.

How significant are these achievements? What do they tell us about the ability of the union to defend workers' interests? In order to be able to discuss possible answers to such questions we need to know more about the conditions under which the union operates. We discuss the determinants of union power first at the level of production, including the structure of the industry, the size of workplaces, regional concentration and ownership. We look at the age and gender composition of the workforce, pattern of labour recruitment, migration and regional differentiation. Education and skill structure interact with the organization of the labour process in influencing workers' outlook and union strategy in facing the crisis. What does it mean, for instance, that workers retain links with a non-wage economy, both rural and urban, that provides them with supplementary income and escape routes?

Some of the features of industry and labour force differ significantly between Kano and Kaduna. Kano is a pre-colonial city with an indigenous merchant class that has taken a strong interest in the textile industry; by contrast, Kaduna is a colonial new town, dominated by state and transnational capital. Industry in both places is the recipient of long-distance labour migration. Kano, however, also has a densely populated rural hinterland which is closely tied to the city in the exchange of commodities and labour. Comparison of the two cities provides a basis for exploring how structural differences have consequences for workers' ability to protect their interests by collective means.

In discussing the political determinants of union power we focus on the effects of the centralization and amalgamation of the union that was imposed by the state in 1979. We argue that, although intended as a means of greater state control, the new structure enhanced the capacity of the union to respond to the crisis. We also show how the union was able to advance its position politically also in Kano, where resistance to unionization had been most persistent.

We conclude with a case study of a major industrial dispute in a Kaduna factory which provides an illustration of the general argument.

THE CRISIS HITS THE WORKERS

Falling employment

The years 1980–6 were years of mass redundancy. The downward trend started in 1980–1 in response to a sharp increase in the minimum wage in a market situation already exposed to heavy competition from cheap, smuggled, imported goods. It acquired new impetus as a consequence of the 1982 squeeze on the importation of raw materials. A survey made by the textile employers' association (interview Eburajolo, November 1985) shows that in 1984 one quarter of a sample of 47 factories employed below 50 per cent of their full labour force. Only about one third employed over 75 per cent, while the overall reduction in employment for the sample was about 40 per cent. If generalized to the whole sector it would mean 40 000 jobless in an industry of a mighty 100 000 workers. Membership in the union fell from 70 000 at the end of 1980 to 45 000 five years later (NUTGTWN, 1986).

In many factories the reduction was effected by going from three to two shifts per day, while complete closures were rare. The erratic and insufficient supply of raw material also resulted in the common application of compulsory leave and temporary closures, sometimes with and sometimes without pay – often with only part pay. Workers were made to take their annual leave of two to four weeks sometimes as much as two years in advance. Sometimes such compulsory leaves would last for many months.

Falling income and benefits

For those who were lucky to remain employed, the prospects for maintaining their income were moot. A wage freeze was imposed by the state in 1983. As costs of living went up, real wages deteriorated so that in 1986, according to the union, an increase in wages of 40 per cent would be required to restore the 1983 levels of real incomes (NUTGTWN, 1986).

With vast numbers of unemployed pressing at the factory gates, care was taken not to provoke the management. Particularly where traditions of organized, collective action were weak, as in many factories in Kano, there was a definite attitude of lying low. The acceptance of poor conditions of compulsory leave was a case in point. NTP in Kano, one of the smaller family-owned companies, could for instance get away with three months' leave on 50 per cent pay in 1986. Even a large multinational like UNTL in Kaduna compensated only 75 per cent when they sent workers on a compulsorily extended Christmas leave. The conditions of the collective agreements could not be effectively enforced everywhere, especially not in the newly unionized companies in Kano.

In some companies annual bonus payments were cancelled, as in the case of Bagauda in Kano in 1986, without workers putting up much of a fight. In KTL, the large old factory in Kaduna, tolerance towards the small incentives and bonus granted in 1986 was remarkable, especially as it was only two years since the workers had successfully defied management in a major industrial action to which we shall return below. The scope for active bargaining had clearly been reduced.

Increasing workload

Some factories used the situation to step up the workload in a process that the union termed 'overloading'. Frustration in the large Kaduna factories in 1987 was great at this process, causing some workers to leave because they found the new working conditions unacceptable. Thus in UNTL the number of workers per loom in the weaving section went from one operator on eight machines in 1968 to one on 24 in 1985, and further stepped up to one on 36 machines in 1986; this according to union sources. They claimed that the output of cloth in the factory had not gone down in spite of a reduction of the workforce by over 400 workers from 1985 to 1986. Union officials in KTL, also in Kaduna, quoted a similar development: one over-looker and one assistant on 16 looms plus one weaver and a spare weaver on 12 looms in 1982 had been replaced by one overlooker and no assistant on 30–34 looms plus one weaver on 10–12 looms with no spare weaver in 1987.

Companies were raising labour productivity in order to reduce the damage caused by the crisis. The consequence, at least in the short term, was to add to the general fall in employment. But they also took advantage of the crisis to introduce changes in the labour process and in the intensity of work that otherwise would have met with greater resistance.

UNION RESPONSES TO THE CRISIS

Nigerian textile workers suffered and they continue to do so. But this is not the whole story. There was also resistance. The positions of the workers were defended and some of the losses and damages were contained. Let us first consider the attempt to reduce the fall in employment.

Protecting employment

In the early 1980s large numbers of workers were laid off by outright redundancy. Individual factories in many cases show a sudden drop in their labour force around 1981, indicating large terminations at one stroke. Since then such cuts have however been restrained, despite the deepening crisis of the textile industry. Union policies contributed importantly to this restraint.

Although permanent lay-offs have continued in some of the smaller plants, reductions in the larger ones since 1983 have been primarily by what the employers call 'natural wastage'. The major part of this has been voluntary termination for old age and other reasons. The Employers Association prides itself on the 'humaneness' of its members in this respect (interview Eburajolo, August 1985). The need to retain the skill acquired by the workers at hand would account for some reluctance to reduce the labour force below a certain level. Another important reason for the restraint, however, was the union's efforts to make it more expensive and difficult to lay off workers.

In 1983 the textile union was able to negotiate a considerable rise in the compensation paid to those made redundant (NTGTEA and NUTGTWN, 1983). One and two weeks' pay in compensation per year in employment were thus added for workers with under and over five years of service, respectively. The cost of retrenching a worker after ten years' service, for instance, was thus raised from 50 to 70 weeks' pay. Especially as companies were financially weak, many preferred to hold on to excess workers, hoping for better times, rather than paying them off in an expensive redundancy exercise.

A related gain in this field was an amendment in 1984 to the collective agreement, that introduced the right to gratuities even for those who were dismissed for absenting themselves from work for over three days without 'acceptable cause' (NTGTEA and NUTGTWN, 1984). Dismissal on disciplinary grounds was part of the 'natural wastage' used by companies to dodge redundancy costs. Having achieved more stringent rules on redundancy it was important for the union to prevent employers subverting those gains by terminating in ways that did not oblige them to pay workers full end-of-service benefits.

Containing disciplinary terminations, however, was also a frontier in itself in the fight to protect employment. Union efforts in this field are a major and regular feature of zonal officers' reports. For instance, for UNTL the quarterly report of December 1984 tells us that 35 cases of termination were withdrawn, 25 dismissals (that is, without benefits) were changed to termination (that is, with benefits), 50 cases of suspension were withdrawn and 40 written warnings changed to verbal ones. The impression is given of a stepped up confrontation with management over disciplinary matters. The crisis encouraged employers to impose tighter discipline not just to facilitate lay-offs by cheap 'natural wastage' but also for the same reasons that made them put workers in charge of more looms; that is, the effort to use the crisis for raising labour productivity. Workers in their turn were more anxious than ever to hold on to work and to protect themselves against this offensive.

The use made by many companies of compulsory leave without or with reduced pay was another major area of confrontation. The union closely watched company manoeuvres and hotly debated within itself how much the firms should be allowed to get away with. The union was forced to make careful judgements about the true state of the companies' finances, the level of stocks of raw materials and so on. Companies often threatened a complete close-down if unpaid leave was not accepted. Were they bluffing? On some occasions the union forced a show of hands, as in the KTL case reported below, by demanding either full pay or closure with full redundancy benefits, being well aware of company difficulties in financing the latter.

Some cases of blatant abuse were successfully fought. One instance was the blanket factory, Chellco in Kaduna, whose market is seasonal and concentrated in the cooler winter months. Half-paid leaves were regularly extended to four or five months during the slack season. Here pressure was put on the company that it should either close down and allow workers to collect their full benefits, leaving them to look for other employment, or diversify production. Some of the temporary close-downs were thus prevented. Discussions were afoot in 1987 concerning alternative production lines. The union was pushed to seek solutions to the problems of the company, based on its knowledge of the textile industry in general.

The partial success of union efforts to limit lay-offs may be gauged by comparing levels of employment and capacity utilization. Whereas employment seems to have been reduced by some 40 per cent, capacity utilization fell much more. The General Secretary in his report to the 1986 congress (NUTGTWN, 1986) spoke of capacity utilization in the industry as a whole of 30–45 per cent or a reduction by 55–70 per cent. This was confirmed by our survey of factories in

Kaduna and Kano. The organized response of the textile workers to the crisis made it difficult for the companies to cut down employment at par with reduction in actual production.

Dodging the wage-freeze

The government-imposed ban on wage increases in 1983, in a situation of fast-rising consumer prices, was a central issue for the Nigerian labour movement as a whole. For the Nigerian Labour Congress, the national body, the removal of the wage-freeze was the key demand in confronting the state. To the individual industrial unions the challenge was to find ways of circumventing the freeze. In the following years the annual fight for the end of year bonus became one important frontier. At the time when the wage-freeze was introduced the annual bonus varied between as little as a week's extra pay in some companies to as much as three months' in others. Although managements continued to maintain that this was a non-negotiable benefit and as such could not be included in any collective agreement, much of the wage struggle came to focus on the bonus. Strikes and go-slows were commonplace in the months before Christmas. Managements' reference to low profits and hard times were not always readily accepted by the workers. Negotiations were carried out at the level of the individual branch but with assistance from union zonal officers. Concessions by one company could be used by other union branches in claiming equal treatment. The union position was normally that one month's extra pay was a non-negotiable minimum. The struggle therefore concerned obtaining as much as possible above that level.

The firms, being under heavy pressure, sought government support in order to resist workers' demands. In 1985, a government decree limited the bonus to a maximum of one single month's pay. In companies where not even this level had been reached, the issue remained in the forefront. Defence of the one month has also in many cases required concerted continued efforts. Elsewhere the frontier shifted to efforts to raise other benefits that could bring some compensation for the continuing fall in real income. Some of these were also outside the collective agreement and were negotiated branch-wise in very much the same way as the bonus. These were termed 'incentives' and included an increasingly complex set of payments in the form of commodities, services, and even cash. A most important one was 'gifts' of cloth produced in the factory to be given out on such occasions as *Sallah* (a Muslim holiday), at Christmas, or at the time of the annual leave. The connection with the bonus could be seen in the way that the value of such incentives was expressed by the unions in percentages of a month's pay. Other incentives were allocation of uniforms and certain consumer items such as soap and bread for a snack. In 1987 one demand on the frontier was for a free meal a day.

The struggle to obtain payments in kind on top of frozen wages and bonuses was supplemented by union efforts to secure cheap commodities for their members through special deals with state distribution agencies and other wholesale dealers. Employers would be made to contribute by providing finance, transport, and storage. Vegetable oil, a key item in Nigerian cooking, was a principal staple of this company-supported trade. The distribution of scarce commodities through the union, however, soon ran into difficulties, including allegations of misappropriation and profiteering voiced by warring factions in union branches. By 1987 the central cooperative department set up by the union to handle this trade was dormant.

Another avenue for seeking compensation for falling incomes was negotiations over the adjustment of wage and salary structures. This was made a main target of central union work in 1987. In many of the major companies, negotiations were concluded on the introduction of a system of incremental rates that allowed workers to increase earnings despite the wage-freeze. An important issue was the effort to remove the upper 'bar' to increments at the top of a particular wage level. In one Kaduna company, Arewa, for instance, the removal of the bar had been hotly contested by the union at least since 1984 according to zonal secretary reports. Achievements were measured in terms of numbers of promoted workers, but the goal was to have the bar removed, which was also finally attained with the support of the central union. A related issue was job definition. Here ways around incremental bars could be found by redefining jobs and placing them in higher grades.

The wage-freeze also gave added force to a spate of demands relating to working conditions, hours of work, overtime and other inconveniences both inside and outside the workplace. Unlike bonuses and incentives, which were exclusive subjects for branch negotiations, claims for heat, dust, and noise allowances and for canteen subsidies were handled at the local branch level, with varying success. Some other benefits were, however, negotiated as part of the collective agreement between the national textile union and the textile employers' association, including medical care, and housing and transport allowances (NTGTEA and NUTGTWN, 1979, 1983, 1984, and 1987). The picture, here too, is one of piecemeal and partial success in attaining compensation for the deteriorating levels of living.

A major achievement was the introduction from January 1985 of a five-day week without reduction in pay; 40 working hours spread over five days were to replace, for the whole industrial sector, the previous six-day week of 44.5 hours. Although it was also a way of cutting employment, it simultaneously represented an increase of 10 per cent in the effective hourly wage rate.

The collective agreement on working hours was not adhered to by all companies, particularly not in Kano where many of them were not even members of the employers' association. Some companies reduced break-times in compensation, and added a half-hour of work here and there. Union officials report cases of companies that continued to work Saturdays without paying overtime, concealing their defiance of the agreement behind closed gates and windows. On the whole, the five-day week with full pay has been enforced. Union insistence on overtime rates for Saturday work, however, has continued to be a cause of conflict.

The reduction in working hours was not the only field where the union had to struggle for the full implementation of the collective agreement. While housing and transport allowances have been commonly granted, conditions of health care and severance pay were contested issues in many local negotiations. In general, implementation was more successfully enforced in the large multi-nationals in Kaduna with their older unions than in the smaller and typically family-based companies in Kano, where union activity was more recent and more strongly resisted by management. We return to these regional differences below.

The Secretary-General of the textile union, addressing the National Delegates' Conference in November 1986, was confident that the 1987 round of negotiations at both the central and branch level would achieve an effective increase in overall benefits, including bonuses, incentives, increments and a wide range of allowances that were equal to a wage increase of some 30 per cent or more – despite the wage-freeze. It seems as if the central negotiations that year lived up to those expectations. It remains to be seen whether the local negotiations were equally successful. The bonus and incentive talks were in full swing when we made our most recent visit in late 1987; union officials were optimistic.

The sharp increase in consumer prices in 1987–8, due to the combined impact of massive devaluation and a poor harvest, has since upset the situation. The gains of the 1987 negotiations were swiftly eroded. As the full effect of the Structural Adjustment Programme was only beginning to be felt, unions were likely to be fighting an increasingly difficult uphill battle. The dramatic confrontation at the national level over the price of petrol in 1987–8 signalled also the stepping up of state repression of unions that placed fresh obstacles in the way of union work.

Looking back at the first phase of the crisis (1981–7), we are struck by the degree of success met by workers' unions in this defensive battle. We have seen evidence of a lot of tough and imaginative bargaining at both the national and branch level and some real achievements in limiting the damage caused by the crisis. To what extent these can be sustained in the next, post-devaluation phase is a different matter.

DETERMINANTS OF UNION POWER AT THE LEVEL OF PRODUCTION

The crisis has hit the workers hard. The union has fought to defend employment, income, and working conditions. What is the basis of its ability to do so? We shall first look at structural determinants in the organization of production and the composition of the labour force. We shall also compare the two northern textile centres – Kano and Kaduna – in this respect. The comparison suggests that certain structural features are more conducive than others in providing a basis for unionization and the collective defence of workers' interests.

We may consider the size and concentration of the workforce. Theories of working-class formation, organization and consciousness have long suggested that size matters. Large concentrations of workers become a physical force, developing their own culture and ideology, capable of sustaining organization and leadership. Also important is the composition of the labour force in terms of age and sex, its social and regional characteristics as related to its origin. It steers reproductive needs and influences the scope, unity, and legitimacy of collective action. The level of education, skill, and stability on the job, further, affects consciousness of rights and self-identification as workers. Skill also has implications for workers' control over the work process.

The structure of the labour force is determined partly by the general social environment from which labour is recruited, partly by the organization of production in the individual enterprise or the industry as a whole. The two interact. The position of the industry within the economic system and its conjunctures, including access to inputs and markets, affects the conditions under which wage labour is reproduced. The organization of the industry in terms of technology, the labour process, ownership and finance sets conditions for workers' strategies, both individual and collective. We conclude this part by discussing the way in which the shifting scope for alternative employment options outside the textile industry has affected workers' bargaining power.

Comparing Kano and Kaduna

It does not take close scrutiny to discover that conditions of employment, remuneration and service in the textile industry are generally much better in Kaduna than in Kano. In reporting above on the impact of crisis and union responses we touched on some of these differences. They can be illustrated, for instance, by the level of the bonus received in 1987. In Kaduna all factories attained one month while in Kano less than half of the factories did. Incentives were generally lower in Kano and lay offs and temporary closures without compensation more frequent. Only a few of the factories in Kano were members of the employers' association and adherence to collective agreements was weak. In Kaduna all companies were members and agreements effectively enforced.

Union rights were not respected in Kano to nearly the same degree as in Kaduna. As will be discussed below, unionization in Kano lagged far behind Kaduna where most factories have well-organized branches, some dating back to the 1960s. There are exceptions and variations, but the general tendency is clear.

Why is the difference between the two cities so marked ? We report here on comparative work in progress, based on interviews with managements, unions and a sample survey with individual workers that we made in 1985 and 1987 focusing on four factories each in Kano and Kaduna. It is a preliminary account of some of the basic features that could be observed. Lubeck's major study of Islam and urban labour in Kano (1983 and 1986) provides a wealth of additional information that has yet to be incorporated in the analysis. The same goes for Main's (1985) survey data on redundant Kano workers. For material on Kaduna, see also Hinchliffe (1973). We begin by briefly outlining the broader setting of the two cities and their textile industries. (A fuller outline of the structure of the textile industry in Nigeria is contained in Andræ and Beckman, 1985).

Kaduna is a colonial city that was established early this century as the capital of Northern Nigeria. It retained its importance during the early post-colonial period because of northern political dominance of the new federation. State investments were purposely directed to enhance this position. The state structure has since been broken down from the original three to the current 21 states. But Kaduna continues to be the unofficial capital of the North with a population of perhaps a million by 1980. Numerous federal, regional and state agencies, and the regional headquarters of banks, insurance companies and other commercial houses makes it primarily an administrative centre. However, its industrial status has grown fast. Its industrial base is characterized by large companies based on state and multinational capital, sometimes in combination. It has a petroleum refinery, a motor vehicle assembly plant, and a brewery. But it is the textile industry that dominates, with a concentration of nine, partly very large firms.

Four of the nine textile factories are integrated mills with spinning, weaving and finishing processes. State involvement is strong in all of these and dominates one, KTL, which also has Nigerian management. Two of the others have Chinese capital participation and management: UNTL and (the temporarily closed down) Nortex. One is Japanese run: Arewa. These integrated mills are all large, with potentially between 3000 and 8000 workers each.

Two smaller factories are closely related by ownership and management to one of the larger mills, UNTL. One spins, Unitex, one only prints, Supertex. They have 700 and 350 workers at full production. The remaining three factories, Chellco and Dagazau, and the Blanket Factory are smaller weavers with Indian owner and management participation. All have well below 1000 workers at full capacity.

The three functioning integrated mills had all been established by 1965, KTL as early as 1957, as one of the first in Nigeria. The two smaller Chinese run factories use the premises of one older company, Norspin, that was closed down in 1980. They started production in 1982 and 1983, respectively. Chellco, the Indian blanket factory, started in 1980; the two other smaller industries also started their production of carpets and blankets in the 1980s.

Kano has a very different history and current structure. It is an old commercial and cultural centre, with the largest traditional market in West Africa, a terminal of many centuries of prosperous trans-Saharan trade. It has a large informal trading and manufacturing sector. It is an important centre of Hausa culture and of Muslim learning with a probable population of well over one million by 1980. The modern industry that grew up in the post-war era was based on local merchant capital, including partly indigenized 'Levantine' (mostly Lebanese) family firms. The oil boom of the 1970s boosted further development along this line and family capital is still very strong. But the boom also brought in multinational companies of the import-substitution kind, flour mills, breweries, pharmaceutical and chemical industries plus some metal working industries and assembly plants. There also remain some primary processors like sawmills, tanneries, and a number of dormant vegetable oil mills. Kano is the capital of Kano state, one of the most populous states in the federation, including a densely populated hinterland, that has been under permanent and intense cultivation for centuries.

The textile industry in Kano is made up of 19 factories. It contains one integrated spinning, weaving and finishing mill, with a capacity to employ 1600 workers. This is the newly established Gaskiya, with all Nigerian capital, but Indian management. Established in 1985 it reached nearly 1000 workers in early 1987. One other mill, an old blanket factory, NTM, once had a capacity for 1500 workers, but recently has employed 400–500 workers. The typical size of the remaining mills is smaller. They either spin or weave or make embroidered lace. Most were established in the 1970s. Only two of those that are presently functioning were started before then. Apart from Gaskiya, two more factories were established in the 1980s. As many as nine factories have substantial Levantine interest and management, some with a background in textile trade, and some second generation Nigerian citizens. There is one Indian owner, in Terrytex, and one of Egyptian origin, in Norspin. The second major owner group is local Kano merchant and industrial capital. We find a number of the well-known Kano families participating in the industry: Gashash in NTM, Dandawaki in NTP, Dantatta together with Lebanese interests in UTIL and USL, Badamasi in Gaskiya and Ishiaku Rabiu in Bagauda. There is one Kano-state owned factory, KTP.

Numbers and concentration of workers

As was suggested above, at times of peak, pre-crisis production altogether some 100 000 workers would have been found in the actual textile manufacturing industry (thus excluding garment manufacturing). They were found in factories of frequently over 1000 workers, in one case as many as 8000 and always over 100. The Nigerian textile industry is concentrated in Lagos, Kano and Kaduna. Between them they house some 80 per cent of total capacity in the industry, with variations for different processes. The rest is scattered over smaller cities, mainly in the southern states, where only Aba and Benin City have more than one factory each.

The concentration of as many as 12–16 000 textile workers in a small number of large companies in Kaduna has ensured a high degree of political visibility. When the workers take to the streets in protest, as they did in 1980 and in 1984, their sheer numbers impress. Concentration facilitates agitation, unified action and organization. There is also a geographical concentration within the city. The distance from one factory to the other is in most cases not more than a 15 minutes' walk within the industrial area of Kaduna South. The majority of the workers live in housing areas adjacent to the factories.

The concentration of big textile industry has justified Kaduna having the headquarters of the national textile workers' union, housed in an impressive five-story building of its own. Having the national headquarters has in turn helped in maintaining a high level of effective unionization. Numbers means money in terms of members' dues. It allows the union to maintain, train, and equip a substantial body of cadres. Kaduna workers are well represented among the national cadres and have easy access to their services.

Numerical strength and concentration is less in Kano. The combined workforce of the 19 factories reached some 5000–6000 at the most in 1987, or under more favourable circumstances possibly 10 000 within the established structure. The workforce is spread over many small factories. Only the new Gaskiya plant nears the large size common in Kaduna. The remaining ones have 100–500 workers only. Many are in the Bompai industrial area, but intermingled with many other types of industry. Workers live more scattered than the Kaduna textile workers. Union members are fewer, absolutely and relative to the workforce. They are less powerful as the small factories cannot support their own paid union officials. As they are further from union headquarters the influence of organized unionism is weaker. One paid locally based organizing secretary for Kano is their link with national headquarters, apart from the roving zonal officer, who visits from time to time and is called in for important negotiations. Naturally the Kano union branches are less in a position to draw headquarters' support in their day-to-day struggles with management and authorities.

Age, gender and origin

The demographic structure of the labour force in the Nigerian textile industry is a source of strength. A nearly all-male workforce, in ages typically between 25 and 40, makes for unified expectations for a living wage that covers the reproduction of a whole family. Politically and socially such demands have high legitimacy. The same is true of their demands for security in employment and reasonable conditions of termination. In this respect the similarities between Kaduna and Kano prevail. More older workers are found in Kano, where, as we shall see below, a considerable component of local labour is found. The experience of labour history elsewhere suggests that male homogeneity goes with a higher level of organization and unity.

Heterogeneity in terms of regional origin, ethnic and religious background can be a source of division. In the factories studied this threat is real, above all due to the large component of migrants that are found in both cities. In Kaduna a majority of the workers come from the non-Hausa areas of the Middle Belt; that is, to the south of the city. Others come from areas still further away in the southern states. The divisions on such lines are visible. There is a clear element, for instance, of ethnic or regional competition in union elections. Union executive committees at the branch level may be tilted in favour of one group or the other, even if broad coalitions rather than 'winner takes all' seem to be the rule.

In Kano, the old commercial city, the local component of the workforce is large. There is thus an additional source of division between, on the one hand, the Kano state indigenes, with their common muslim religion and Hausa language and, on the other, the outsiders. Industrialists report pressure from Kano state officials to give preference to state indigenes when employing or laying off workers. The combination of a large local labour force and a strong local component in management and ownership has set the scene for special relations between management and workers. This is seen for instance in the way in which local labour is recruited through networks of patronage between the leading Kano families and the surrounding villages. It creates a relationship of dependence and 'trust' that creates openings for community based or individual strategies by workers and employers.

Education and skill

The educational background of textile workers differs importantly between the two cities. In the Kaduna factories a fairly high level of 'western' education is the rule. Primary school is a prerequisite for employment. All workers can read and write in English. Some secondary education (usually uncompleted) is not unusual. Further educational aspirations, for teacher training or clerical, technical or commercial work are common. Many workers attend evening classes or take correspondence courses. Education helps them to be better informed.

The Kano textile workers, as we have seen, include a large section of long distance migrants with characteristics similar to those that dominate Kaduna. But there is also a major group of workers of Kano town or rural Kano state origin, whose background is rather different. Many of these workers have not been to 'western' schools, and do not speak or read English. Some are entirely illiterate, but most have some Koranic education. Some are literate in Hausa and Arabic. Many remain subjected to the traditional authority structures of Hausa society, as more or less incorporated by and adapted to the colonial and post-colonial political economy. Their type of education makes them more exposed to cultural values that are supportive of these structures. The clientelism that we have noted in both recruitment and managerial strategy is facilitated. Differences in education create obstacles to effective unionization. It reinforces other cultural divisions, and allows locally rooted employers to exploit the distinction between 'us' and 'them'. Union organizers, with their fine English, can be branded as outside troublemakers who seek to destroy relations of respect and understanding between workers and management, based on the values of Hausa society.

Education affects consciousness. But it also has implications for skills and the differentiation of the labour force as based on skills. Skill affects the bargaining strength of the workers, especially when trained personnel is scarce. The level of skill required in the textile industry is modest for the majority of workers. The highest-skilled category are the technicians for maintenance and repair of machinery.

Those who require no training at all are, however, very few. Most workers operate machinery that has to be kept running if productivity is to be kept up. Workers' training and experience therefore represent an important asset to the company that has to be handled with some care. Our interviews with managers show that preservation of skill is an important factor behind the reluctance to reduce the labour force, despite the absence of raw materials or other inputs necessary for the productive utilization of the labour at hand.

Investments in training on the job are greatest in the large factories, and thus more important in Kaduna than in Kano. The large firms are also the ones who regularly send personnel for external training; for example in polytechnics. They are therefore more sensitive to the loss of skill that goes with large redundancy. They will also be less prone to use large-scale terminations as a weapon in fighting industrial disputes. The numerous unemployed job seekers at the factory gates will be less of a threat to union strategy when confronting the employers. Conversely, the lower level of skills in the small Kano factories makes workers more easy to replace and more vulnerable to intimidation by management.

These are features of workers' bargaining power well known from elsewhere. Higher skills give workers greater technological control in the labour process which can be used in industrial action. When, for instance, skilled machine operators who control several machines decide to go slow or obstruct in other ways, the consequences for production will be felt more acutely. A number of go-slow actions were documented in connection with pressure for revision of wage structures at Arewa, the big Kaduna plant, in 1986.

Coherence in the work process in this industry within the blowing, spinning, and finishing stages, made it vulnerable to stoppages and enhanced workers' bargaining power. The weaving process with its more additive form is less exposed to this form of workers' power. Again it would be the large integrated factories in Kaduna, with their complex combination of independent processes, that would be most vulnerable to such obstruction. The smaller single-process plants that dominate the Kano industry are much less sensitive to such threats. We can thus see how skill structure, size and types of production processes combine to influence workers' power in the two cities.

Industry may seek to counter such forms of increasing bargaining strength on the part of the workers by changing the technology. This has not occurred to any noticeable extent in the Nigerian textile industry over the last decades. The efforts to raise labour productivity, by for instance putting workers in charge of more looms, as discussed above, has rather strengthened workers' control. Similarly, the introduction of more efficient rotors for spinning and shuttleless looms for weaving will have made for greater vulnerability in both cities. It has been reported from other industries (cf. Waterman, 1983, on the Lagos port workers) that differences in skill go with differences in forms of employment and job security. Unskilled workers are more likely to be employed on a daily paid, casual basis, with a minimum of job security and other benefits that go with 'permanent' employment. In the textile industry, casual, daily paid labour has been largely eliminated, much as a result of union efforts. The distinction between skilled and unskilled workers as a source of division within the labour force has therefore been reduced.

Again, however, a difference in this respect can be noted between the two cities. While casual workers are rare in Kaduna, workers in many of the smaller Kano plants are still on temporary contracts, sometimes after as many as ten years of employment or more. While also marginally related to skill structure, this difference reflects the generally weaker position of organized labour in Kano. The crisis, however, seems to have encouraged the resurfacing of casual labour also in Kaduna. Union officials complain that managers avoid taking on fresh permanent workers when production occasionally picks up. They prefer to hire temporary hands that can be sacked as swiftly as they were taken on when, for instance, stocks of cotton are exhausted. Although the union may be tempted to tolerate such practices as long as it does not affect its permanent constituency directly, it still raises a threat as the division between the two categories of workers can also be used by managements to undermine the union.

Alternative employment options

We have argued above that workers' skills, especially in the large Kaduna factories, with their more vulnerable production processes, are an important source of bargaining power. The argument, however, presumes the existence of alternative outlets for those skills outside the factory in order for any threat of withdrawal of labour to be credible. If the skills are exclusive to a particular industry or if such other outlets do not exist the effect may otherwise be the opposite. Workers are 'captured'. They risk losing the return to their industry-specific skills if and when they place their jobs at risk in confronting management.

What are the alternatives open to the textile workers? While the skilled workers face problems of their own, the question relates to the workforce as a whole. What is the evidence of mobility between different jobs and industries? The question includes the scope for non-wage employment in both the urban and rural economy. How desperately will workers hold on to their jobs, succumbing – especially in times of crisis – to material and political degradation? How readily will they stay on and fight? Under what circumstances will they opt out?

The Nigerian working class is in the process of formation. Rural-urban migration has been central to this process, especially in the period of rapid expansion of wage employment in the 1960s and 1970s. By the time the crisis struck in the early 1980s, the process was old enough for a working class core to have consolidated itself. We may think of this in terms of stability on the job and self-identification as workers. Still, it was a matter of a first generation of workers where most had come directly from a peasant family background. In the case of both Kaduna and a good portion of the Kano workers the road to wage labour had been via their primary school training. Already by completing this training they had built up expectation of a life that could not be met inside the village economy.

Yet the consolidation was far from complete. Factory work was seen by many merely as a station on the way to other, preferred jobs in the wage economy. An extremely high mobility on the job, documented for Arewa Textiles in Kaduna for the late 1970s, was explained by personnel officers partly as a question of seeking promotion between factories within the textile industry. But it was also a movement into further training and into office work, after attending evening classes.

Mobility was not limited to the wage economy alone. Savings from industrial work could be profitably used for trading and other business, including mechanical workshops, small mills, transport, and so on. Expansion in the 'formal' economy had created flourishing opportunities in the 'informal sector' which, among other things, offered greater freedom and control over one's own labour but, above all, the prospects of success and advancement unattainable by an ordinary worker. Industry-related activities, such as tailoring and trading in textiles, could serve as a bridge into full-time work outside the factories. Some earnings were also channelled back into farming, commonly in the home village where family land and family labour could be mobilized, but also on vacant plots in the urban surroundings. While this may primarily have been for own consumption, it also provided a scope for commercial production, especially as food prices rocketed.

Before the crisis, opportunities outside the factory gate were many and mobility was high. At one level, this enhanced workers' bargaining power. They could press for radical improvements of pay and working conditions knowing that they would not be stranded if such strategy failed and they were put out of work. This, we think, was reflected in the 1980–1 campaign for a massive wage increase at the national level. On the other hand, high mobility and wide scope for individual solutions outside the factory were not conducive to effective unionization. They detracted from collective solutions and from the consolidation of working class consciousness and identity.

The crisis has dramatically changed this situation. Since opportunities elsewhere have been blocked, the tendency is to hold on to the job one has got. Voluntary mobility has drastically declined with the contraction of the markets for other activities. In this way the crisis conserves the factory workers that are able to stay in their roles as such. This does not necessarily mean an end to 'straddling' or involvement in non-wage work alongside the factory work. On the contrary, workers are more desperate to find such supplementary sources of income as they are unable to sustain themselves on the sharply eroded factory wage. It is no longer primarily a question of exploiting commercial opportunities that may provide a profitable exit from the factory. It is an intensification of self-exploitation, working long extra hours each day on poorly rewarded secondary work in order to survive.

The only side-line that has offered some genuine relief has been farming for home consumption, an activity unaffected by the collapse of commerce. There has been a scramble by workers for vacant plots, more successful in Kaduna than in Kano (not to speak of Lagos). Kaduna as a colonial town was established in a sparsely populated region and there is still uncultivated land within the reach of the city worker. Kano on the other hand is at the centre of a densely populated and intensely cultivated area with few such openings except for those with traditional access to land or with money to buy their way. Many workers from villages not too far from Kano told us that they would go home to farm on weekends.

Some of those who were forced out of work have also been forced back into farming in their home areas, because they have failed to find an alternative income in the town. This is an ultimate escape route and is spoken of as such by the workers we interviewed. Most Kaduna workers had a rural background to which they claimed they could return, even if it was not an option that they would settle for freely. Part of the Kano workers had a Kano urban background and no such rural exit. Kano town, on the other hand, with its unbroken history of crafts and commerce, offered more escape routes into the urban informal sector than Kaduna with its dominant bureaucratic-industrial orientation.

More than ever, then, workers in both Kaduna and Kano see themselves as workers and want to be able to survive as such. It is not by any means certain that they will be allowed to do so. The ultimate escape routes back into the village economy are still there, and most workers believe they will retire to the village and the family farm at old age. But the wider range of alternative opportunities in the informal economy has been eroded by the same crisis that has cut the ground under the textile industry. The informal economy is no longer supportive of workers' bargaining power by competing with industry for labour. Instead, it is relegated to its familiar role as a source of subsidy for labour costs in the formal sector. Workers continue to come to work despite the fact that they cannot live on the wage they are paid. Their bargaining power has been undermined and exploitation intensified.

POLITICAL DIMENSIONS OF UNION POWER

In setting the conditions for union defence of workers' interests, determinants at the level of production interact with those at the level of politics and the state. The Nigerian state has intervened dramatically in the trade union movement and regulated its mode of operation. Has it obstructed or facilitated union work? How has it influenced union response to the crisis? Has the crisis affected the process of unionization? In discussing these questions, we also observe important differences between Kano and Kaduna.

State intervention in the unions

For whom is the union? Burawoy (1985) suggests in the Zambian case that unions wade in and obstruct workers' struggles in the interest of state and capital. Africa is full of cases where the state has either created unions or deprived them of whatever autonomy they may once have had. Are Nigerian unions any different? The National Union of Textile, Garment, and Tailoring Workers of Nigeria (NUTGTWN) was constituted by the state in 1979 as the sole recognized union for this industry. It was one of the industrial unions created as part of the general overhaul of the trade union movement enforced by the state in the late 1970s. It was an amalgamation of one former national union and several independent company unions, previously affiliated to separate national organizations, each in turn with their own international supporters. At the national level, amalgamation meant the establishment of one central labour organization, the Nigerian Labour Congress (NLC), which all the new consolidated unions had to join. The NLC in turn was barred from affiliating to any international labour centre, except the all-African Organization of African Trade Union Unity (OATUU).

As part of this restructuring exercise, the government gave legal backing to the check-off system whereby union fees were deducted from wages by management. It revolutionized the finances of the industrial unions and permitted an increase in the number of paid officials. Management was compelled to recognize the union and effectuate the check-off if half of the workers in the company so demanded.

The union negotiates collective agreements with the textile employers' association, including procedural agreements which are binding on the members. Negotiations are carried out at the company level over the implementation of the optional aspects of the collective agreements and over issues specific to the individual company, including bonus and incentives. Much negotiation at the branch (company) level, as we have seen, concerns terminations, dismissals and disciplinary matters.

The amalgamation and centralization of the textile union have strengthened its bargaining capacity both centrally and in the individual company. It has allowed for the taking of collective decisions based on uniform demands backed by a united national body with a centralized leadership structure. Gains made in the best organized branch unions have been translated into national policies and enforced via collective agreements in companies which previously had refused to deal with unions at all. The improved financial situation has permitted the training of cadres to make them more effective negotiators. The recognized social status and prestige of the National Secretariat and the Secretary General in particular has allowed authoritative interventions in local disputes to force the compliance of recalcitrant managements.

The new union structure with its well-funded zonal offices made a particular impact in companies that had either resisted unionization altogether or where the local union branch was too weak to protect branch officials against company reprisals or to ensure that they were given sufficient time off to attend to union matters. These were rights that unions had achieved in the major Kaduna factories already in the pre-amalgamation period. In the small Kano factories such concessions by management were rare. In most of them, victimization of union leaders and activists was common. Zonal and district officers therefore came to play a vital role in forcing managements to the negotiation table and in offering support for the branches. As experienced unionists and with the backing of the national secretariat, such officers could face the managers with the authority of the national union. As full-time union employees they could not be easily victimized. The crisis of the textile industry gave added weight to this supportive role played by centrally paid union officials. The crisis, as we have seen, weakened the bargaining power of the workers. The threat of closures and massive redundancies allowed managers to activate clientelist practices of labour control and other divide and rule methods in order to obstruct local union work. Support from outside was critical to the survival of the union inside such factories.

The restructuring of the trade union movement was imposed by the state at a time when the oil boom had greatly enhanced workers' numbers and bargaining power. It aimed at creating more 'responsible' unions that would listen more readily to government advice. With the coming of the crisis, however, the unions were able to put the new system to good use for rather different purposes. They used it to prop up union activity in a conjuncture when workers' bargaining power was under severe strain. The new, amalgamated textile union was thus able to offer an organized defence of workers' rights, with the formal backing of state legislation.

The defence of union rights

Centralization under state auspices gave a boost to unionization. It is suggestive of the strength of the new textile union that it has succeeded in advancing the frontiers of unionization, in spite of the crisis. Today only a few textile companies seek to block the formation of union branches altogether. Still, there is a big difference between Kaduna and Kano in this respect, reflecting some of the structural features discussed above, including the size and ownership of the factory, the structure of the labour force, and the mode of labour recruitment.

In Kaduna, unionization was fully achieved in the 1970s and proceeded continuously as new factories were opened, although not entirely without struggle. In Unitex, for instance, there were reports of withdrawal of increments and promotions for elected officials. In Chellco the whole of the first elected leadership was sacked. In the latter case relations continued to be bad. However, by 1987 all factories in Kaduna recognized unions and their officials.

The real frontier was in Kano. In the 1970s only three or four of the companies were organized, and only after tough struggles. In the 1980s, efforts to obtain the support among the workers required for the formation of a union were pursued in company after company. It often took months of agitation by the district organizing secretaries outside the company gates. The job of persuading managers to recognize the union followed, often involving some show of force by the workers. Managers would counter by calling in the police, leading to the dispersal of the workers with teargas, and the arrest of union officials.

Madratex, Nigerian Braiding Co, and Nigerian Spinners and Dyers (NSPD) were such cases. In Madratex a union was formed, but as the collective agreement was to be implemented it was again dissolved after management pressure on the workers to renounce it. Only in 1986 was a union established under more peaceful conditions. In the case of NSPD, all attempts have failed so far. No union branch has yet been maintained beyond the first month. As soon as one has been formed it has again been denounced, as happened again in 1986. Under such conditions it must be considered an impressive feat that by 1987 only three of the 19 factories remained to be unionized, particularly as only four were members of the textile employers' association.

Recognition of union rights according to the procedural agreement was also supposed to ensure the job security of union officials. This has been largely achieved in Kaduna. The largest branch unions have paid officials for chairman, secretary and treasurer and the right for them to enter the premises at any time – rights that were contested at earlier stages, as they are still in Kano in some cases. Here union officials are not given paid leave and much of the organizing work is done from the district office of the union. The acceptance of the right of the district staff to deal with local branch matters continues to be a frontier in the struggle.

How can the differences in unionization be explained? Some of the features have already been indicated above, including differences in the size of companies and the pattern of ownership and labour control. An important aspect not touched before, however, is the difference in the role played by the local agents of the state, including the police and the courts. In Kano these have been frequently mobilized on the side of managements that resist unionization. Union organizers have been chased out of town either by threats of personal violence or by court order. Unionists have been treated as trouble makers, disturbing public peace or inciting to lawlessness. Factory owners in Kano, being part of and closely integrated with the local ruling class, have had easy access to the authorities. The union has rarely bothered to call on state support, even when knowing itself to be in the right according to the official law of the land.

In Kaduna, the industry was dominated by transnational or state ownership in large companies, with integrated production processes, more impersonal forms of labour recruitment, and a more educated labour force. As we have seen, these were factors that combined to facilitate unionization. Workers were less easily intimidated. They were under pressure to accept collective action rather than personal favours from management.

Again, the political dimension was important. The large foreign firms and state companies of Kaduna were under greater pressure to accept the labour laws of the country. Most managers were foreigners and had less personalized relations with local law-enforcing agents. As foreigners they were vulnerable to the mobilization of nationalist sentiments. Most came from societies where unions are an inevitable part of the workplace. They had experience of dealing with unions.

Yet, even in Kano, union persistence seems to have brought some signs of change at the political level. When Gaskiya started production in 1985 with some 900 workers in a modern factory, the management refused to recognize the union that was first formed. The elected officials were sacked. However, on this occasion, the union succeeded in enlisting the support of the representative of the Federal Ministry of Labour for new elections to be held. The manager was made to recognize the union and the collective agreement. Again, Gaskiya – for Kano conditions – was a special case, both in terms of size and the advanced production process. The latter had prompted the company to recruit experienced workers from Kaduna. They carried their commitment to the union along with them.

Despite continued resistance, Kano has seen major advances in unionization in the very period that witnessed a deepening crisis for the industry and a decline in workers' bargaining power. How can this be? We have already suggested that part of the explanation lies in the state imposed union reforms that immediately predated the crisis. They were used by the union to create institutions capable of challenging the clientelist system of labour control in the Kano factories. One may add that the union, while incapable of preventing the decline in employment and barred by the wage-freeze from an all-out wage struggle, sought an outlet for its newly-gained organizational strength in the consolidation of its political position, upholding union rights, and advancing the process of unionization.

THE CASE OF KADUNA TEXTILES LIMITED (KTL)

This chapter has been a discussion of unions and workers in the textile industry in the face of crisis. We wish to conclude with an example of acute confrontation in one factory, the Kaduna Textiles Limited (KTL). It is intended as an illustration of some of the propositions about the union's ability to protect workers' interest that have been discussed above, including its determinants at the levels of production and politics.

In explaining the outcome of the KTL dispute, however, we attribute importance to a factor that has not been raised previously: the autonomous militancy of the workers, that is, militancy outside the union framework, and its place in union strategy. The militancy can be explained in terms of the structural characteristics of the labour force and the wider political economy.

The January 1984 events

In January 1984, the KTL workers took the General Manager hostage and marched on Government House in Kaduna to protest the attempted imposition of half-pay 'to save the factory from closing down' (Ahmed, 1986; Bangura, 1987). KTL was the second textile mill in Nigeria to start production, in 1957. By the late 1970s it was facing major difficulties due to aging machinery, changing demand, competition from newer plants and smuggling. It ran heavy losses in the early 1980s and was hit severely by the increase in the official minimum wage (AWC, 1983). Employment which peaked at almost 5000 in 1979 was down to 3600 by 1984. In 1982 workers were forced to accept advanced annual leave because of shortage of cotton. Periods of compulsory leave were again imposed in 1983.

By mid-1983, the financial crisis of the company was acute. Management threatened a complete close down. The union therefore agreed to forgo 50 per cent of pay on the understanding that full pay would be restored from January and that part of the pay forgone would be treated as savings and paid back in 1984 (NUTGTWN, 1984).

The company, however, did not meet its obligations. In December 1983 it threatened again to close down unless the half-pay arrangement was continued. Management simultaneously sought to pressurize the owners, the NNDC, a major state finance conglomerate, to release funds to prevent violence: 'The only way to avert any serious violent reaction of workers and possible damage to the company's assets and perhaps even assaults on Management staff is to assure employees of full settlement of all their entitlements on closure' (KTL, 1983).

The union rejected the extension of half-pay, 'a nonsensical piece of nonsense', insisting that the company was free to close down 'provided they pay workers all entitlements before the gates are closed' (NUTGTWN, 1984). The union knew of course, that there was no such money and that it therefore might be a lesser evil for the company to keep paying wages until the problem of long-term financing and raw materials had been solved.

The union applied to the police for permission to stage a demonstration to the New Nigerian Development Company's (NNDC) headquarters and to the State Governor's Office. There had been a military coup at New Year and the new leaders had made bold promises to attend to workers' grievances. The new Military Governor in Kaduna in particular had sought to convey a radical, pro-workers image. But the police permit was refused (Ahmed, 1986). The Managing Director made an attempt to side-step the union by appealing to the workers directly at a mass meeting to accept half-pay to avoid close down. He was booed and jeered at. The workers took to the streets, carrying the MD along as hostage to present their case to the Governor.

The workers were confronted by heavily armed riot police who were allowed to 'liberate' the captive MD on condition that there would be no further police interference. Once the MD was set free, however, the police attacked again. After hours of street battle workers regrouped and marched on the Police Headquarters to 'smash it' and to recapture the MD. Adams Oshiomhole, the General Secretary of the national textile union, tried to stop another bloody confrontation but was beaten up by some workers who thought he was a government agent before he was recognized and rescued by others. In the end, the workers were beaten and dispersed. Some were arrested and given short prison sentences (Ahmed, 1986).

The Management of KTL had been given a golden opportunity to 'solve' the workers' problem, now with massive backing by the police. The company dismissed all workers, offering to re-employ only those who had been 'screened' and who signed an undertaking to accept an indefinite 25 per cent reduction in pay. The company invited new workers to apply. Some 4000 turned up at the gates. The union, however, appealed successfully to the workers not to submit themselves to screening or to sign any undertaking. Picket lines were at least partially effective.

In the end, management was forced back to negotiate with the union. An agreement was signed where screening was dropped and no workers would be dismissed or victimized. Workers accepted the 25 per cent cut for nine months on condition that it was treated as a compulsory saving and paid back in 1985. The union demanded and obtained an assurance on finance from the owners (NNDC, 1984).

Union power: interpreting the KTL case

Was it victory or defeat for the workers? There were elements of both. But there was more of victory. It is true, workers had to accept a continued temporary pay cut for a long period. But it had been reduced from the original 50 per cent to 25, no longer for an indefinite period and with an agreement on repayment. It was actually paid as agreed.

There were other elements of victory: workers had resisted company blackmail; they had defied the state (the police) and got away with it. No disciplinary measures could be imposed by the company despite the unlawful actions of the workers and the manhandling of the manager. The company was forced to take back even those who had been sentenced by the court. The attempt by management to bypass the union was successfully resisted.

A basic source of strength was the collective agreement between the textile unions and the employers at the national level which made it expensive to sack workers. The fight to raise and uphold redundancy benefits and gratuity payments had circumscribed management's room for manoeuvring. However, the significance of such 'constitutional' achievements was reinforced by the willingness of workers to take to the streets and engage in 'unconstitutional' struggles in their defence.

Of critical importance was the ability to organize the picket, in defiance of the police, that prevented the company from placing conditions on re-employment as well as from hiring new hands to replace those who had been sacked. Had the picket failed, the credibility of the union would have been destroyed and workers might have scrambled for re-employment on any terms (cf. Bangura's study of the Bauchi automobile workers in this volume). The ability to enforce the picket rested on a combination of union leadership and rank and file militancy, including the willingness to physically prevent workers from entering the factory gates, in the intimidating presence of armed police forces.

Let us look at some of the structural determinants that may have influenced the outcome. KTL was an old company. It had an experienced workforce with a high level of literacy and skill. The latter is likely to have affected the outcome of the confidence trick when management decided to sack all workers. The purpose was not to hire entirely new ones. It was intended to intimidate the old, experienced workers to re-submit themselves for employment on conditions decided by the company.

But literacy, skill, and a high level of unionization does not explain the militancy with which workers were prepared to confront management and police without consideration of the legal consequences. Such defiance also reflects the structural conditions of a working class that has only been partially made to succumb to regimentation. In Nigeria, as in much of the third world, wage labour constitutes islands in seas of petty commodity production. This places constraints on the subordination of labour under capital. The diffusion of independent ownership of means of production sustains a culture of autonomy and resistance.

The union was unable to fully control the autonomous militancy of the workers. The thrashing meted out to the Secretary General was in that sense symbolic, even if it was unintended. However, the union could also make good use of this militancy when confronting management and the state. The union claimed that it was against lawlessness but that major concessions were necessary to placate the workers if violence were to be avoided. In this sense, the union offered to mediate between the irate workers and the authorities.

The KTL union was experienced and had played an important role in national union politics in the pre-amalgamation period. It had been forced to join the new national union in the centralization exercise. The 1984 events suggest that it benefited from membership of the NUTGTWN. The company was run down and therefore particularly badly hit by the crisis. Workers' bargaining power was at a low point. If left to fend for itself, the local union might have easily succumbed to management pressures. Now, the National Secretariat played a critical role in boosting branch resistance, also threatening to bring out other Kaduna workers in solidarity with the KTL workers. Such threat carried some credibility as the textile union played a key role in the State Council; that is, the regional coordinating body of the Nigerian Labour Congress. State imposed amalgamation had thus put new weapons of self-defence in the hands of the workers.

The size and importance of the company made the dispute politically visible. The principal owners, the NNDC, were the most prestigious northern ruling class institution. It was equally closely watched by the public. The political dimension is also significant when explaining why the police was restrained from breaking up the picket lines. While this may partly be attributed to the indecisiveness of the state in a period of transition, following on the recent *coup d'état*, it also suggests a realistic assessment of the balance of forces. Here not only the militant mood of the workers had to be taken into account. The state would also have to consider the consequences of violent confrontation in a city where the union was well entrenched and could muster the support of tens of thousands of workers.

In the period of our study, Kano did not experience any industrial action on the scale of the Kaduna events of 1984. The very absence of a major confrontation, however, reflects the difference between the two cities. In Kano, a fragmented industrial structure, a labour force penetrated and divided by clientelistic patterns of recruitment and labour control, the dominance of indigenous factory owners with their close ties to the local state and law enforcement agencies and with a strong record of anti-union policies, were all factors that combined to reduce the scope for successful workers' struggles of the KTL type. Not only did it produce a weaker union. The scope for autonomous militancy by the workers was also undercut by clientelism, reflecting both the structure of ownership and management and the social background of many of the Kano workers. It did not preclude outburst of militant protests. But it made organized industrial action more difficult to sustain.

Conditions in Kano, however, were not immutable. Unionization, as we noted, made important advances, despite the crisis. With the opening of the large, integrated Gaskiya factory a new element was introduced with repercussions for industrial relations. It may well provide Kano with the core of skilled, conscious, and well-organized workers that the large integrated mills once did for Kaduna, and a basis for further penetration of this hostile environment by the union.

REFERENCES

A. Y. Ahmed, 'The Development of the Working Class and Trade Union Movement in Nigeria and the Demonstration by Kaduna Textile Ltd Workers', BSc diss. Dept of Political Science, ABU, Zaria (1986).

G. Andræ and B. Beckman, 'Labour and Industrial Crisis in the Third World: The Case of Nigerian Textiles and Cotton. Project Proposal and Outline', *AKUT* 30, Uppsala (1984).

—— *The Wheat Trap. Bread and Underdevelopment in Nigeria* (London: Zed Books, 1985).

—— *Industry Goes Farming. The Nigerian Raw Material Crisis and the Case of Textiles and Cotton* (Uppsala: SIAS, 1987).

AWC, 'AW Consultants Ltd, Kaduna Textiles Ltd, Financial analysis and appraisal of operations' (Kaduna, 1983).

Y. Bangura, 'Industrial Crisis and the Lessons from Kaduna Textile Limited and the Workers' Demonstraton of January 1984', Paper at the Conference on Planning Transitions, Nigerian Political Science Associaton, Ahmadu Bello University, Zaria, 17–22 May (1987).

M. Burawoy, *The Politics of Production. Factory Regimes under Capitalism and Socialism* (London: Verso, 1985).

K. Hinchliffe, 'Kaduna Textile Workers: Characteristics of an African Industrial Labour Force', *Savanna*, June (1973).

KTL, Managing Director of Kaduna Textiles Ltd to Chairman of New Nigerian Development Corporation, 15 Dec. (1983).

P. Lubeck, 'Industrial Labour in Kano: Historical Origins, Social Characteristics and Sources of Differentiation' in M. B. Barkindo (ed.), *Studies in the History of Kano* (Ibadan: Heinemann, 1983).

—— *Islam and Urban Labour in Northern Nigeria* (Cambridge: Cambridge University Press, 1986).

H. A. C. Main, 'Responses to Inequalities: Workers, Retrenchment and Urban–rural Linkages in Kano', Commonwealth Geographical Bureau

Workshop on Spatial Inequalities in Development; Bayero University, Kano (1985).

NNDC, Managing Director of New Nigerian Development Company to General Secretary of NUTGTWN, 24 Feb. (1984).

NTGTEA and NUTGTWN, Nigerian Textile, Garment and Tailoring Employers' Association and National Union of Textile, Garment and Tailoring Workers of Nigeria, Procedural and collective agreement (Kaduna, 1979).

—— 1983, 1984 and 1987, Amendments.

NUTGTWN, National Union of Textile, Garment and Tailoring Workers of Nigeria, General Secretary to Military Governor, Kaduna State, 18 Jan. (1984).

—— National Executive Council, Report on activities by General Secretary to 3rd Tri-ennial National Delegates Conference (Kaduna, 1986).

P. Waterman, *Aristocrats and Plebeians in African Trade Unions? Lagos Port and Dock Worker Organization and Struggle* (The Hague: The Author, 1983).

INTERVIEWS

V. Eburajolo, Executive Secretary, Nigerian Textile Garment and Tailoring Employers' Association, Kaduna, August and November (1985).

A. Oshiomhole, General Secretary, National Union of Textile, Garment and Tailoring Workers of Nigeria, Kaduna, January (1987).

7 Steyr-Nigeria: The Recession and Workers' Struggles in the Vehicle Assembly Plant

Yusuf Bangura

On 10 October 1985, the workers of Steyr-Nigeria in Bauchi force-marched the managing director of the company out of the factory premises and told him not to return to the factory until he was ready to negotiate with their union officials. Other management staff, local and foreign, either took to their heels or went into hiding to avoid coming into contact with the highly provoked and agitated workers. The workers were protesting against the deteriorating conditions of work and management's anti-labour rationalization policies, following the decline of the Nigerian economy and the massive reduction in import licences, necessary for the importation of parts. Similar demonstrations took place a week before, on 4 October, at Peugeot Automobile of Nigeria (PAN) in Kaduna and a few weeks later at Volkswagen of Nigeria (VON) in Lagos in December 1985.

These demonstrations brought to the fore a hitherto hidden, but important, dimension of the operations of vehicle assembly plants in Nigeria. Public debate had primarily focused on the failure of such plants to transfer technology to Nigerians, improve upon their local content supply, and maintain a stable and reasonable price for their products. Indeed, the astronomical price increases of the vehicles generated a barrage of criticisms against them, with many middle-class Nigerians calling for their closure and the re-introduction of the policy of direct importation of fully built-up cars. The demonstrations established a connection between technology transfer, local content supply, stable prices and workers' rights. The workers' stand was quite clear and emphatic: strategies of adjustment and rationalization would have to take into account the interests and rights of the workforce, which stood at well over 15 000 in 1986, excluding those in the support and allied industries.

RATIONALIZATION AND ADJUSTMENT

The assembly plants must rank among the hardest hit of the industries in the recession. The life-line of the industry – import licences – has been shortened with the collapse of oil revenues. Companies continue to record losses. In fact, most of the plants operate below 25 per cent capacity. Steyr, for instance, operated at 15 per cent installed capacity between 1986 and 1988.

Nigerian industries have introduced various rationalization and adjustment measures to sustain their pre-crisis profit levels. When austerity measures were announced by the government in April 1982, the Nigerian Employers' Consultative Association distributed a circular to its members suggesting ways of responding to the crisis without resorting to mass retrenchment. The measures included an embargo on new appointments, reduction of overtime and work days, elimination of shifts, retrenchment of temporary staff and suspension of expenditure on employee welfare services. Whilst most of these measures have been introduced by the auto plants, the deepening crisis has called for an even more stringent and comprehensive package.

Management strategies have varied but, at bottom, they are primarily aimed at resolving the crisis on the backs of the workers. The labour force is to be drastically reduced to an 'optimum' level to correspond to the availability of parts. Compulsory leaves can then be introduced when there are no parts to hand. Part of the retrenched staff can be held in reserve, to be recalled for higher productivity work when the parts arrive. This way, annual production targets can be reached very quickly at reduced cost since the reserved workers enjoy no benefits and the permanent workers can be sent home without pay after the parts have been exhausted. The Procedural and Collective Agreements provide that workers may not be paid if there is no work.

Peugeot and Volkswagen, with big labour forces, have combined compulsory leaves with progressive retrenchment because of the high cost of paying benefits in one fell swoop. Steyr has adopted the more standard approach of an initial massive retrenchment since such an exercise did not entail a high retrenchment bill. Its staff strength was reduced by about 44 per cent from 744 in 1981 to 418 in 1982. The retrenched junior staff were given four months' salary benefits whilst the senior staff received six months' pay. There was a gradual reabsorption of some of the workers, with the entire staff gravitating between 539 in 1984 and 518 in 1985. It appears that the management has decided to peg its staff numbers at around 500 barring any major upset in future allocations of import licences which stood at an annual average of ₦10m between 1985 and 1987. More adjustment measures, such as temporary lay-offs, had to be adopted by Steyr in 1983 as the supply of parts dried up. Compulsory leaves or drastically reduced work days have become notorious in most of the auto plants. Temporary lay-offs started in PAN in 1982, intensified in 1983–4 and deteriorated further in May/September 1985. Volkswagen of Nigeria has shut down at least eight times between 1981 and 1986.

Steyr introduced a package of austerity measures to cover the period 1983/84. Junior staff were placed under austerity measures from 1 October to 30 November 1983, which entailed their receiving only 50 per cent of their basic salary. Virtually the entire factory was closed from 2 December 1983 to 9 January 1984. The apprentice training programme was suspended for four months and even though the management tried to reach a compromise with the workers by paying all staff their full December salaries during the closure, the annual bonus for 1983 was cancelled. Moreover, management insisted that the four working days during the closure of 2–5 January would be deducted from the January salaries of all staff. Staff numbers for the period 1981–85 are shown in Table 7.1.

As part of the rationalization programme, automobile plants have tampered with the range of parts that are to be assembled locally, so that they come in partially assembled instead of in the completely knocked-down condition stipulated in the technical agreement.

Table 7.1   Size of staff force at Steyr-Nigeria, 1981–85

	1981	1982	1983	1984	1985
Junior staff	630*	324	356	417	394
Senior staff	n a	71	75	84	84
Management	n a	6	6	6	5
Expatriates	n a	17	22	32	35
Total	744	418	459	539	518

* Estimate

Source: Steyr-Nigeria Personnel Department

Allegations that this has been done at Steyr are rife among the union officials and workers. According to the Secretary of the defunct in-plant union, John Pam, who went through the three-year training programme of the company, 'there are times when the engine is already assembled. Then all you do is to put the tyres, do repairs and test the engine'. In fact, workers refer to the 'CKDs', completely knocked-down parts, as 'PKDs' (partially knocked down). Union officials maintain that this practice became acute after 1983. No doubt such a policy must have contributed to the adjustment process and the streamlining of the labour force.

WORKERS' RESISTANCE

Workers' response to the national industrial crisis has varied between industries. But overall relations of domination which generally characterize workers' management relations are being reinforced by the patronizing ideology of the ruling class, the limited extent of the capitalist sector and the low level of political and organizational work within the unions themselves. Workers are consistently told by their employers and state officials to be thankful for being on the payroll when millions of Nigerians are jobless.

The economic crisis has deepened those prejudices. Nigerian workers have been quite dynamic, however, since colonial times in fighting for their historic rights and defending threatened gains. In fact, it was as a result of this tradition of spontaneity and resilience that the Nigerian state has devised various strategies of labour control and subordination culminating in the restructuring of the trade union movement during the period 1975 to 1978. This restructuring altered the affiliations of the previous labour centres and their respective trade union units by regrouping the latter into 42 industrial unions, in the process strengthening some of the old unions and weakening the others. Most of the unions that made up the Automobile, Boatyard, Transport Equipment and Allied Workers Union of Nigeria (ABTEAWUN) were relatively new when the Nigerian Labour Congress (NLC) was established in 1978. The national union has been forced, therefore, by the constraints of finance and lack of seasoned unionists to give considerable initiative to in-plant branches.

Workers in the textile, automobile and construction industries have been adversely exposed to the crippling effects of the depression. This should not be surprising given that the construction boom depended on high government patronage whilst the textile and automobile industries have relied upon a guaranteed supply of foreign exchange to import raw materials and parts. Workers in these industries have, therefore, experienced more stoppages, compulsory leaves, deferment of salary payments and retrenchment than most other Nigerian workers. But no major industrial dispute has been recorded in the construction industry because of the low level of unionization there. Strikes, go-slows and demonstrations are, however, rampant in the textile (see chapter 6) and automobile industries. Workers demonstrated, for instance, in Kaduna Textile Limited in January 1984 against the deferment of salaries and other benefits and at PAN and Steyr in October 1984.

THE PROBLEMS AS PERCEIVED BY STEYR WORKERS

The events that gave rise to the October 1985 crisis started to unfold in February of that year. The immediate problems were housing, transport allowances, the annual increment and bonuses which were progressively being undermined in the company's adjustment measures. Workers' resistance to the 1982 retrenchment exercise was low-key since the union was still in its infancy and no strategy had been worked out to cope with the crisis; such was also the case with the 1983/84 austerity measures which the workers and their union representatives grudgingly accepted. That particular experience, however, exposed the workers to the realities of having to contend with periodic closures and attendant assaults on bonuses, facilities and hard-earned wages.

The union reviewed the industrial scene in late 1984 and decided as a priority to fight for the revision of the workers' handbook by including it along with the other outstanding demands in their negotiations with management. They reckoned that negotiations on the other outstanding areas would be fruitless without a serious revision of the workers' handbook – the contract of employment – which was drawn up solely by the company in 1979 before the branch union was formed. The areas in the handbook which dealt with terminations of employment and dismissals were considered to be obnoxious since they had been used by the management to get rid of labour without having to pay any benefits. Terminations had become rampant in many factories as management tried to avoid the payment of heavy retrenchment benefits. The union insisted, therefore, on strengthening its contractual position by instituting a collective and procedural agreement that would spell out the rights and duties of management, and guarantee workers jobs during the recession or at least ensure that workers got their salaries even if the factory were to be closed periodically because of lack of parts. The revision of the handbook, restoration of bonuses and annual increments, and the provision of housing and transportation were to form the backbone of workers' demands in 1985. The union had resolved that the restructuring programme of the industry should not be carried out at the expense of labour alone.

CRISIS IN LABOUR–MANAGEMENT RELATIONS

Pending the revision of the handbook, the union signed a temporary agreement with management to restore the yearly increment which had been suspended during the 1983/84 austerity measures. The increment was to be added to the January 1985 salaries. Management's failure to honour this agreement prompted the union to schedule a labour–management meeting in February to discuss the increment and the other outstanding issues such as the handbook, housing and transportation. Management maintained that there was a serious financial problem facing the company which called for a major cut back on facilities and benefits. It alleged that the company incurred a loss of N7 million in 1984 and a debt of N30m in November 1984 and that although the debt was reduced to N16m in 1985, the company still operated an overdraft of N35m. In the circumstances, it maintained that the payment of annual increments and bonuses and the provision of staff cars were unreasonable. The union asserted that they were not consistently informed about the actual liquidity of the company, and that the annual increment was a right which their earlier agreement had guaranteed.

Management's intransigence led to a work-to-rule for three days. A plea was made to call off the industrial action and an agreement was temporarily reached. Management was to give the yearly increment by July 1985 when 'the financial position would have improved' and would look into the other outstanding problems. An agreement was signed after the company secretary publicly addressed the workers stating the terms of the agreement. The workers went back to work.

Union elections were held on 6 June which resulted in a new executive taking office with the exception of the vice-chairman and treasurer, who were re-elected. The need for an effective union response to the problems of workers was emphasized during the election campaign. The new executive had pledged not to let the workforce down in the outstanding negotiations. Management was, however, getting worried about the increasing radicalism of the union. Previous acts of militancy over confirmation of appointments had been firmly dealt with in 1980, leading to the termination of employment of 11 workers. Relations between the union and the management were strained by that incident, prompting the local NLC to set up a commission of enquiry on the dispute. Such bitter memories resurfaced in June 1985 as union officials accused the personnel manager of putting obstacles in their way to getting introduced to the managing director as the new union officials. They had to book a direct appointment with the managing director to discuss the outstanding problems of the workers.

The company's decision to buy three new 505 and four 504 Peugeot cars convinced the union and the workforce that the company's financial position had improved. They were made to believe that the old cars were sold to management staff at drastically reduced prices instead of returning them to the car pool. Workers were outraged by these discoveries. They added weight to the union's agitation as to why workers should not continue to bear the brunt of the austerity measures.

After several meetings with the managing director, a temporary agreement was reached which allowed the management to look into all factors affecting labour–management relations with a view to solving them 'in the near future'. However a publication appeared in *Sunday Triumph* in September 1985, in which the managing director was alleged to have given an interview threatening the imminent closure of the company. Tension was high the following day at the factory as workers besieged the union officials and insisted that they should demand from management the true situation in the company. The union gave the management a week's grace since, as it reasoned, such a major decision as closure would not be announced on the pages of newspapers without discussions with the union.

The union wrote the managing director in early October 1985 demanding an immediate meeting to discuss the alleged closure and other outstanding issues. Union officials reckoned that the story was deliberately planted in the newspaper to get the workers and the union to scale down their demands. The managing director replied that he would not be able to see the union officials until mid-October.

He maintained that he had just returned from Austria and had other pressing issues deserving his attention for the rest of the week, that his deputy was already in Lagos trying to obtain the approval of credit lines to secure the importation of parts, and that he had to prepare for a Finance Committee meeting of the Board of Directors scheduled for the following week.

The union officials felt slighted by this decision. They were under tremendous pressure from the workforce to clarify the newspaper report and reach an early settlement on other important issues. The workers had become restless about their deteriorating conditions of work. The bus service had been withdrawn for two weeks, and workers had to trek long distances to work or pay high transport fares. All attempts to get the personnel manager to prevail upon the managing director for an early meeting failed.

A meeting of the sectional representatives was therefore called by the union to discuss some limited pressure that could get the managing director to change his stand. The meeting decided on a work-to-rule on 10 October. The union officials went back to the personnel manager on that day to get him to prevail upon the managing director to schedule an early meeting to prevent an escalation of the dispute. But the managing director stuck to his guns. The union executive, undeterred by such intransigence, went back at around 1 p.m. to see if negotiations could be held as situation reports showed that the workers were getting restive about the management's arrogance and insensitivity. But all of the principal officers were away and did not return until around 2.30 p.m.

By this time, however, the workers had decided to go beyond the work-to-rule. Apparently without the knowledge of the union officials, who were in the offices trying to revive the negotiations, the workers had determined to demonstrate their disgust at the managing director's behaviour. They walked directly to his office, marched him off the premises of the factory and told him not to return until he had learned to behave himself and negotiate with the union officials. Acting on the advice of the union, the workers returned after the incident and stayed on the job until closing time at 5 p.m. Some senior members of staff had, however, phoned the police and asked for protection. The police commissioner of the state arrived at the factory but found the workers already on the job and advised that the peaceful atmosphere be maintained. Management had been completely humiliated. Workers' power had been demonstrated and the mask of authority removed.

CONSTRAINTS ON WORKERS' STRUGGLES

Even though management's authority was deflated and useful lessons drawn about the centrality of the workforce in production the workers did not take over the company. Steyr's operations involve a heavy capital outlay tied to the operations of the parent company and the availability of foreign exchange to import the necessary parts. Steyr workers could not have taken over the factory and run it successfully without a national revolution and solidarity with the workers at Steyr–Daimler Puch AG in Austria. The workers' action was limited, geared mainly towards the achievement of two objectives: to protest against the arrogant posture of the managing director whom many believed was a racist and to strengthen the hands of the union officials by demonstrating to management the extent to which the workers could go in defending their interests.

Management was determined to forestall the workers' show of strength and impose its authority. Given the ease with which such authority had been dislodged there was a strong temptation to use extreme measures to restore the *status quo ante*. The following day, 11 October, workers reported for duty hoping that management would have drawn the appropriate lessons and would be ready to discuss with the union. To their dismay they found the factory gates locked, with a big signboard saying that the company was closed until further notice. There were also two units of armed policemen guarding the company premises. Management had decided to close the company in order to resolve the crisis on its own terms.

The battle lines were thus drawn, but it was a battle which had now put the workers on the defensive since they were not allowed to regain possession of the factory. Management was in full control of the premises and could dictate the new terms of re-entry. Union officials recognized this weakness. They instructed the workers to report for work every day at 7.30 a.m. as a way of putting pressure on the authorities to reopen the company. Workers' power at this stage of the crisis could only be effective if the workers were allowed to be at the workplace.

The Bauchi state branch of the NLC, under the leadership of Shehu Abdullahi, waded into the crisis and rendered support to the branch union since the national secretariat of the ABTEAWUN was unable to send officials to Steyr sufficiently quickly. The NLC wrote to the chairman of the board of directors of Steyr-Nigeria and the military governor of Bauchi state expressing great concern about the punitive measures of the company which amounted to a lock-out, outlawed by decree 68 of 1968, and appealed to both bodies to prevail upon the management of the company to reopen the factory and settle outstanding issues with the union. A series of negotiations was also held with Steyr management, all aimed at bringing pressure to bear on the policy makers to reopen the factory gates which had by this time been besieged by workers for about a week. A heated public debate also developed about the relevance of the assembly plants in the country, given the high prices of the vehicles. The plants were clearly receiving a bad press.

The union had hoped to cash in on this bad publicity by drawing attention to the industrial relations aspect of the plants. For his part the minister of industries was worried about the possibility of a generalized crisis at the assembly plants which could trigger off a general strike. He visited the various plants to study the situation and settle the crisis. He disapproved of the workers' actions and accused the union officials of sabotaging foreign investment in the country. But he also called on management to open the factory immediately and set up a committee that would include the union officials to help in pointing out the culprits. The union's participation in the work of the committee, however, was blocked since on this same day, 18 October, the company served the union officials and other active members of the workforce with letters of dismissal, backdated to 10 October.

A total of 17 workers were dismissed, including six members of the new executive: Musa Abubakar (Chairman), John Pam (Secretary), Sunday Adeyemi (Vice Chairman), Patrick Mobutu (Public Relations Officer), Goddefry Dackas (Treasurer) and Jibrin Atokolo (Assistant Auditor). The Auditor and the Assistant Secretary were absent from work and the Financial Secretary, Ladele Umaru Gurkuma, was not mentioned. No reason was given for his exemption. In addition, several ex-union officers were also dismissed: Samuel Ishiaku (Auditor), Bako Doga (Assistant Secretary), Evans Jones (Chairman), Garba Inuwa (Financial Secretary), Auto Yekhen (ex-Financial Secretary), Gambo Ali (ex-Assistant Auditor), Usman Agude, Moses Nyipwo, Samuel Kajange and Adamu Mato (all floor members). The seventeenth worker was a former chairman of the union who had in fact graduated to the senior staff scale. His contract was terminated. It would seem the authorities were determined not only to crush the executive but to wipe out all vestiges of unionism in the factory.

The board of directors of the company held a meeting on 17 October and resolved that the factory would open on Monday, 21 October. All employees were instructed to reapply to the office of the managing director for re-employment. The company maintained that 'any employee who had not applied by the following Friday for re-employment should consider himself/herself automatically terminated from the company'. The application form for re-employment sought to reverse whatever gains the workers had made since the factory was established. Management would decide on the position where the re-employed worker would now be placed and the worker would agree unconditionally to terms of employment as specified by the company and comply with all rules and regulations imposed. Management could now change the contract of employment without even referring to the contentious workers' handbook.

The workers were enraged. The situation was tense. The union, fully supported by the workforce, resolved to resist the re-employment conditions. Security forces moved in and arrested seven top union officials and activists. The arrested officials were dispersed into various cells and detained for three days. They were later prosecuted with six others after a bail of ₦400 had been granted to them. The arrests were aimed at breaking the link between the union and the workers to get the latter to obey the injunctions of the company and return to work on Monday, 21 October.

It was difficult to break the solidarity of the workers. The NLC officials filled the vacuum created by the arrests and instructed the workers not to accept the anti-democratic conditions laid down for re-employment. Other activists emerged from among the ranks of the workers to coordinate the resistance with the NLC. The NLC chairman wrote the managing director a strongly worded letter protesting the arrests and the anti-worker conditions of re-employment and urged that the proposed enquiry be allowed to take place without prejudice. Since it was management that was now keen on resumption, workers' power lay in resisting it. All workers were urged not to return to work until their union officials had been released and reinstated. They were also instructed not to sign the re-employment forms. Not a single worker turned up for work on 21 October, the day the factory gates were re-opened. A few who wanted to report for duty were dissuaded by well-organized groups of activists, positioned strategically on the main road leading to the factory. A stalemate ensued for about three days.

The board of directors was astute in giving a whole week for the re-engagement of the workers since it reckoned it would be difficult to break workers' solidarity in a day or two. Workers had completely lost faith in the integrity of management. They looked solidly up to their union officials and the local NLC for leadership and direction. But the security forces had tried to penetrate the ranks of the workers by identifying the militants and separating them from the general workforce. The arrest of the unionists was part of that strategy. Management's injunctions were given the widest publicity in the media. The failure of national union officials to arrive on time afforded management the opportunity to suspend its negotiations with the local NLC by insisting that the latter had no *locus standi* in the crisis. The forces ranged against the union were now formidable with the state and federal governments, security forces, the local media and notable personalities in the town putting up a well articulated campaign to intimidate the workers into submission. Apart from the NLC and a few other local workers' unions only the BACAS (Bauchi College of Arts and Science) branch of the Academic Staff Association (among the non-workers' associations) openly supported the Steyr workers.

The members of the senior staff association in Steyr were initially included in the re-engagement exercise. However, the policy makers realized that some members of the association could be used to bring pressure to bear on the resistant workers. An agreement was reached with the senior staff association exempting them from the conditions of re-employment, thus securing their loyalty to the company.

There is a strong patronage element in the mode of recruitment in Steyr and many other Nigerian companies. Very rarely do companies employ labour purely on the basis of advertisements and interviews. In any case, there are no employment bureaus to act as a link between companies and prospective labour. The slow pace of capitalist development, the over-supply of labour and competition for jobs are responsible for such a situation. Workers invariably end up being employed through patronage structures, with senior relations on the job, well placed bureaucrats, politicians and business persons playing the role of godfathers. The situation is compounded in small cities like Bauchi where inter-personal relations are very strong. This is reinforced by Steyr's quota system of employment with the catch-ment area, Bauchi, having a 43 per cent share of the labour force. Those of Borno, Gongola and Plateau are 2.3 per cent, 4.2 per cent and 6.7 per cent respectively. The remaining 43 per cent is open to national competition. A good number of the workers in Steyr owe their employment to senior relations in the company.

There was a two-pronged strategy of breaking the workers' resistance after the senior staff had been exempted from the re-engagement exercise. First, senior members of the company, at times acting in concert with other local personalities, held private meetings with identified individual workers and persuaded them to return to work and ignore the 'empty union posturing'. They claimed that the union had been disbanded and that management was actually determined to strike off all erring workers from the payroll after 25 October. They also pointed out the difficulties of getting new jobs in a recessed economy and played on the psyche of the workers by claiming that three-quarters of the workforce had already filled the forms. To prevent a possible confrontation with the hard core of the militant workers, senior members would volunteer to submit the forms to the managing director.

Why would the company devise such divide and rule tactics if, as the chairman of the board of directors boasted, 'there are millions of Nigerians more qualified than some of them, roaming the streets and corridors of offices in search of whatever jobs are available to them'? The point, of course, is that there is a limit to the policy of mass dismissals. Some of the more technical positions could not be filled at short notice since they required years of training. The company had, in any case, cut down its training programme because of the recession. Furthermore, the survival of patron–client relations demand, at times, cautious and moderate approaches to crisis-management. The safest policy, therefore, was to persuade the workers to return to work.

The second part of the strategy was the use of regionalism. Since the union officials were predominantly northerners it was impossible to use the standard divisive argument that southern unionists wanted to hold down the development of the north. This time the argument was reversed and personalized: 'Northern unionists want to frustrate the ambitions of individual southern workers in the company since northerners could always get jobs in their areas. Southerners have struggled hard to be employed under the company's stringent quota system; the recession works against southern immigrant labour in the north; and, in any case, most of the northern workers have already filled the forms and handed them over to their senior relations in the company'.

The union was unable to counter these retrogressive initiatives. It was difficult to know which workers had succumbed to such pressures since most of the activities were done in private. Some of the affected workers reported to the union and the NLC some of these activities but there was little they could do to those who complied. The union leadership had been intimidated by the security agents. Propaganda work became difficult to sustain. Pay day was also just around the corner. Management issued a statement on 24 October, just a day before the deadline expired, stating that 'all employees of Steyr who by Friday 25 October 1985 have submitted their applications for re-engagement will be paid their full salary for the month of October 1985', even though there had been no work for about two weeks. Furthermore, those who had submitted their application '*in accordance with Board directives*' and who were subsequently notified in writing about their re-engagement by Friday 25 October would be regarded as having been continuously employed by Steyr-Nigeria Limited with '*no break in their service to the company*' (italics in original).

Most workers were worried about their October salaries. Since these were now guaranteed by the management, many felt that they should secure them and continue the struggle from within, especially as the latter part of the company's statement created the impression that many workers had already signed the forms. There was no strike fund to sustain the resistance.

Many other workers who genuinely wanted the industrial action to continue requested from the NLC an alternative to the management's bait. The NLC branch, of course, lacked the financial resources to support a prolonged resistance. Since the national union was not around and the local branch had been incapacitated, it was difficult for the NLC to urge the workers to hold on. A good number had actually returned to work by Thursday, 24 October. Those holding back could not be assured of an alternative. By Friday, most of the workers were back at work. The resistance had collapsed.

POST-RE-EMPLOYMENT DEVELOPMENTS

There were very serious constraints on the workers' struggles in this case. Localized union struggles had been difficult to sustain nation-wide since the recession set in, in 1981. The problems of rationalization which triggered off the October demonstrations had affected all the auto plants and many other manufacturing industries in the country. Pockets of industrial dispute accompanied these rationalization programmes. The demonstration at PAN on 4 October 1985, for instance, influenced that of Steyr a week later. Auto workers had hoped to attract easy public sympathy since the public debate on car prices and technology transfer was weighted against the assembly plants. The workers had hoped to get the public to accommodate the workers' plight in the debate and persuade the companies and government to take into account workers' rights in the rationalization programme.

The tragedy of the October demonstrations was that there was no national inter-plant coordination of the workers' struggles against management's rationalization package. The national union lacked the resources to play an effective leadership role in the general crisis and the branch unions were unavoidably too busy coordinating their own local disputes. As it happened, the national secretariat failed to maintain a presence in either the PAN or the Steyr demonstrations. Most of the work was done by the NLC and the local unionists and activists. The branch union at PAN was, in fact, split as workers accused a section of the branch secretariat of collaborating with management.

National coordination of strategies, buttressed by propaganda and public education was missing. The opportunity offered by the two major demonstrations at PAN and Steyr to wrest concessions from management and influence the rationalization programmes was lost. There was no way the auto plants could have survived a general assembly plants strike without some major concessions to the workforce. Instead, the individual unions were left to face their employers who have always relied on inter-plant management cooperation through the Nigerian Auto Manufacturers' Association and state resources to deal with their workforce.

The workers in Steyr went back to work without management meeting any of their demands and in consequence a serious blow was dealt to trade unionism in the company. There was no viable organ left to defend workers' rights and interests. Instead the disbanded union and the national secretariat became saddled with two outstanding court cases and an industrial dispute. The first is a criminal case filed by the management against the dismissed workers on charges of disturbance of public peace, grievous hurt and assault. The second is a civil case filed by the disbanded branch union against management for wrongful dismissal. Finally, a trade dispute has been filed by the national secretariat of the union at the Industrial Arbitration Panel.

Workers, however, continued to identify with the dismissed unionists even after their acceptance of the obnoxious conditions of re-engagement. In fact, several attempts were made at the beginning to withdraw their check-off funds and give them to the unionists as a way of sustaining them until the three cases were resolved. One of the remaining unionists, the financial secretary, Umaru Gurkuma, withdrew ₦1000 and ₦900 separately from the union account on 2 December 1985 and 3 February 1986 respectively. He was, however, issued with a query by the personnel manager on 25 February 1986 to explain who authorized the withdrawal and account for the expenses incurred with the money. The union had made the mistake of keeping its dues in a separate code in the company's account instead of opening a separate bank account in town. Given the new situation in the company there was little the remaining unionists could do to ward off what actually amounted to gross interference in workers' rights in the disbursement of their check-off. The query was heeded.

The workers also agreed to make voluntary donations to a Dismissed Workers Support Fund. Contributions ranged from ₦2 to ₦5 per worker per month. Management got to know about this and issued a warning to the workers to discontinue the practice. Even so, contributions continued until December 1985.

Union power had now collapsed. But management wanted the national secretariat of the union, which was anxious about the blocked check-off dues in the company accounts, to organize elections for a new branch executive. Management insisted that otherwise the check-off would not be passed on to the national secretariat. The national secretariat resisted this, since holding elections would undermine the civil case in court and the industrial dispute at the Industrial Arbitration Panel. The term of office of the disbanded executive was to expire in 1988.

Meanwhile, workers' problems remain. Dismissals and terminations of employment are rife. The morale of the workers is low. The company was, in fact, closed down by the summer of 1986 because of the non-availability of parts, but most probably also because of the anticipated high cost of production that would accompany the introduction of the second tier foreign exchange market. There was no union to negotiate the terms of closure, a situation making workers even more insistent on the reinstatement of their branch officials. Many of the workers interviewed were themselves willing to serve the union and continue the struggle from where the sacked unionists left it. A more pliable union was constituted in 1987.

CONCLUSION

The current crisis has demonstrated that most of the assembly plants are not viable after all. The policy makers failed to carry out a proper appraisal of these plants and of how they fit into an industrialization strategy. They easily succumbed to the pressures of the technical partners who were more concerned about finding an outlet for their products. As Diaku (1982) argued, there was neither a legal framework for enforcing the terms of the contract nor an efficient institutional mechanism for checking the performance of the plants against policy targets. What is more, the establishment of an intermediate and capital goods sector with a high local content did not take place before the plants were established. The awkward situation therefore arose where both the assembly plants and the so-called local content suppliers were dependent upon the state for the importation of parts and raw materials. With the collapse of oil revenues and the rationing of import licences, both sectors of the industry faced very serious shortages, necessitating rationalization policies that affected both labour–management relations and the prices of their products.

Various proposals have been articulated by the Nigerian public concerning the future of the assembly plants. These range from complete closure (reintroduction of fully built-up cars) to privatization (so that government funds can be spared this unviable enterprise) to standardization of the auto parts and specialization in the generation of local research to allowing the realities of the market to take their toll on the less efficient ones.

These proposals fall within the short- to medium-term perspective and have direct implications for labour. In fact, they take a purely technicist position without any regard for the role of labour in the rationalization programme. The execution of these programmes could lead to more retrenchment, reduced work days, compulsory leaves, forced saving, curtailment of bonuses and increments and the suspension of workers' facilities. Such policies are responsible for the frequent industrial disputes in the plants. Government's own rationalization programme which may be based on the standardization of the auto parts does not deviate from this anti-labour perspective. The primary objective, it would seem, is to simply increase the local content supply without jeopardizing the profit levels of the companies. But the capacity of the government to enforce controls has been extremely weak. What it fails to take into account is that the workers can effectively monitor the operations of these companies locally, starting from the clearance at the ports to the actual production and sales stages. My own experience with some of the workers is that they know a great deal about what goes on in these industries and could produce better results than INTERPOL, at least at the local level, if major concessions were made addressing their specific demands and rights. As it is, most of them are not prepared to expose the dubious activities of these companies because they believe that the state's and management's interests converge and workers will be penalized if, as happened in Steyr, they challenge the unpatriotic activities of the plants.

Whatever position finally emerges, workers in these industries have to devise appropriate strategies to respond to the crisis. The Steyr case shows that the national union needs to do much more in providing effective leadership to the general workforce. Propaganda, self-education, inter-plant union coordination, and effective strategies of bargaining and industrial intervention have to be set in motion if the labour force is not to be depleted.

But workers' responses should not stop at the defensive level. Obviously, the future of the assembly plants is bleak. Most of them are not viable. The introduction of the second tier foreign exchange market is likely to lead to the permanent closure of most of the plants or a massive reduction in turnover as their products go out of the reach of ordinary Nigerians. The industrialization strategy itself which established the plants was defective. Undoubtedly, Nigeria does not have the economic base for the production of cars, trucks and tractors. A more efficient public transportation policy should have been devized to depress the need for private vehicles.

In contrast to the chaotic pattern which has prevailed heretofore, a rational and peasant-based agricultural policy would have determined whether to operate just one closely monitored tractor plant or import the product until the appropriate infrastructure and support industries had been established. Workers, of course, need to think about the long-term strategy of transforming the economy to serve popular needs and make it more self-reliant. The final position might very well be that assembly plants are not needed at this stage of the country's development. Many Nigerians have made this point but they have not advanced any suggestions about what to do with the 15 000 or more workers in the industry. Workers will support closure only if alternative employment and new training facilities can be provided. Most of the workers interviewed support the orthodox policy of providing sufficient foreign exchange for the importation of parts. They are genuinely worried about their jobs.

A rational and progressive long-term strategy involves mass-based political education, the forging of broad alliances among workers from various industries and the public service, and democratic links with other vital sectors of the society like the peasantry, the progressive intelligentsia and various sectors of the urban poor who have been seriously affected by the adjustment programme of the state and capital. These are the forces that will transform the Nigerian economy and phase out the vehicle assembly plants without subjecting the labour force to the dictates of bourgeois rationalization.

REFERENCES

A number of interviews or discussions were held with union and company personnel during the course of research for this paper. These include Mr A. D. Dzarma, Deputy Technical Manager, Steyr-Nigeria, 8 May 1986; Mr Haroun, Deputy Personnel Manager, Steyr-Nigeria, 8 May 1986; officers of the in-plant union, John Pam, Secretary, Musa Abubakar, Chairman, Samuel Ishiaku, Auditor, 1984, and Patrick Mobutu, PRO, 6 and 7 May 1986, Monday Maji, Deputy National President of the Automobile, Boatyard; Transport Equipment and Allied Workers Union of Nigeria, 12 February 1986.

Company and related documents

S. Adbullahi, Chairman, and Y. L. Zambuk, Secretary, to the Managing Director, Steyr-Nigeria Ltd. NLC/BASC/MD/Vol. 1/15/85, 22 October 1985, 'Austerity Measures' 1983/84 by Steyr-Nigeria, 26 September (1983).
M. Abubakar and J. Pam to Managing Director, 'Booking of closed door Meeting', 7 October (1985).
M. Wadzani Gadzama, Chairman, Board of Directors, Steyr-Nigeria, 'Press Conference', Bauchi, 25 October (1985).
'Local Automotive Component Manufacturers – Steyr-Nigeria, Bauchi, 26 April (1985)
'Staff Grievances and Junior Staff Demands'; 'Letter of Dismissal', Steyr-Nigeria, Bauchi, 26 April (1985).
'Important Notice', Steyr-Nigeria Ltd., 20 October (1985).
'Application for Re-Employment', Steyr-Nigeria Ltd., n.d.
'Clarification of Terms of Re-engagement with Steyr-Nigeria, Ltd., Applicable to All Employees, 24 October (1985).
Workers' Handbook, Steyr-Nigeria Ltd., n.d.

References relating to the automobile industry

I. Aremu, 'Automobile Plants: Issues in Workers' Protests', *The Triumph*, 30 October, 8 November and 13 November (1985).

L. Bhutto, 'Multinational Corporations in the Third World: a Case Study of Steyr-Nigeria Ltd.', mini-project, International Studies, Ahmadu Bello University (1983).

K. von Bothmer, Managing Director, Volkswagen of Nigeria in *African Guardian*, 24 April (1986).

I. Diaku, 'Vehicle Assembly Plants in Nigeria', *African Development*, lll, 3 (1982).

M. Harouna, *The Progress Achieved So Far in Steyr-Nigeria Commercial Vehicle and Agricultural Tractor Plant, Bauchi from 1979–1982*, dissertation Ahmadu Bello University (1983).

Morley, 'Vehicle Assembly Plants', *Guardian*, 12 March (1986).

Teriba *et al.*, *The Structure of the Manufacturing Industry in Nigeria* (Ibadan: Ibadan University Press, 1981).

'Car Crisis: Consumers Pay the Price', *African Guardian*, 24 April (1986).

'Spotlight on Apapa Industrial Area, *Sunday Concord*, 16 April (1986).

'Volkswagen of Nigeria, Why Local Content Achievements are Minimal', *Business Concord*, 21 March (1986); *Business Concord*, 25 February 1986.

Government documents

Financing Memorandum for Steyr-Nigeria Ltd., Federal Government of Nigeria, September (1977).

Fourth National Development Plan, 1981–85, (Lagos: Federal Government Printer, 1981).

The State of the Nigerian Economy, National Economic Council Report, Federal Ministry of National Planning, February (1983).

Other materials

Academic Staff Association, BACAS, Bauchi, Press Release, 'Our Views on the Current Crisis in the Steyr-Nigeria Ltd.,' October (1985).

Nigeria Employers' Consultative Association, 'Recent government economic measures and the level of employment: suggested measures to prevent or minimise reduction in the workforce,' NECA/C2/CON, 24 December (1982).

Report of the five man team appointed by the Bauchi State Council of the Nigerian labour congress to look into the Steyr company controversy, Unpublished report, 21p., February (1980).

Map 7 Chile: Major Towns and Copper Mines

8 Trade Unions and Democracy – Chile in the 1980s

Bosco Parra

LABOUR AND DEMOCRACY IN 1987

By *labour* we mean in this chapter the trade union movement organized in the Comando Nacional de Trabajadores (CNT) which has coordinated since 1982–3 the most important labour organizations of employees and workers in Chile. It has continued the tradition of the Central Unica de Trabajadores (CUT, dissolved in 1973), in order to unite all the wage workers of the country with a perspective of social transformation and internal ideological–political pluralism. By *democracy* we mean here the system of government based on plural representative institutions commonly called 'bourgeois democracy'.

The first five sections present the subjective perceptions of democracy held by the trade union movement, its engagement with democracy and the means of struggle that it has utilized in order to bring back democracy in Chile under the regime of Pinochet.

In the next section, and based on the description already made, I discuss the meaning that could be assigned to the concept of 'social mobilization' and in the conclusion I outline the general political struggle of the labour movement against the dictatorship. The bulk of the chapter refers to the anti-dictatorial struggle as it stood out in October 1987. A postscript, taking into consideration the post-Pinochet situation, was added in 1990.

THE DEMOCRATIC INTEREST OF THE LABOUR MOVEMENT

Why does the trade union movement struggle for democracy? 'Because this is the only system that can permit an effective respect for our interests', answers the CNT (1987). This is an historically-based answer. In the Chilean case, both the 'marketplace bargaining power' (MBP) of the workers and the 'workplace bargaining power' (WBP) were strengthened by the democratic political regime in power until 1973. The 'MBP refers to the bargaining power of workers when they sell (individually or collectively) their labour power'. Chilean history illustrates the apparently general tendency of the democratic system to offer possibilities of political meditation which to some degree correct the 'downward tendency of labour's MBP', determined by the very process of capitalist accumulation (Arrighi, 1983).

Since the democratization measures of the 1920s, the Chilean Parliament has regularly produced laws which tend to improve the conditions under which labour is sold on the market: for example, the determination of legal minimum wages, compulsory wage adjustments, systems of social security, and so on. The initiative for this legislation has come not only from workers elected to Parliament, but also from political centre parties with workers in their rank and file, stimulated by the electoral need to gain political prestige in the world of labour.

This legislation resulted in measures by governments and right wing political parties, which gave the privileged category or status of 'white collar' or 'employee' to the more professionally qualified workers, while seeking the fragmentation of the workers' movement and the control of key sectors of the economy (such as the copper industry or the heavy steel industry). Legal measures allowed therefore significant sectors of wage-earners to start their collective negotiations at a rather high level. By 'workplace bargaining power' I refer to the bargaining power of workers when they have actually entered the capitalist labour process. It is based on the circumstance that the 'increasing connectedness of work roles and the weight of indirect labour costs make capital vulnerable to work stoppages and passive resistance, even on the part of small numbers of workers.' (Arrighi, 1983).

The capacity to engage in everyday struggle at the workplace was strengthened in the Chilean case by the existence of legal institutions of democratic–parliamentary origin. The Labour Code promulgated in the 1920s, following a model of 'cooptive democratization', attempted to prevent workers from organizing on a national scale, by legalizing only trade unions in each individual factory.

A factory with a minimum of 25 workers was entitled to have its own union directed by five workers of the same productive unit.

Union leaders had legally guaranteed job security – the so called 'fuero sindical'. As a result of this the different forms of daily 'labour resistance' were no longer illegal informal ones but aquired a significant degree of legal legitimacy. Some direct legal support became operative on the shop floor itself, *in situ.*

As the industry was modernized through the process of import-substitution in the 1930s and the development of state-owned industry of the 1940s, the strategic significance of this legal capacity for direct union influence on the process of production acquired additional importance. Modernization, as we know it, implied an increasing concentration of the technical process with the subsequent emergence of 'key points' which have command over the whole labour process. The direct connection between the workers who operated those 'key points' and the legally-protected union leaders tended to maximize opportunities for trade unions to exploit the internal pressure.

The general democratic atmosphere at that time also allowed everyday factory struggles to get external support from the political representatives of the workers' movement, such as members of Parliament and Municipal Councillors. The prestige of those political agents allowed them to present the workers' demands to employers or authorities, with a high degree of legitimacy.

This positive linkage between workers' corporate interest and the political–democratic game is clearly apparent for the workers' movement from more than half a century of concrete experience. This differentiates the workers' organizations from the relationship that exists between other social actors and representative democracy. Other social actors may not share this positive appreciation of a system of political mediation through representative democracy. To the employers, political mediation through representative democracy seems harmful, since the dictatorial model guarantees them complete freedom from such political interference with the laws of supply and demand in determining the conditions of the labour market.

At the opposite end of society, the idea of a political power which is both exclusive and monopolistic in nature tends also to develop. For the unemployed, connected to the *movimiento de pobladores* (the movement of shanty-town dwellers), the absence of an established practice of direct negotiations between their organizations and the state has contributed to the conception that the power that will replace Pinochet should be a 'dictatorship of the proletariat' representing their interests and objectives.

THE SPECIAL DEMOCRATIC CAPACITY OF THE TRADE UNION MOVEMENT

The privileged relation between the trade union movement and representative democracy created a 'democratic capacity' that has begun to characterize its internal activity. It takes a particular skill to produce consensus between the different political tendencies which operate within the movement. It requires, in my view, a commitment in spirit and method of operation that is really democratic, renouncing claims to exclusive exercise of power. Thus, the power aspirations of the Communist and the Christian Democratic leaders in the trade union movement are significantly less exclusive, less sectarian, and less hegemonic than those of their fellow leaders in the party political sphere.

Therefore alliances are more easily formed in the trade union than in the political sphere. The ideological menace represented by the Communist thesis of the dictatorship of the proletariat is cooled down in the trade union world by the Christian Democratic leaders' experience that the practice of Chilean Communists has been democratic in essence. This was later confirmed by the Communist Party's rejection of armed struggle as a means to achieve power.

At the same time, the Communist trade union leader can verify that his Christian Democratic colleague understands that his own power depends on the support that the former can give him. The understanding of this necessary interdependence is absent in the activities of Christian Democracy in the general political sphere, where they still propose a clear-cut alternative: Christian Democracy or Communism.

This situation helps to explain actions that in the actual atmosphere of the Chilean opposition seem unexpected, such as the offer by the left-wing majority of the Confederacion de Trabajadores del Cobre (Copper Workers' Confederation), after their elections of March 1987, to give the presidency of that organization to a Christian Democratic leader. This offer was not accepted, however, because of internal problems in that party.

AN AUTONOMOUS ROLE OF THE TRADE UNION MOVEMENT IN THE DEMOCRATIC STRUGGLE

The interest and the capacity we have mentioned contrast deeply with the actual orientation in 1987 of the national political process. The trade union movement, which depends for its further development on the functioning of representative democracy, was forced to watch how the dictatorship's potential for survival seemed to be growing stronger. This resulted in a certain political opportunism in sectors of the opposition, thus confirming that 'certain political sectors are more concerned with giving guarantees to employers than with defending the demands of the workers' (CNT, 1987).

While unions renounced their hegemonic claims in the interest of unity they discovered that the political opposition remains split precisely because different opposition parties seek to secure privileged conditions for themselves in the post-Pinochet era. The obvious conclusion that some union leaders draw from this is that they should therefore strive to secure gradually a relatively 'high degree of autonomy in the specific political sphere' (CIASI, no. 7, 1987). This search for autonomy appeared especially suggestive when it manifested itself during a period when the left-wing political parties were taking important steps to improve their coordination in the political sphere.

THE STRATEGY FOR AUTONOMY

On what basis and with what method does the trade union movement seek to achieve its role as proponent of greater political autonomy? First comes the need for completing the process of reconstruction and unification of the trade union movement, creating a new united Central Organization (CIASI, no. 6, 1987).

As is well known, the established CUT was outlawed by the Pinochet dictatorship. Basic trade union structures lived through a very hard period of dispersion. To overcome this period of setbacks involved first the starting of the Coordinadora Nacional Sindical in 1975, followed in the 1980s by the building of the CNT, Comando Nacional de Trabajadores, which brings together the top leadership of several national trade union organizations through political agreements among the principal partisan tendencies.

The CUT heritage thus came to manifest itself in a new central organization integrating all wage earners, from both the productive and service sector units, respecting at the same time the principle of political pluralism within a general perspective of social transformation according to class interests. This process of unification strengthens the instruments of struggle proposed by the trade union movement (CIASI, no. 6, 1987; CNT, 1987).

One such instrument is a 'social contract' which can be defined as the acceptance by the entire society, including the employers, of the legitimacy of the workers' demand to put an end to the present relation between the gains of the employers and the wages of the workers. This task is tackled, for example, by using the initiatives put forward by the Catholic Church towards 'national reconciliation', which, in order to be implemented, required a 'social contract' as the workers understand it. The social contract could simultaneously serve as the basis for a 'political agreement' among all those struggling for democracy. To impel the general process of democratization, the trade union movement insists upon 'social mobilization', which as I understand it consists of the so-called 'protestas', constituting visible violations of the dictatorial public order, carried out without the use of weapons, and taking the form of street demonstrations, strikes, partial work stoppages, barricades and other minor actions.

THE PROCESS OF TRADE UNION UNITY

The present process of unification presents, in my view, more favourable characteristics than the one that had earlier resulted in the creation of the CUT in 1953. In the first place, the most important sector of Chilean workers – the copper industry – are now not only participating in the CNT, but have also played a significant role in its creation. Let us not forget that their support for CUT had always been precarious – and that the behaviour of a significant part of its members was a key element in the fall of the Allende government, in which the CUT leadership was represented at the cabinet level. The present mobilizing capacity of today's CNT is due fundamentally to the active presence of copper workers' representatives in its leadership.

The unification taking place among the agrarian workers has also favourable repercussions. The recently created Confederacion Nacional Campesina gathers together 180 agrarian trade unions. The capacity of this organization will be a key element in the organization and mobilization of the 230 000 workers today employed in fruit exports, which is already one of the most dynamic sectors of Chile's new capitalist agriculture. The over-exploitation of these workers is made possible by the existence of temporary work contracts, which prevent them from organizing themselves and from holding collective wage negotiations. If some of the initiatives to strengthen the present mobilizing capacity of the agrarian workers (CIASI, January–March, 1987) being undertaken by some minor mining unions catch on and spread it would help to repair some grave historical insufficiencies. In the past, there was practically no relationship between the 'active army' of workers and the unemployed. By now, such a relationship tends to establish itself. If it was the state that prohibited such a relation in the 1920s, not allowing the unemployed to join the trade unions, it is now the same state that favours such an affiliation by means which produce different effects from those expected.

In its efforts to discipline and use the unemployed labour force at a low price, the dictatorship implemented various minimum wage work programs, paid for by the state. These also reflect a certain Chilean state culture which has, traditionally, required every government to take measures to deal with 'extreme poverty'. In this way structural unemployment takes on a wage form, the only way in which these groups, wrongly labelled 'marginalized', can become visible to the traditional trade union organization.

Paradoxically the dictatorship contributed to this tendency of integrating the unemployed. While aiming at breaking up the workers' unified organizations at the factory level (which excluded the unemployed), the dictatorship allowed the development, at the municipal level, of various trade unions with a right to register unemployed.

In short, we are witnessing a process of centralization that encompasses both the larger and more important workers' organizations and a more diversified set of situations within which the proletarianized labour force can express itself. As this tendency is consolidated so the trade union movement will be able to achieve a greater degree of autonomy, a greater capacity for dialogue with other actors, and a higher level of prestige, all of which will in turn enable it to reach even more intense levels of social mobilization.

SOCIAL MOBILIZATION

For analytical purposes it seems essential to differentiate between: (i) the formation of a potential for struggle, and (ii) the effective realization of that potential in the conflict. The first refers to a socio-political process, while the second refers to problems of organization and methods which I will analyse here in some detail.

The option of non-armed social mobilization assumes that the trade union movement builds its strategy on the idea that the fundamental resource of the working class in the struggle is that which Perrone describes as its 'disruptive potential' (Perrone, 1987: 253). In this case, the effect would be a situation of ungovernability, where the state does not succeed in adjusting the functioning of society to its plan of domination.

What does a conflict between a social movement and the state apparatus involve, when the former seeks to produce a situation of ungovernability? I believe that it will result in at least two controversies. Firstly, it will lead to a controversy over the control of the territory. The various discussions about the concept of the state should not allow us to forget the basic idea that the state ceases to exist when left without a territory. In any conflict 'against' the state as opposed to conflicts 'within' it, the objectives reached by the anti-state side can be measured by the degree to and the form in which the inhabitants of the state territory cease to be controlled by the state's apparatus of domination. And the second controversy will be about control over the technical infrastructure on which the public administration rests. A state without an administration does not rule, and an administration without a technical base cannot operate.

The territorial controversy: a people's and workers' democratic commune

How can the proletariat challenge the state's control over territory? In my opinion by regulating the daily life of the urban popular community in such a way that it lives according to an 'order' that is contrary to the dictatorial 'public order'. A 'popular order' in the workers' urban community is primarily the strategic centralization of the various forms of 'realization' of the labour power or capacity of different fractions of the proletariat. This happens when all of those forms are linked up in such manner as to get control of the urban territory.

Autonomous realization of labour power may take place when industrial workers declare a strike and carry out urban protests such as the occupation of streets, building barricades, and so on. The industrial worker complements his/her wage with self-managed economic activities, such as building his/her own home. The unemployed face, on their own, the reproduction of their labour power through survival activities within the so called 'informal sector'.

Viewing this situation from a functionalist perspective, one would discern a heterogeneous group having no special significance; or even an example of 'self-exploitation' on the part of the proletariat. Instead, we discover both a homogeneous set of actions (all of which are expressions of the only unexpropriable means of action available to the proletariat – its capacity for labour) and a specific potential target (to control the city, to prevent the state from using the streets, the buildings and urban technical facilities). The conjunction of such different forms of autonomous activity constitutes the basis for ensuring:

- the functioning of urban services which make possible the independent life of the city, and
- the stoppage of the city's services to the state.

If one wonders in which concrete form this centralization of the autonomous realization of the labour power could take place, the *movimiento de pobladores* (movement of the shanty-town dwellers) gives the answer. The united meeting or Congress of the *pobladores*, held in Santiago in April 1986, formulated two observations that seem essential to me:

- the *pobladores* movement should consider itself allied with the trade union movement in the urban sectors of the country, and
- the territorial agreement should be directed against one of the main supporting pillars of the dictatorship, namely the municipalities (SUR, 1986).

Such proletarian centralization could be realized through an alliance of the trade union and the *pobladores* movement in a people's and workers' democratic commune. This integrated organization operates at the same level at which the dictatorial state cannot prevent its own fragmentation while trying to fragment the popular movement: that is to say at the municipal level.

The strategic significance of a people's and workers' communal authority at the municipal level

Let us assume, to begin with, that such a communal workers' authority allows the constitution of a set of physical forces that is able to sustain the struggle into the future. By such a system of forces, we mean an organic configuration which relates the constant and autonomous generation of energies to the constant energy consumption in the urban conflicts. This could be done by a popular commune which succeeds in integrating both self-managed working capacity and politics; that is to say, succeeds in integrating economic organization and conflict. It integrates production with strikes and protests.

This matter is of particular importance in Chile, because state legislation has from the very beginning prevented the trade unions from building strike funds. Putting these problems side by side implies accepting the existence of 'praxeological regularities'; that is to say of problems and principles common to all conflicts (Puig i Scotoni, 1980: 63).

All conflicts involve a more or less prolonged consumption of physical force. A non-armed conflict involves the consumption of physical force, especially when weapons are replaced by social mobilization, which consists in fact of various forms of work. This consumption of energy demands an independent renewal capacity protected from the opponent. Military rationality deals with this problem by distinguishing between battle and service units, and by requiring constant tactical and strategical consideration of how to get the latter to the battle fronts. To our knowledge, the physical nature of the non-armed social conflict is not very frequently considered in revolutionary theory; and it is probably the failure to do so that explains, to some extent, the asymmetry of conflicts with the state.

The state has among its resources not only the weapons themselves, but also a military 'physical' way to analyse situations of social confrontation. This allows it to discover ways of weakening popular rebellions or uprisings without the need for indiscriminate use of arms.

It should not surprise us if this underestimation of the physical nature of the conflicts could explain part of the contradictions which often appear between a 'masculine' tendency towards the left and a 'feminine' tendency towards the right. As long as the organization of daily life – that is to say of the physical–biological basis of the social process – is exclusively in the hands of women, it may happen that in face of conflict, women react negatively; they tend to consider only the 'logistical' dimensions of the clash, and withdraw their participation when they find that they will not be able to hold out in the long run. The communal integration of both daily life and politics produces a collective actor that overcomes the feminine/masculine contradiction. In other words, one 'feminizes' oneself when discovering the physical–biological dimensions of the conflict.

Before leaving this subject of the configuration of a system of forces, I must mention a basic assumption about the concrete operation of such a system which refers to the need for separating, both in time and space, the civil actions of the masses from the armed actions of military groups. The existence of the latter is accepted with enthusiasm by some people, while others, including trade union leaders, are more inclined to reject them. The important thing to take into account is that tactical military rationality teaches both of them to avoid any situation where fire is given from the inside of a concentrated group of unarmed people. Even the more offensive of military tactics try at every moment to establish an optimal relation between attack and defence, between the necessary risk and the need for survival: *se ataca porque se tiene defensa* (we attack because we have a defence). A weapon in a man's hand allows him to attack, because the weapon also defends him.

The civilian who fights at the side of someone who possesses a weapon cannot establish this relation. In the end the repressive fire-power reaches everybody – and only those with weapons in their hands can defend themselves against the fire-power. The repetition of this experience leads unnecessarily to the demobilization of the unarmed. The masses are, in the long run, a group of individual actors who make rational calculations of survival. A minimal point of agreement between the military and the civilian, non-armed forces of the people should be the separation of operations in time and space.

Considering further the strategic significance of a people's and workers' communal authority, let us assume also that it allows the people to combine the forms of struggle which are typical of an active army of workers with those typical of a relative surplus population. In the Chilean case the political commune could replace trade unions as the common organization for both armies. This could be done as long as the *pobladores* movement implies an integration between *strikes* – the specific form of struggle by active workers – and *street clashes* – the specific form of struggle of the unemployed, especially the young people.

The integration of these two forms of struggle into urban protests comes to be a superior expression of both. With the removal of the nature of workers' strikes as a political instrument, they become part of a larger whole, rather than the superior expression of it. The 'urban protest', as an integration of various proletarian struggles, finds its highest level when it becomes sustained or protracted. Again we find here the same praxeological constraints: to sustain prolonged physical efforts implies, apart from distinguishing between logistic and battle units, being able to divide the forces between a 'bulk' characterized by its recurrent rythm of action and a 'vanguard', capable of keeping itself in movement when the main force is resting.[1] Not only the armed force, but also the civilian force and the non-violent force require some sort of militia (Oppenheimer, 1971). From the point of view of a theory of conflict, the absence of any attempt to face this problem is one of the most evident methodological deficiences in the Chilean experience.

Let us finally assume that the communal organization of the proletariat could generate a certain cultural homogeneity of the labour force and in this way raise the bargaining capacity of the trade union movement.[2] The integration of politics with the self-managed reproduction of the labour force could improve daily life for the unemployed. The level of demands of this sector moves from a purely natural minimum level of subsistence towards a properly urban and modern level. The demands for collective consumption grow. In this way the political 'uniformity' of consumption leads to cultural homogeneity of work even where the proletarianized labour force has yet to achieve the full status of the wage-work. This homogeneity, in line with the Arrighian model, would diminish the negative influence of the 'marketplace bargaining power' upon the 'workplace bargaining power' of the active workers.

The dispute over the control of technical infrastructure

As I have said, the logic of ungovernability presupposes obtaining control of the technical infrastructures from the public administration. This is a question of concern to engineers and other technicians, and for those 'middle sectors' that within modern fields of communication, such as energy, computer systems, and so on, exercise functions of 'command' and technical 'control'.

From the perspective of the independent functioning of society *vis-à-vis* the state apparatus, what is required is more complex than the simple disruption of those systems through strikes. It is then indispensable to have the participation of a direction which knows how to combine movement and standstill of the systems. From an organizational and strategical point of view it is a question of associating assets coming both from 'workers' and 'professionals'.

In the Chilean case it means being able to strengthen and know how to use the *Asamblea de la Civilidad*; an interesting manifestation of strategic spontaneity that came into being as a result of the protests of 1983 and gathered together the trade union movment, the students, the *pobladores*, and the professional corps.

An analysis of the trade union movement's new role must take into consideration how it affects the *Asamblea de la Civilidad*, ways in which it tries to achieve compatibility with it, and ways in which it is capable of providing definite strategic objectives for it.

CONCLUSION: THE TRADE UNION MOVEMENT AND THE DEMOCRATIC STRUGGLE

A dictatorship which deprives the people of their political liberties and restrains access to the public services which – in relation to historical conditions – are necessary for the assured reproduction of their labour power, constitutes a government that reduces society to a 'state of nature'. By such a 'state' I mean here, in accordance with Locke's formulation, 'any condition where no legitimate government exists' (Wienfield, 1984: 551). From this perspective, even if the theory of Locke is not accepted as an explanation of the origin of the state, it may well be used as a list of the political operations which become rational for the social actors whom the dictatorship expels from the political system, reducing them to such a state. The first of these operations will be 'to join and unite into a community, for their . . . greater security . . . and make one body politic, wherein the majority have a right to act and conclude the rest' (Locke, 1977: 279).

Under these conditions the struggle for democracy consists of the (re)foundation of a democratic 'political society', where self-built liberties and services are governed by their own authority rather than by the authority of the state. For the trade union movement – a social actor which must defend its interests through the unification of the proletariat and the endless reiteration of the democratic game – the (re)foundation of political society implies the building of two sets of popular–democratic authority. One is the people's and workers' authority which unifies – at the communal level – the different proletarian factions, adding to the logic of the industrial branch ('resemblance') the political–strategic logic of territoriality ('proximity'). The other authority is national–popular, unifying the workers' organizations with the technical professional groups. Through these two popular–

democratic authorities the organized proletariat ensures first its class autonomy and, secondly, the reiteration of the democratic game; that is, ensures the operation of the democratic political constitution.

The proletariat ensures the latter when it confers a concrete material sanction upon the norm that military power should be subjected to civilian power. This concrete material sanction is the ungovernability of military dictatorship. Neither the liberal theory nor the liberal practice of constitutional law contemplates this sanction, either because it is generally unnecessary for the preservation of bourgeois domination (frequently constitutional crises are produced intentionally so as to liquidate the workers' movement by military means), or impossible as the bourgeoisie lacks the material resources necessary to match the weapons of the military. This marks a difference between the bourgeoisie and the proletariat, in as much as the latter, through the productive and conflictual realizations of its labour power, can reorganize the urban ground, thus neutralizing the military.

While securing its own autonomy and the enforcement of the constitution, the workers' movement transforms the liberal–democratic state into a space where it can operate with freedom of action;[3] that is, with the possibility to pursue the realization of its own project of transformation. We are facing a dynamic equilibrium: only by accepting the non-monopoly of political power – in other words, by accepting shared political power – can the workers' movement secure its military non-annihilation.

And the political parties? Describing an anti-dictatorial struggle obliges us to recall two circumstances. The first circumstance is that political parties lack political power of their own. If by power we understand an actor's capacity to transform the external conditions in a direction favourable to its interests (Dahlström, 1987: 59), then we should take into account that in a dictatorial situation the resources for transformation, which have their origin in the state, are monopolized by the repressive apparatus. On the other hand, those resources which are autonomous and direct can only be displayed by social movements. The very character of civil society assigns to those movements situations from which they can coordinate the population's massive capacity for work in order to develop actions that bring about the inactivity of the government. The parties cannot by themselves achieve that privileged position.

The second circumstance to recall is that, while noting how important social movements are, we still have to count upon the political parties. For the parties act not only as operators of the social movement (Castells, 1983: 277), linking with the other structures of society; before doing this they have contributed to the constitution and organization of that social movement as such. To the extent that they create social movements, the parties create power for others. Thus, they alienate themselves. But perhaps the political virtue of the modern prince is to accept certain alienations – and to know how to use them.

POSTSCRIPT: LABOUR AND DEMOCRACY IN 1990

After the above had been written, democratic forces in Chile came up with an agreement which allowed an electoral victory over the dictatorship, both at the 1988 plebiscite, and at the presidential elections in 1989. These advances were made in the absence of social mobilization. The trade union movement's political incidence proved less than that expected by its leadership in 1987–8. Transition itself is taking place under a significant degree of military control. The main task for the global democratization movement is to gain independence from that control.

Under the present conditions, a strategy for the trade union movement which restricted itself to being a contractual actor in the negotiations with the employers for improvements in their particular situation would probably meet with the following risks: (i) support given to it by an insufficiently democratized political system could prove precarious; (ii) self-restriction by the trade union leadership during negotiations, in order to diminish the global costs of democratization, could appear both insufficient to the process's political leadership, and excessive to the long postponed legitimate demands of its bases.

The democratization of the city councils intended by the Aylwin regime could provide the trade union movement with a much further-reaching strategy, allowing simultaneously both political and social advances. It could consist of the following steps:

(a) A platform of 'local development' which would contemplate the cooperativization and technification of the 'informal' sector, and the supply of budget resources from the government. On this basis the following could be achieved: (i) a fusion of the interests of the 'relative surplus population' with those of the employed industrial army, and

(ii) an alliance of the proletariat in general with sectors of the bourgeoisie, and petite-bourgeoisie, who are oriented towards the internal market.

(b) The local-council democratic power thus established could make an alliance with the executive and legislative powers elected by the people, and give origin to a 'democratizing system'. This system, having monopolized the conditions for governability in the country, could pose a credible threat of generalized civil disobedience to any dictatorial government, and that way neutralize the threats of intervention now coming from the armed forces.

A transition thus initiated could head for a democracy much more profound than the previous ones, since it would support not only the demands of the employed industrial army, but also those of the 'relative surplus population'.

NOTES

1. Parra (1985: 20). The expression 'vanguard' is not used here as a synonym for party, nor as leadership, but rather in its military sense: a militia working for a decisive force, in this case for the civil population.
2. Arrighi (1983: 56): '. . . the most important determinant of the trend in the "actual" bargaining power of labour is its cultural homogeneity, particularly with regard to the conditions of labour-power reproduction'.
3. 'Freedom of action'. Another praxeological constraint is to look for security conditions, to pursue in any case the realization of its own plan. 'At the end of the war there will be one victorious and one defeated party. The difference is that one of them will remain free to act . . .' (Foch, 1918: 96).

REFERENCES

G. Arrighi, 'The Labor Movement in Twentieth-century Western Europe', in Wallerstein (ed.), *Labor in the World Social Structure* (Beverly Hills, London: Sage, 1983).
M. Castells, *The City and the Grass Roots* (Berkeley: University of California Press, 1983).
Centro de Investigacion y Asesoria Sindical (CIASI), *Informe trimestal*, no. 6 (January–March 1987).
—— *Informe trimestral*, no. 7 (April–June 1987).
Comando Nacional de Trabajadores (CNT), *Mensaje a los trabajadores y al pueblo de Chile, del Consejo Directivo Nacional* (1 May, 1987).

E. Dahlström, 'Maktanalysers kontextuella och ideologiska förankring', in O. Petersson (ed.), *Maktbegreppet* (Stockholm: Carlssons, 1987).

F. Foch, *Des principes de la guerre* (Paris: Berger-Levrault, 1918).

J. Locke, *Two Treaties*, II, section 95, quoted here after J. W. Yolton, *The Locke Reader* (London: Cambridge University Press, 1977).

M. Oppenheimer, *Stadsgerillan – en sociologisk analys* (Stockholm: Wahlström & Widstrand, 1971) (translation of *The Urban Guerilla*, 1969).

B. Parra, *Dimensión operacional del proceso de democratización en Chile* (Santiago de Chile: Publicaciones Pedro Manrique, 1985).

L. Perrone, *Positional Power and Propensity to Strike. Politics and society* (1983), p. 12, quoted from O. Petersson (ed.), *Maktbegreppet* (Stockholm: Carlssons,1987).

P. Puig i Scotoni, *Att förstå revolutionen* (Understanding the revolution) (Lund: Zenit, 1980).

SUR Documentacion, *Hechos Urbanos*, no. 55 (1986).

R. D. Wienfield, The reason for democracy, in *History of Political Thought*, vol. 3 (1984).

9 World-Scale Patterns of Labour–Capital Conflict

Beverly Silver

THE WORLD LABOUR MOVEMENT IN THE 1980s[1]

Two trends stand out in a survey of the world scale patterning of labour unrest in the 1980s: the weakening and subsequent decline of militancy among workers in the advanced capitalist (or core) countries *and* the simultaneous emergence of strong and effective labour movements in numerous newly industrializing (or semi-peripheral) countries. Thus, while workers in US mass production industries have been on the defensive as companies close plants and cut real wages, a wave of worker militancy in the summer of 1987 shook the South Korean economy, and won major concessions from employers and the state. And while British mine workers were decisively defeated after a long and bitter dispute, deepening the overall crisis of the labour movement, black South African miners have, through a series of extremely disruptive strikes, become perhaps the most strategic force directly and indirectly challenging the apartheid structure. Poland, Brazil, Spain and other examples would only further illustrate the point: that is, by the 1980s the centre of gravity of world labour unrest had shifted from its historical epicentre – the core countries – to the semi-periphery of the world economy.

The two trends discussed above – a weakening of labour *vis-à-vis* capital in the core and a strengthening of the former *vis-à-vis* the latter in the semi-periphery – are intimately and causally linked. The late 1960s upsurge of labour militancy in the core, together with the intensification of world market competition as Western Europe and Japan caught up with the US economic lead, led to a squeeze on profits which drove core capitalists in search of ways to lower costs and to re-establish firm managerial control in the workplace. The strategies pursued (that is, disinvestment in the geographical and industrial locations which were labour strongholds in the core; the re-orientation of production in these branches to areas with cheaper supplies of labour through either direct investment or subcontracting;

217

the expanded use of labour-saving technologies) progressively wea-kened workers' bargaining power in the core. This weakening was perhaps most visible in the US as the corporate strategy of local disinvestment/overseas investment was first launched in the 1950s – partly in response to the militant workers' struggles of the 1930s and 1940s, which succeeded in firmly establishing unionization in the country's mass production industries and ensuring processes of wage-level determination that made the US factory workers' wages among the highest in the world. By the 1970s, following the upsurge of labour militancy, western European foreign direct investment and subcontracting also took off. And, faced with steadily rising real wages and the exhaustion of their rural latent reserve army of labour, Japanese capitalists pursued a vigorous policy of sending labour-intensive production to its neighbouring countries.[2]

Partly as a by-product of these processes, new working classes were created in the semi-periphery which occupy strategic positions within the world-scale division of labour. To be sure, many of these workers were drawn into production in ways that left them with little effective bargaining power *vis-à-vis* either their employers or the state: for example young women drawn into highly labour-intensive export production platform sweatshops where high labour turnover rates and high profit rates are perfectly compatible. Here profitability is based on the payment of very low (below subsistence) wages and the continuous expansion/contraction of the number of workers em-ployed in response to world market demand. Thus, workers are obliged to subsidize their wages and counteract their economic insecurity through non-wage sources of income – for example retaining ties to rural households to which they can return during spells of unemployment and which have non-wage income derived from subsistence and/or petty commodity production. Because production is not capital-intensive, employers can easily move production elsewhere if the workforce becomes militant. And because of the unskilled nature of most of the work, capitalists lose little by merely firing protesting workers. In these cases, the move-ment of capital out of the core (through foreign direct investment or subcontracting) creates and *reproduces* a semi-proletarianized wage labour force with little effective bargaining power.[3]

However, another significant group were drawn into jobs using relatively capital-intensive mass production technology. Here, em-ployers are pushed and pulled into creating a stable industrial working class. They are pulled by their need for an experienced workforce. While mechanization decreases capital's dependence on the skills of the old-style craftworker, it creates new skilled and semi-skilled positions learned on the job. Furthermore, given the capital-intensity of production, very high levels of labour turnover and absenteeism can become costly in terms of idle or underutilized equipment. Thus mass production capitalists have pursued strategies – like Henry Ford's 'Five Dollar Day' – designed to create a stable, dependable workforce.

More fundamentally, capitalists have been pushed by worker militancy into providing the wages and working conditions necessary for their workforce to survive as fully proletarianized wage earners without access to non-wage sources of income. As we have argued elsewhere (Arrighi and Silver, 1984), the detailed division of labour associated with capital-intensive mass production technology enhances the 'workplace bargaining power' of labour by increasing the vulnerability of capital to workers' direct action at the point of production. For example, with continuous flow production, a relatively small number of strategically placed activists can bring an entire plant's production to a halt. And with the increasing centralization and integration of production, the damage that can be done to an entire corporation by a strike in one of its key plants and the disruption that can be caused to a nation's economy by a strike in a key corporation or industry also increases.[4]

While the processes of centralization are generally less advanced in the semi-periphery and periphery, the bargaining power of workers is often additionally enhanced by dependence on a single industry for foreign exchange earnings. Relatively small groups of workers linked to the major export earning industry or to transportation (docks, railways, airports) have the capacity to disrupt the entire economy.[5] Thus, in the South Korean 1987 summer of labour unrest, car exports fell by two-thirds from their normal rate; meanwhile the strike in South Africa's gold and coal mines was costing the corporations between $10 and $15 million dollars per day.[6]

Such disruptions have often called forth heavy-handed repression by the state, but under the pressures described above, cooptation through the extension of tangible material benefits has increasingly supplemented or replaced pure repression as the central labour control strategy. Thus, for example, the rapidly mechanizing South African mining industry of the 1970s and 1980s (which for decades had forced an unstable, migratory existence onto its black workers) began taking steps to stabilise the latter by, for example, allowing some of the black mineworkers *and their families* to live near the mines, paying them as full proletarians; that is, wages sufficient to support a family without access to non-wage sources of income (Pycroft and Munslow, 1988).

The above discussion illustrates that the labour movements within different nation-states are linked in fate by the existence of a world-scale division of labour. The geographical mobility of capital (felt simultaneously in one area as 'deindustrialization' and in another as rapid industrialization) is one of the global processes that forge that link. The flows of trade and labour migration in the world economy are two others. Unless we look at the labour movements in Sweden, Brazil, Poland, and so on, from the level of the world economy, we are unable to see the important causal links among them. Just as 'development' and 'underdevelopment' have been interpreted as two sides of the same world historical process, so too we can (and should) reinterpret the 'strength' and 'weakness' of the different national labour movements across the globe as part of *a single world-scale historical process of labour–capital conflict* linked to the evolution of the capitalist world economy as a whole.

CURRENT TRENDS IN WORLD-SCALE HISTORICAL PERSPECTIVE

The world-scale evolution of labour–capital conflict since the beginnings of the modern labour movement in the late nineteenth century can be divided into two distinct phases: (i) from the crisis of British hegemony to the end of the struggle for world hegemony (1870 to the Second World War), and (ii) from the establishment of US hegemony to the present.

The striking characteristic of the first phase is that labour–capital conflict in the world as a whole rose continuously and rapidly (with short-term fluctuations) throughout the period.[7] This rapid rise was punctuated by two major explosions of labour militancy after each of the two world wars. In contrast, in the second phase, the overall level of labour–capital conflict in the world has been relatively stable since the end of the post-war explosion, fluctuating around a high but constant trend.

In the first phase, the centre of gravity of worker militancy was decisively the core countries of the world economy, with an occasional notable outburst from the semi-periphery (for example, Russia, 1905,

1917) or periphery (for example, China, 1926) having signficant weight in the world total. In contrast, during the second phase, the centre of gravity has progressively shifted to the semi-periphery of the world economy (as discussed in the preceding section). Worker militancy in the periphery (the poorest countries), while never accounting for a major percentage of total world worker militancy, becomes significant after the First World War, in large part following the same geographical path traversed by the decolonization struggles.

Finally, the first phase is characterized by the strong and growing politicization of workers' struggles across the globe; that is, the emergence and spread of working class political parties with the goal of obtaining (through insurrectionary or electoral means) state power. By contrast, worker militancy in the second phase was often outside the control of established unions and working class parties (for example the spread of wildcat strikes in the 1960s in the West) or in direct confrontation with working class parties in power in the East (from East Germany in 1953 to Poland and Yugoslavia in 1988) and nationalist movements in power in the periphery (for example, Nigeria, 1971; Botswana 1975; Zambia, 1981).

From the crisis of British hegemony to the Second World War

What accounts for the major characteristics of the first phase; that is, the rising levels and increasingly explosive nature of conflict and the growing politicization of that conflict? The intense inter-capitalist competition of this period (as Germany, the US and others caught up with the 'workshop of the world') drove capitalists to seek ways to lower costs and reduce competition. The strategies pursued – for example mechanization, centralization of capital, state-sponsored protectionism of the home market and imperialist expansion abroad – directly or indirectly attacked the wages and working conditions of the world's workers. The latter, in turn, responded with growing militancy and organized attempts to control state power.

The intense price competition of the late nineteenth century Great Depression (1870–96) squeezed capitalist profits as prices tended to fall faster than money wages, leading to steadily rising real wages. In an effort to eliminate this intense price competition, capitalists responded with mergers, cartels and a general move toward monopolistic regulation of markets. By the last decade of the century, the profit squeeze had been turned into an inflationary squeeze on workers' real wages as prices began to rise faster than money wages. Workers could no longer count on price competition in the market to protect or increase their real wages. Instead, they were compelled to combine their efforts in the struggle to counteract the combination of capital. And as states became more and more involved in the competition among capitalists – for example through imperialist expansion – expenditures for armaments and war made both inflation and worker militancy more explosive.[8]

The intense price competition of the late nineteenth century also drove capitalists towards increasing productivity through mechanization and a greater technical division of labour. These transformations in the organization of production constituted a direct attack on the working conditions, economic security and lifestyles of craftworkers. The latter responded with militancy, increasingly wedded to anti-capitalist political parties and ideologies. Craftworkers resisting downgrading and deskilling 'formed the front line of industrial class battle' – for example in the armaments/metalworking industries during the First World War, where the intense pressures for rapid mechanization in all the belligerent countries encountered the resistance of skilled manual craftsmen who were 'self-confident, combative, and often politically conscious' (Hobsbawm, 1984: 169).

The resistance of the craftworkers impelled capitalists to find alternative supplies of labour. The intense competition and rationalization of production had swelled the industrial reserve army by squeezing out inefficient producers in industry and agriculture. The transformation of agriculture, in particular, created large supplies of cheap labour for the newly created semi-skilled positions in industry. These (often partially proletarianized) supplies eventually enabled capitalists to overcome the resistance of the craftworkers by progressively marginalizing the latter from industrial employment.

Thus, these responses by capitalists to the late nineteenth century squeeze on profits – centralization of capital, mechanization and the incorporation of new supplies of cheaper wage workers – attacked the 'marketplace bargaining power' of workers. Inflation ate into wages, while mechanization made craftworkers' skills obsolete. The large supplies of 'peasant workers' further increased the competitive pressures in the labour market. Workers responded with militancy inside and political organization outside the workplace.

These trends spread generally, albeit unevenly, within the core and semi-periphery of the world economy. The weaker the economic bargaining power of workers, the greater the tendency to compensate by seeking state power. And the smaller the working class within the total population of the nation-state, the greater the need to forge inter-class alliances, and hence the greater the tendency to strengthen the political arm of the working class movement. Thus, within the overall trend towards the increasing politicization of class conflict, the tendency was stronger in the semi-periphery (for example, Russia, Spain, Italy) than in the core (for example, United States, Britain) of the world economy.

Finally, while the imperialist expansion of the core powers had an ambiguous impact on the working classes within the expansionary states themselves, it accentuated the main features of the first phase of labour–capital conflict (rising levels of strike activity, radicalization of demands and forms of struggle, and growing support for working-class parties) in two ways. First, the imperialist expansion led to two world wars in which class conflict was delegitimized in the first years of each war leading to a downturn in worker militancy – but whose economic and social hardships culminated in world-scale explosions of worker militancy as well as major revolutions (Russia, China) towards the end of each.

Second, the incorporation of new areas and peoples into the capitalist world division of labour created new working classes in the periphery – principally in primary commodity-producing export enclaves and allied transport sectors. The labour supplies for these export enclaves often had to be elicited through coercion and violence, the indigenous peoples forcibly separated from the means of production and subsistence. This forced proletarianization pro-voked intense conflicts in the periphery in the first decades of the twentieth century.[9]

Worker militance in the export enclaves themselves spread in the 1920s, 1930s and 1940s. The enclaves often occupied strategic positions within the resource needs structures of the imperial powers. Thus, as the Second World War *and* worker militancy in the periphery heated up, Britain, in an effort to avoid major wartime disruptions, introduced trade unions and conciliation and arbitration mechanisms throughout its Empire (Brown, 1988; Burawoy, 1982).

The spread of worker militancy in the periphery contributed to the growing worker militancy in the world economy as a whole albeit on a much smaller scale than the core and semi-periphery. It also contributed to the growing politicization of labour–capital conflict on a world scale, although from different causes. Increasingly, labour–capital struggles in the periphery overlapped and allied with broader-based nationalist struggles – whether against the colonial state (Africa, Asia) or against foreign control of the country's basic resources (Latin America). The major outbreaks of labour unrest – from the nitrate mines of Chile to the ports and textile mills of China and India – fed into and off larger anti-imperial struggles for state power.

From the establishment of US hegemony to the present

The strategies pursued by capitalists and core powers from 1870 to 1945 in order to overcome the squeeze on profits thus only transferred the crisis from the economic to the political realm – that is, wars, revolutions and explosive labour militancy. Even in the economic sphere, the strategies pursued only succeeded in turning the late nineteenth century crisis of falling prices and profits into the underconsumption crisis of the inter-war Great Depression.

US hegemony brought an end to the political and economic crisis of world capitalism, and to the escalating, explosive and highly politicised labour–capital conflict of our first phase. The *Pax Americana*, by bringing to an end the cycle of world wars and colonialist expansion – and thereby an end to the accompanying extreme dislocations in economic and social life – eliminated one of the main sources of the politicized explosiveness of world-scale labour unrest. The overwhelming military supremacy of the US at the close of the Second World War, combined with the shift to nuclear weapons technology, assured an end to wars between the major powers. Even within the context of the eventual US–USSR nuclear duopoly, full-scale war among the major powers, unless it were to mean the complete destruction of the world, was no longer possible.

The US-backed decolonization process also eliminated one of the main sources of the explosiveness, politicization *and* effectiveness of the struggles of the small working classes in the periphery. With each success in the anti-colonial struggle, the cross-class alliance of the nationalist movements dissolved. Once the nationalist movement (whether capitalist or socialist in ideology) controlled state power, workers' struggles invariably lost much of their former legitimacy and support from other classes in society (cf. Post, 1988).

The de-escalation in labour–capital conflict was also brought about by concessions to the (core) working class which were embedded in the social-economic policies of the new hegemonic power. The exercise of Keynesianism on a world scale, the globalization of the New Deal, the spread of Fordist mass consumption norms – these interrelated policies took into account what Polanyi (1957) has called 'the fictitious nature of the commodity labour'. Under British hegemony, labour had been treated like any other commodity – whether its services were bought and at what price were determined by 'the self-regulating market'. As we saw above, however, when 'the self-regulating market' determined that real wages should plummet, unemployment should skyrocket, or people's customary living and working conditions be dramatically reorganized, labour did not respond as an inanimate object or passive commodity. Rather, worker protest escalated. The new post-war hegemonic order offered a New Deal to the core working classes – rising consumption levels and a social welfare floor in exchange for acceptance/ cooperation in the total restructuring of production along the lines laid out by the most advanced sectors of US corporate capital.[10]

By the end of the Second World War, this corporate restructuring of production (what Chandler called 'the organizational revolution') had made the greatest advances in the US. Among the processes involved were: a separation of ownership from management; a separation of conception from execution; the vertical (as opposed to horizontal) integration of production within the firm; an increasingly complex division of labour and mechanization; and a transition from a three-tiered structure of the labour force (capitalist entrepreneur, skilled craftworker, unskilled manual worker) to a two-tiered structure (managers, semi-skilled operatives).[11]

In the US this transformation in the organization of production was made possible by the incorporation of large supplies of immigrant labour from eastern and southern Europe into the newly created semi-skilled positions in industry. Employers were thus able to bypass the established craftworkers and their resistance to the deskilling process. When the transformations culminated in the over-production crisis of the Great Depression and the worker militancy of the 1930s and 1940s in the US, the redistributive, mass consumption and social welfare aspects became the finishing touches to a new model of social relations which would be exported by the new hegemonic power to the rest of the core over the post-war period. The export of this model via the Marshall Plan and US multinational corporations served to transform world-scale labour–capital conflict.

As in the US at the beginning of the century, the post-Second World War 'organizational revolution' in the rest of the core was made possible by the incorporation of large supplies of newly or partially proletarianized workers into the semi-skilled positions in industry – for example the internal latent agricultural reserve army of labour and/or immigrants from less developed regions (for example, from southern Europe to northwestern Europe). The restructuring of production meant high levels of unemployment through the 1950s, but this unemployment was very unevenly distributed among different sectors of the labour force. Expanding employment opportunities were available to the newly proletarianized workers entering the sectors using the new methods and technologies. At the same time, the marketplace bargaining power of workers in the sectors using the old methods and technologies was further undermined. Thus, the craftworkers – the backbone of the explosive and politicized labour movement of the first phase – were marginalised from production, and the impact of their struggles was likewise increasingly marginal.

A new working class was created with a different history and world-view from that of the old. They were the bearers of an entirely different culture from the workers that had grown up, worked and struggled within the craft labour system. Their world-view was consumerist rather than productivist. Their attitude toward industrial employment was purely instrumental.[12] Initially, these new working classes were less predisposed to militancy than the old working classes. They did not have the craftworker's cultural resistances to doing the Taylorized tasks required of the semi-skilled operator. The pay they received was generally higher than any alternative available to them, such as in unskilled manual labour or agriculture. In many cases, these new workers saw themselves as part-lifetime proletarians: they had entered wage employment with the intention of staying only long enough to save enough money to set up a small business or buy a piece of land or pay off a debt. Thus, onerous conditions of work and pay take on a different connotation, if seen as temporary rather than a lifetime commitment. Often the new labour force was made up of young single men without families to support; or, alternatively, individuals with ties to rural households which could subsidize their wage income. Futhermore, until the new techniques of production had become generalized (at all input/output levels of the industry) there was little pressure to speed up production to the maximum. Finally, since these jobs did not require the possession of scarce skills, as long as unemployment remained high, these workers possessed little marketplace bargaining power.

Thus, the restructuring of production took off, based on the incorporation of these new supplies of relatively cheap and non-militant labour. However, the very incorporation of these new supplies into the wage labour force unleashed processes which over time undermined the basis of their cheapness. Part-lifetime proletarians found themselves to be full-lifetime proletarians as the advance of 'big business' closed off the escape routes from wage-labour, as well as the possibility of subsidizing wages through ties to rural households and their non-wage sources of income. Young, single male labour forces grew older, married and became heads of households with families to support. Exposure to 'consumer culture' raised expectations about wage levels as former luxuries became necessities and new necessities were created. The generalization of the new technologies allowed (indeed, demanded) a speed up at work. And the unprecedented boom in core countries unleashed by world-scale Keynesianism and the new hegemonic order, dried up the reserves of cheap labour in the core and created tight labour markets. With a combination of strong workplace and marketplace bargaining power, the once cheap and non-militant labour force was able (and willing) to engage in radical and effective strike actions.

However, these strike waves did not cumulate and escalate as they had in our first phase. One of the strengths of world-scale capitalism in our second phase – and which accounts for the stable (rather than escalating and explosive) trend in labour–capital conflict – is corporate capital's ability (organizationally and technologically) to plan and execute production on a world scale. Thus, each time reserves of cheap labour are dried up in a given region, corporate capital responds by re-orienting their investments to new areas which still have large reserves of non-wage labour. This process has the effect of containing the labour movement in the region from which capital has emigrated, but strengthening the movement in the areas to which capital migrates. The result – in our second phase – has been waves of labour unrest which counterbalance each other, rather than cumulate on a world scale. They thus 'add up' to a high but stable world trend, rather than an escalating and explosive one.

Thus, the wave of workers' struggles in the US in the 1930s and 1940s (where the transformations of the 'organizational revolution' had advanced the farthest) provided an incentive for the transnational expansion of US corporate capital to areas which still had large reserves of non-wage labour. The massive US foreign direct investment in manufacturing in western Europe in the 1950s and 1960s (and the competitive response of western European capitalists and states to this 'American challenge') had contradictory effects. On the one hand, it weakened the old craftworker-based politicized labour movements in western Europe. But, it created, then strengthened (over time), the new working class in the mass production industries; meanwhile it contained the bargaining power of this same group within the US. As the reserves of non-wage labour dried up in western Europe and the rest of the core, and as these workers began to express their newly found strength in a wave of strikes beginning in the 1960s, corporate capital again re-oriented production to areas which still contained large reserves of non-wage labour.[13] Thus, in southern Europe (Spain, Greece and Portugal) a similar sequence to that described was repeated – but the strike waves in these countries erupted in the context of the anti-dictatorial struggles of the early 1970s. Strike waves, combined with the general intensification of competition and crisis of profitability of core capital in the 1970s, prompted an even broader movement of capital towards less developed regions. The processes were repeated on an expanded scale until we arrived at the situation described at the beginning of this chapter.

ALTERNATIVE FUTURE SCENARIOS

We are now left with the question of the likely future evolution of world-scale labour–capital conflict in the next 10 to 20 years. A first possibility is that, faced with growing industrial conflict in the semi-periphery, *capitalists once again will decide to widen the circle of their investments, incorporating the labour supplies of the poorest countries of the periphery into the global division of labour in mass production industries.* To some extent, such a trend is already visible (for example in the recent surge of Japanese foreign direct investment in Southeast Asia). However, such a strategy is fraught with difficulties deriving from the extreme poverty of the periphery (for example poor infrastructure, lack of mass consumer markets). Unless this re-orientation of investment (and wage employment opportunities) from the core to the periphery is accompanied by a similar *and* drastic redistribution of world income, capitalists will once again be solving the squeeze on profits (real wages rising faster than productivity) with strategies leading toward an underconsumption crisis.

A second possibility is that *capitalists will vigorously pursue the new technological advances in automation in order to bring much of the industrial production from the semi-periphery back to the core countries of the world economy.* Such a trend is already visible, for example in the textile industry where automated plants located in core countries can produce more cheaply and efficiently than plants located in the semi-periphery and periphery, despite their higher labour costs. However, the automation route – solving the problem of labour control by eliminating workers from production – can solve temporarily the squeeze on profits only at the cost of further undermining the political legitimacy of capitalism among the growing numbers of unemployed in the core created by the automation and 'deindustrialization' strategies combined.

Finally, whatever strategy is pursued, *industrial conflict in the semi-periphery will be difficult to bring under control*. The conflict (from South Africa and Brazil to South Korea and Poland) is taking place in the context of demands for fundamental economic and political democratization. The poverty of these countries rules out solutions which have been viable in the core, such as: (i) a 'political exchange' with unions and/or working class parties in which the latter two agree to help discipline the workforce in exchange for rising levels of real wages and consumption for the workers and recognition/political legitimacy for the union and party; and (ii) restructuring the labour force by concentrating the higher status (corporate brain) jobs in the country and sending the lower status (execution) jobs to more peripheral areas via the organizational networks of multinational corporations based in the country. The first option would require an emulation of core consumption standards for the majority of the working class – an unfeasible solution barring a dramatic redistribution of world income from core to semi-periphery. The second option is limited not only by the poverty of the semi-periphery (which constrains their ability to develop multinational corporations), but also by their position further down the totem pole of world wage levels (making it more difficult to find places to which labour-intensive production can be relocated that would be both politically feasible and cheaper than home production). Thus, the applicability of 'core' solutions is limited. At the same time, the movements for economic and political democratization cannot be easily repressed.[14]

Thus the current crisis of world capitalism cannot be easily resolved by a continuation of the post-Second World War pattern of successive incorporations of new supplies of cheap labour. The historical limits of our 'second phase' of labour–capital conflict have been reached. Given the intractability of the crisis (and the contradictory effects of the current 'solutions' on the world's workers), we may well be on the verge of a return to the explosive and escalating pattern of our first phase. Whether the geographical epicentre of the coming explosions will be in the core, semi-periphery or periphery, and what exact form the movements will take, depends on the world-scale decisions of capitalists and struggles by workers which are currently in progress.

NOTES

1. The arguments and evidence presented in this chapter are in part based on preliminary results from an ongoing investigation by the Research Working Group on World Labor at the Fernand Braudel Center. Our research team seeks to analyse and explain the world-level patterning of labour unrest from 1870 to the present, and to study the interrelationship between labour–capital conflict and the historical evolution of the modern world-system. In order to provide the empirical base necessary to pursue these objectives we are conducting a major data collection project based on newspaper reports of labour unrest around the world. For earlier statements of the group's theoretical orientation and research objectives see Research Working Group on World Labor (1986) and Arrighi and Silver (1989). For preliminary empirical results with special reference to long waves see Silver (1989). The members of the Research Working Group on World Labor are Giovanni Arrighi, John Casparis, Jamie Faricellia Dangler, Melvyn Dubofsky, Roberto Patricio Korzeniewicz, Donald Quatert, Mark Selden and Beverly Silver. I would like to thank Giovanni Arrighi, Inga Brandell and AKUT in Uppsala for their comments and suggestions on an earlier draft of this chapter.
2. On the emergence of Japanese multinational corporations, see Ozawa (1979). On the decline of labour's bargaining power in the US, see for example Craypo (1981), and 'Labor's Lost Strength', *New York Times*, 10 May 1988, which reports that '. . . the bargaining power of American labor, both union and non-union has so diminished that no one knows just how low the unemployment rate must fall before workers can insist on higher pay and get it'.
3. On this kind of foreign direct investment and subcontracting, see for example Froebel, Heinrichs and Kreye (1980), and Nash and Fernandez-Kelly (1983).
4. We have derived the concept of 'workplace bargaining power' from Marx (*Capital*, volume I and *The Communist Manifesto*). See Arrighi (1978, 1982), Arrighi and Silver (1984), and Arrighi, Hopkins and Wallerstein (1989). For analogous derivations see Eduard Bernstein (cited in Gay 1962: 240–1), Tronti (1971), Bologna (1972), Phelps-Brown (1973), Coriat (1979), Edwards (1979), Perrone (1984), Wallace, Griffin and Rubin (1989).
5. See Bergquist (1986) and Brown (1988) for studies on the strategic position of export production workers in Latin America and West Africa, respectively.

6. See 'South Korea's Costly Summer', *New York Times*, 17 September 1987, D1; and 'African Miners Agree to Continue Disruptive Strike', *New York Times*, 27 August 1987, A1.

7. This description is partly based on the preliminary results of research in progress by the Research Working Group on World Labor of the Fernand Braudel Center (see note no.1).

8. The argument (and data) on this transition from a deflationary to an inflationary pattern (and the impact on strike activity), is further developed in Arrighi and Silver (1985).

9. See Arrighi (1973), Burawoy (1982) and Cohen *et al.* (1978) on the forced proletarianization in Southern Rhodesia, Zambia and the Congo, respectively. See Yun (1988) for Western Malaysia.

10. On the globalization of the New Deal, see Schurmann (1974) and Arrighi (1982); on Fordist mass consumption norms, see Aglietta (1979); on the limits of the spread of Fordist mass consumption norms to the periphery and semi-periphery, see Lipietz (1987).

11. For the various aspects of this transformation, see Chandler (1977) on vertical integration; Braverman (1974) on the separation of conception from execution; and Arrighi (1986) on the transition from a three-tier to a two-tier structure of the labour force.

12. For case studies which substantiate the characterization of the 'new working classes' as put forth in this and the following paragraph, see Arrighi and Piselli's (1987) study of Calabria and Chapter 5 in this book; and Piore's (1979) study of migrants to the United States.

13. For a more detailed account of the causal links between the 1930s–1940s wave of labour unrest in the US and the 1960s–1970s wave in western Europe, see Arrighi and Silver (1984).

14. For case studies of the constraints facing semi-peripheral states in their efforts to come to terms with strong labour movements, see the articles by Korzeniewicz (Argentina), Martin (South Africa) and Silver (Israel) in W. G. Martin (ed.) (1990).

REFERENCES

M. Aglietta, *A Theory of Capitalist Regulation: the US experience* (London: New Left Books,1979).

G. Arrighi, 'Labor Supplies in Historical Perspective: A Study of the Proletarianization of the African Peasantry in Rhodesia', in Arrighi and Saul (eds), *Essays on the Political Economy of Africa* (New York: Monthly Review,1973).

—— 'Towards a Theory of Capitalist Crisis', *New Left Review*, no. 111 (1978).

—— 'A Crisis of Hegemony', in Amin, Arrighi, Frank and Wallerstein (eds), *The Dynamics of Global Crisis* (New York: Monthly Review, 1982).

—— 'Custom and Innovation: Long Waves and Stages of Capitalist Development', in DiMatteo, Goodwin and Vercelli (eds), *Technological*

Change and Social Factors in Long Fluctuations (Berlin: Springer Verlag, 1989).

—— T. Hopkins, and I. Wallerstein, 'Rethinking the Concepts of Class and Status-Group in a World-System Perspective', in Arrighi, Hopkins and Wallerstein, *Antisystemic Movements* (London: Verso, 1989).

G. Arrighi and Beverly Silver 'Labor Movements and Capital Migration: The United States and Western Europe in World-Historical Perspective', in C. Bergquist (ed.), *Labor in the Capitalist World-Economy* (Beverly Hills: Sage, 1984), pp. 183–216.

—— 'Labor and Long Waves', paper presented at the Second Annual Forum on the History of the Labor Movement and of the Working Class, Paris, June 26–8 (1985).

—— 'Global Patterns of Labor Movements', *Cahiers du GEMDEV*, no. 12, June (1989).

G. Arrighi and F. Piselli, 'Capitalist Development in Hostile Environments: Feuds, Class Struggles, and Migrations in a Peripheral Region of Southern Italy', *Review*, X, 4, (1987).

C. W. Bergquist, *Labor in Latin America: Comparative Essays on Chile, Argentina, Venezuela and Colombia* (Stanford, CA: Stanford University Press, 1986).

S. Bologna, 'Composizione di classe e teoria del partito alle origini del movimento consiliare', in S. Bologna *et al.*, *Operai e Stato* (Milano: Fetrinelli, 1972).

H. Braverman, *Labor and Monopoly Capital: The Degradation of Work in the Twentieth Century* (New York: Monthly Review Press, 1974).

C. A. Brown, 'The Dialectics of Colonial Labour Control: Class Struggles in the Nigerian Coal Industry, 1914–1949', *Journal of Asian & African Studies*, XXIII (1988), pp. 1–2, 32–59.

M. Burawoy, 'The Hidden Abode of Underdevelopment: Labor Process and the State in Zambia', *Politics & Society*, 11, no. 4 (1982), pp. 123–66.

A. D. Chandler Jr., *The Visible Hand: The Managerial Revolution in American Business* (Cambridge, MA: Harvard University Press, 1977).

R. Cohen, J. Copans and P. W. Gutkind, 'Introduction', in Gutkind, Cohen and Copans (eds), *African Labor History* (Beverly Hills: Sage, 1978).

B. Coriat, *L'Atelier et le chronomètre* (Paris: Bourgois,1979).

C. Craypo, 'The Decline of Union Bargaining Power', in Gordon, Thurow, Craypo and Killingworth (eds), *New Directions in Labor Economics and Industrial Relations* (Notre Dame, ID: University of Notre Dame Press, 1981).

R. Edwards, *Contested Terrain: The Transformation of the Workplace in the Twentieth Century* (New York: Basic Books, 1979).

F. Froebel, J. Heinrichs and O. Kreye, *The New International Division of Labour* (Cambridge: Cambridge University Press, 1980).

P. Gay, *The Dilemma of Democratic Socialism* (New York: Collier, 1962).

E. Hobsbawm, 'The "New Unionism" in Perspective', in *Workers: Worlds of Labor* (New York: Pantheon,1984).

A. Lipietz, *Mirages and Miracles: The Crises of Global Fordism* (London: Verso, 1987).

W. G. Martin (ed.), *Semi-peripheral States in the World-Economy* (Westport, CT: Greenwood Press, 1990).

J. Nash and P. Fernandez-Kelly (eds), *Women, Men and the International Division of Labor* (Albany, NY: State University of New York Press, 1983).

T. Ozawa, *Multinationalism, Japanese Style* (Princeton: Princeton University Press, 1979).

L. Perrone, 'Positional Power, Strikes and Wages', *American Sociological Review*, XLIX, 3, June (1984), pp. 412–26.

E. H. Phelps Brown, 'New Wine in Old Bottles: Reflections on the Changed Working of Collective Bargaining in Great Britain', *British Journal of Industrial Relations*, XI, 3, November (1973), pp. 329–37.

M. J. Piore, *Birds of Passage: Migrant Labor and Industrial Societies* (Cambridge: Cambridge University Press, 1979).

K. Polanyi, *The Great Transformation: The Political and Economic Origins of Our Time* (Boston: Beacon Press,1957).

K. Post, 'The Working Class in North Viet Nam and the Launching of the Building of Socialism', *Journal of Asian & African Studies*, XXIII (1988), pp. 1–2, 141–55.

C. Pycroft and B. Munslow, 'Black Mine Workers in South Africa: Strategies of Cooptation and Resistance', *Journal of Asian & African Studies*, XXIII (1988), pp. 1–2, 156–79.

Research Working Group on World Labor, 'Global Patterns of Labor Movements in Historical Perspective', *Review*, X, 1, Summer (1986), pp. 137–55.

F. Schurmann, *The Logic of World Power* (New York: Pantheon, 1974).

B. Silver, 'Class Struggle and the Kondratieff, 1870 to the present', in A. Kleinknecht, E. Mandel and I. Wallerstein (eds), *New Findings in Long-Wave Research* (London: Macmillan, forthcoming).

M. Tronti, *Operai e Capitale* (Torino: Einaudi, 1971).

M. Wallace, L. J. Griffin, and B. A. Rubin, 'The Positional Power of American Labor, 1963–1977', *American Sociological Review*, 54, 2, April (1989), pp. 197–214.

H. A. Yun, 'Labour Transformation and Capital Accumulation in West Malaysia', *Journal of Asian & African Studies*, XXIII (1988), pp. 1–2, 60–78.

Index